BOB WOLFF'S COMPLETE GUIDE TO SPORTSCASTING

Also by Bob Wolff:

It's Not Who Won or Lost the Game, It's How You Sold the Beer
Andy Bathgate's Hockey Secrets (with Andy Bathgate)
The Drive Within Me (with Bob Pettit)

BOB WOLFF'S COMPLETE GUIDE TO SPORTSCASTING

HOW TO MAKE IT IN SPORTSCASTING WITH OR WITHOUT TALENT

Bob Wolff

SKYHORSE PUBLISHING

Skyhorse Publishing books may be purchased in bulk at special discounts for sales promotion, corporate gifts, fund-raising, or educational purposes. Special editions can also be created to specifications. For details, contact the Special Sales Department, Skyhorse Publishing, 307 West 36th Street, 11th Floor, New York, NY 10018 or info@skyhorsepublishing.com.

Skyhorse® and Skyhorse Publishing® are registered trademarks of Skyhorse Publishing, Inc.®, a Delaware corporation.

www.skyhorsepublishing.com

10 9 8 7 6 5 4 3 2 1

Library of Congress Cataloging-in-Publication Data is available on file.
ISBN: 978-1-61608-081-5

Printed in the United States of America

Contents

CONTENTS

CONTENTS

Introduction

"We'll Begin After A Word From Our Sponsor"

AT AN EARLY age, I was addicted to sports—reading about them and playing them.

My parents didn't watch me play very often. Dad was working in New York City and couldn't return home in time for afternoon games. Mom seemed to have more concern for my safety than for who won or lost. At dinnertime they plied me with questions about the games and were thrilled with every accomplishment I relayed.

My folks always made sure we lived close to a schoolyard, and I spent hours competing on, or against, all of the teams that practiced there, with age making no difference.

I was fast, shifty, and gifted with good hands. Because I was thin, in football I played safety or cornerback on defense, quarterback on offense. I made headlines in high school with long touchdown runs and interception returns.

With his long working hours, my dad never had a chance to watch me play a high school football game, but he got a big kick out of reading about my exploits. My mom never watched me play either, but because she knew I didn't have much weight to protect me, she spent football game days worrying about my safety. "Mom," I said, "I keep running *away* from tacklers, so please don't be concerned." But Mom didn't want to take a first-hand look. She revealed later that she spent game time driving near the school, listening to the roar of the crowd. If she didn't hear the siren of an ambulance, that was a winning game for her. Fortunately, I finished my senior season in good shape physically, and was an All-Star selection in the New York City suburban schools. Except for a few aches and pains sustained while making an occasional tackle as safety man, I enjoyed the fun of scoring touchdowns and winning football games.

The Wolff family

I captained the school basketball team but baseball was my passion. I was selected as one of the city's top young baseball prospects by the *New York World-Telegram and Sun*. I owe a lot to my high school baseball coach at Woodmere Academy, "Pop" LaRue, who every day after practice, would spend hours of his personal time hitting fly balls to me and pitching me extra batting practice. I became his project to succeed in the game.

My folks enjoyed reading about me in the papers, but the only games Mom watched were some night basketball games. After one game, I asked Mom what she liked most about basketball. "The ceremony before the game," was her answer.

Not being aware of any ceremony, I mentally reconstructed what took place. I shook hands with my opponent, then leaned forward to view the number on his back so I'd always keep him in sight. Then we were ready for the center tip.

"The ceremony, Mom?" I asked.

"Yes," she said. "When you bow forward as a courtesy to your opponent before play begins. That's sportsmanship at its finest." I showed my sportsmanship by not changing her view.

This book is a real bow to my parents. I'm thankful for the genes they bestowed. Mom's grace as a singer and dancer, her love of words, and her storytelling ability all have aided my sportscasting. So has Dad's work ethic. He was a relentless perfectionist and I admired the intensity he always demonstrated as a three-sport athlete. Dad's engineering firm, Wolff and Munier, provided the heating and ventilation for many of New York's landmark buildings. Dad concluded his career as deputy commissioner for air pollution in New York City. I told Dad that some of my early broadcasts may have contributed to the air pollution, but Dad assured me that eliminating smokestacks was a greater problem.

My wife, Jane, is more than a partner—she's a one-woman team. Sportscasting is a rather one-dimensional job. To succeed, one has to stay with it every day and night. In addition to providing love and encouragement, Jane's also our chief operating officer and runs the show. She's an amazing woman. You're right, I'm lucky. Our family is a vital part of our life. We bask in their love and accomplishments. We're grateful also to the doctors and dentists who take pride in our longevity. The show goes on and they make sure we're in it.

This book is also a bow to my sportscasting colleagues. I'm proud to be part of this upbeat group. Like all of you, I'm indebted to the hirers—the stations, networks, and sponsors who make this fun job possible. And I'm thankful to all those behind the scenes—the producers, directors, technical crews, stat men, spotters, sales people, agents, publicity people, and all the rest who play such important roles in this business. Above all, a hearty thanks to all the fans who have been our audience, and to the athletes who make our jobs possible.

The athletes provide the stories. Sportscasters add information and identification, sometimes entertainment, and aim at enhancing the viewing or listening pleasure for our electronic friends at the other end. It's nice work if you can get it.

PREFACE

Defining Talent

TALENT IS ONE of those all-encompassing words that has many definitions. In the television business, the performers are referred to as "the talent." I find the upgrade flattering.

One of the definitions that I subscribe to describes a talented person as someone with a "special or creative aptitude." What's not defined is how special or creative that aptitude has to be to graduate from being good at something to being great. You know that TV show, *America's Got Talent?* Frankly, I don't think I'd win that award in my own family.

Like acting, sportscasting requires reading and speaking lines—or ad-libbing them. Sportscasters have some ability or else wouldn't be hired. For most, that ability is to describe or analyze what others are doing athletically. Many of those they talk about are the real stars. Just a small percentage of sportscasters can hold an audience all by themselves. A few have the magnetic quality, content, and presentation to do so. They rate the word "talent" because they are specially gifted. All great sportscasters can make a winning season sound even more exciting, and just as important, or maybe more so, many can make a losing season entertaining. How many can take over a two-hour rain delay and single-handedly make it an entertaining experience? They enhance the product skillfully while maintaining objectivity.

The Wolff sports family

In show business, two names come to mind. Billy Crystal is an excellent comedian, a brilliant impressionist, an entertaining singer, graceful dancer, expert show producer, wonderful writer, and unsurpassed host of awards shows. He's also a serious actor, a devoted sports enthusiast, and has worn well over a long period of stardom. That versatility should put him in a special category. He's a talented man.

For instant energy, it's difficult to top Robin Williams. On talk shows his quick ad-libs delivered in frenetic style, his one-liners, and the general bedlam he creates, provide instant comedic exhilaration. That's talent, too. Some people have great appeal, but no specific talents. One can win with appeal. Regis Philbin wins with his.

There are many good ballplayers, musicians, singers, dancers, and sportscasters—all with a degree of talent. But if they all have talent, what's the designation for those who cause you to shout, "Wow, that's talent!" because their talent stands out?

And sportscasters can be taught. It's an acquired art. As with any other occupation, some have a better knack for it than others.

I won't quibble, though. How about, "one can make it in sportscasting with or without outstanding talent?" Sometimes one just likes the performer, you know. Some who get to the top may exhibit more talent than others, some get there with a combination of abilities that appeal to the hirer. Strong points in many categories.

But I am haunted by this thought. There are well over a hundred sportscasters, writers, actors, and performers whom I enjoy. They do their jobs well as team members, but do not bear the label of artist. They're specialists in what they do and many prove their appeal with longevity. They've contributed to our lives. I appreciate and am thankful for their, should I say, "talent" or "work"? Is their work talent or are they talented in their work? Certainly one can be a popular performer but not be a journalist. One can be an excellent journalist with little electronic appeal. It helps to have journalistic ability, but that's only one phase of the job.

A word or phrase is needed to characterize outstanding sportscasting. In playing sports, it's a "clutch player" or a "game-winner"; in medical praise, a "life-saver"; in the military, a "hero"; in business, a "financial wizard"; in entertainment, a "show-stopper." Some sportscasters enhance more than others. Most do it with talent in a specific way, but others do it without. In the TV and radio business, one survives by being hired.

In 2009, when sportscaster Bruce Beck introduced me as an Emmy presenter with some kind words at a formal dinner in New York City, I walked on stage to a standing ovation. I was touched by this tribute; but in my heart I wasn't sure whether it was for my talent or that, at age 88, I was able to make it unassisted to the microphone. Regardless, I was grateful. So let me be realistic about this fun job of sportscasting. To be a sportscaster, no qualifying tests are required. And if the public believes some have talent, let's not quibble. It beats the alternative. We wouldn't have jobs unless the viewers believed that's what we bring to our work.

One doesn't have to prove himself or herself with grades or entrance exams. Being hired is the key. That can take some enterprise. Doing something that will attract a hirer's attention or selling yourself to a hirer may take a creative approach and plenty of energy. The most talented may not get the job. The job may go to the person who makes the strongest impression. Nice guys have a good chance, but those who aren't nice may also attract an audience. They, too, may be hired.

Remember, this is a business. And once hired, success is measured financially by the size and type of audience one attracts and holds.

There are a lot of sportscasters' names mentioned in this book. There are just as many whose aren't. Most of those I mentioned are those I have worked with or spent time with, hired, taught, listened to, or watched. They all qualify the same way: they were hired.

I can guarantee that I've personally pre-tested my recommendations for how one can succeed in the business.

This book details: "How to make it in sportscasting with or without talent." Fortunately, the end result can be reached either way.

PART ONE
Getting The Job

1: Understanding The Sportscaster's Role

Myth: One succeeds on the airwaves by being accepted as a sports journalist. Truth: One succeeds by personal appeal with the proper mix of theatrics, sports journalism, and entertainment.

TO SURVIVE IN this glamorous business called sportscasting, one should first understand what the job is all about.

Forget all the myths about what it takes: voice, looks, a degree in journalism, athletic ability, or any of the other popular attributes many believe are so essential. One can possess all of these but still have only limited appeal. Conversely, one can have an average voice, a plain look, limited education, and non-varsity status and still be a headline performer. There is something extra that makes the difference. It's called appeal. In show business, people say they've got "it."

Baseball historian and author Curt Smith told me how much he enjoyed hearing Hall of Fame pitcher Dizzy Dean calling ball games. Dean offered a breezy rendition, didn't concern himself with all the players' names, laughed a lot, and, lacking an extensive vocabulary, made up his own words. When this irreverent fun caused educators to rise up in protest, Dean laughed even harder and said, "But they don't know pitching like I do." Diz was a Hall of Fame pitcher with personal appeal. That was enough to draw an audience.

I liked "Old Diz." He and his partner Pee Wee Reese were on CBS-TV, competing on the *Game of the Week* against Joe Garagiola and myself on NBC-TV. Reese was a straightforward, excellent broadcaster but Dean was the star. His good humor, the way he poked fun at his own shortcomings, appealed to listeners. He was, in his own words, a "good ol' country boy."

Joe, my partner, was a quick-witted analyst with great one-liners and a tremendous sense of timing. He stood out among baseball humorists as a natural talent. Versatile and enthusiastic, he also appeared on NBC-TV's *Today Show.* Joe wasn't selling his voice or looks—he had content. He still does. He's an outstanding performer, perceptive and analytical. Joe and I took a more strictly-baseball approach to broadcasting. It was a treat for me to work by his side.

Curt Smith has two books out at present—one about Mel Allen, the other about Vin Scully. With both broadcasters, their voices and their styles made them all-time greats. Their sound was their power. Mel used a rich, warm Southern drawl; Vin has a poetic quality, imparting a musical sound to routine calls.

On the other hand, one of New York's most popular broadcasters was Phil Rizzuto, not because of his voice but because of his emotion and enthusiasm. Phil's excitement at great plays, home runs, and pitching feats delighted his many followers. Fans lined up at the ballpark to shake his hand or to get an autograph. Phil didn't worry about words—or his delivery—five or six "Holy Cows" would be his scream of delight. Phil was the ultimate fan and former Yankee great, cheerleading at the microphone. Homerism in the broadcast booth is frowned on today, but with Phil it was fun.

All of these sportscasters are winners, each in their own way. Being different is an asset in sportscasting as long as you don't stray from accuracy. The viewer or listener has to have faith in the information being imparted.

Joe Garagiola

There are no written standards in sportscasting. It's a wide-open field. If you get a sportscasting job—any job—you're in the fraternity. There is an art to succeeding, though. Getting on the air, if one has that desire, is not that difficult. Whether it be through internships at college, working the public address system at high school games, or putting one's own high school or college shows on cable stations, there are many ways to get started when, in essence, you're helping out. For experience, nothing beats practicing game-calling on your own audio or video recorder.

The biggest step is getting hired to do a job. That may be the biggest obstacle and it demands perseverance. To get hired, you have to appeal to the hirer, who must believe you'll appeal to the listeners or viewers. You're being hired as an electronic friend to the audience. Whether you're in the studio or at the game, your mission is to enhance the viewers' sports entertainment .

A sportscaster is a sports enhancer. That can include a variety of tasks on TV. For play-by-play you need to identify the players quickly and accurately, provide notes about the games and the players, and add insights, strategies, newsworthy stories, and some humor. You'll also need vocal emotion. That's a primary ingredient for excitement.

Is this a performing art? Yes. I teach this in my sportscasting classes. One can't be inhibited behind the microphone. One has to be able to shout "home run" or "touchdown." One more time now, a little louder please.

Is this show business? In a sports way it is, although I prefer the term "natural reaction." As an electronic friend, you're shouting "what

Phil Rizzuto

a play" along with your pal in the living room watching the TV set. If you're his friend you're both getting excited, yelling with the same reaction.

Do you bristle at the term "show business"? Well, consider how your zest—your natural outburst at a ball game or any sports event—is triggered by the emotion of the moment, the artistry of the play, and the roar of the crowd. It happens naturally, the same way one laughs at a joke or applauds in a theater. I get excited all the time by things I like. My emotions just erupt naturally. This helps on TV, but it just amplifies the way I feel. The key word is "naturally." It's not planned. It's certainly not scripted like Hollywood movies or Broadway shows. It's a sports reaction, far different than the common perception of "show business." In the studio, however, with no crowd roar to shout above, one has to speak as if he or she were

at the game, in a more excited tone than that used in normal conversation.

But there's no way to escape the word "entertainment." That's what it is, too.

Let me explain the term "sports journalist." Sportswriters who are outstanding in their craft are frequently referred to as "journalists." But it's sort of an honorary title. Those who write from time to time for community papers or school newsletters often refer to themselves as journalists, too. It sounds more distinctive, and maybe they write well. If one has graduated from a journalism school, one should have the right to use the word.

Most sportscasters don't have journalism degrees, but they do know what makes good stories, which ones appeal to viewers, and how to present them in the time allotted. This is their art. Content is their material. Some are better than others. The word "journalist" is now a generic term used by the qualified and unqualified alike.

In the early days of radio and TV, gathering information, making phone calls, and meeting with others were important and time-consuming parts of a broadcaster's preparation.

Today, with the Internet, the bulk of information is already gathered for you. What's important, though, is to quickly sift through the deluge of background material to focus on what is relevant, what will hold the attention of your viewers or listeners. Journalism is knowing what is important and how to present it.

2: How Does One Qualify?

Myth: The best method is to take college courses in the art.
Truth: Formal education can be helpful, but most achievers are self-taught.

SO YOU WANT to be a sportscaster? Well, do you give scores at school in the morning on the public address system? You qualify. Report late-night scores in Montana with high school results? You're in. Do sports talk radio in Kalamazoo? Of course that counts. Soccer games on campus radio? Join the club.

How do you qualify? By doing it.

It's like being a salesman, a musician, a singer, or a president. There are no prerequisite courses to complete, no tests to pass, no degrees to attain.

How do a few sportscasters get to do the big events and get rewarded so well financially? Because someone hired them. How did the hirers get their jobs? Chances are they had a plan, too. One doesn't go to a school to become a hirer. Some have the knack, some don't.

Here's one key for job-getting when starting out: have a plan of how you can fulfill a need for a station, sponsor, or network.

Of course, once hired, a sportscaster, musician, or singer has to perform well to progress. Same goes for a pro athlete or a comedian.

Presidents are elected, not hired, but they have to be in a position to get the job.

That's where it all begins.

Getting the job is fifty percent of the battle. Of course, then you have to do it. Fundamentals can be taught—that's thirty percent. Then you've got to hold the job, which is the remaining twenty percent.

So how does one begin?

The first step in the plan is learning about yourself. You have to know your strong points and your weak points. This is vital because you have to sell yourself to the hirer on your strong points.

How do you know what your strong points are? Well, you've heard countless TV and radio play-by-play announcers, analysts, studio anchors, reporters, and talk show hosts do what they do. So ask yourself this: if you knew the necessary preparation techniques, could you qualify to work in any one category or perhaps all of them?

Most young sportscasters starting out believe they can top a lot of these veterans in knowledge, speaking ability, presentation, and appeal and can't wait to give it a try. The ability may be there, as well as the desire, but first they have to learn the mechanics.

For the vast majority, they're self-taught.

Some colleges and universities have TV or radio stations. One can learn the engineering tools, the editing process, writing, on-camera techniques, the importance of being newsworthy and accurate, and how to produce shows as well as perform on them. Just as important, these stations offer students a feel for the job, and an indication of what's required. Hopefully, the students also meet some guest lecturers who can serve as future contacts in the business.

That's all helpful, but remember, these are skills. There are not many newscasters or sportscasters with journalism degrees. A degree is helpful, but it isn't necessary. All the practice and training one can get at any level, particularly on the technical side in college, adds to one's knowledge; but there are few schools or colleges designed strictly to graduate major league players—or comedians, or congressmen, or talk-show hosts, or sports anchors, or play-by-play callers. Nor those who hire them.

If the networks want learned men to report the news, why don't they hire college professors with their many degrees? The answer is that they want performers.

Throughout the country, there are stations in cities large and small which have nightly sports segments in their newscasts. Each also has a sports anchor for TV or radio. These segments are usually three or four minutes in length.

For radio, one has to assemble the sports news—mainly scores and highlights—and read it on the air with a pleasant, animated style. It should sound conversational. On TV, it can be read off the tele-prompter. The trick is sounding as if you're not reading. You have to look pleasant and smile along with your co-anchors on the news side. A few add more than that with an engaging personality and friendly banter. This small group with extra appeal or energy, or better comments, can aim for jobs at a higher level. That extra bit of quick-witted amiability is enough to advance. What need are you fulfilling? In a sea of sameness, your style may draw more viewers, and that's what stations are looking for. That's the winning edge—being different with appeal. A good teacher can help one learn this. Some may find they have a natural knack for it.

One learns by doing. Make videos of yourself and critique them. Be honest with yourself. Most top-flighters can evaluate their own performances. If you're not sure, call in a trusted friend, preferably in the business to get an opinion. Employers spend more time looking at tapes than they do résumés.

The words one uses and the manner of enunciating them should have appeal. Any deviation from sameness can leave an impression. Done repeatedly, it becomes one's style.

Along with your audition, many other factors will play a role. One's reputation as a person, ability to get along with others, education, friends in the business, willingness to work hard and work extra hours without grumbling, being likable—these are all part of selling oneself. Does your tape stand out from the crowd? Will it be remembered? Above all, if there's a job available, try to strike a responsive chord with the hirer and discuss your ideas. That's the most important part.

In preparing to climb the ladder, once you feel you're at a professional level, use your best tape as an audition entry. (Make sure you have extra copies, as they are rarely returned.)

When you send an audition entry, if that's needed, aim to do more than just compete favorably. Instead, send one designed to win. It's not enough to duplicate the sameness that will characterize most of the other contenders. Sameness is the formula for most studio sports shows. Performing differently can often be enough to stand out. Performing is the art. Skills are vital. Content is mandatory. Add an appealing personality and getting along with others. That's what's needed.

If auditioning for a sports anchor position, understand what most of the others will send. They'll introduce themselves on camera, go to highlights of one sport, then another, give the other sports news of the day with video highlights, and sign off. Most compete, but can't win. To be remembered, the challenge is to eliminate the sameness and create a quick, strong impression. A distinctive four-minute piece might include a humorous bit either to lead or to close—a short but strong editorial, a quick interview with a probing question, a couple of game highlights (one with excitement at the end), and closing banter with the news anchors. Being remembered puts one in the competition.

If competing for a play-by-play position, conclude that all the others will put in their most hysterical calls: game-winning shots, walk-off homers, and eighty-yard touchdowns. Your tape should also exhibit how you cover the less exciting moments in a broadcast—with strategy, insights, and compelling stories. That complete mixture is more revealing of one's full abilities. High-level excitement is only a small part of any game.

When I was hiring people, I wanted to hear how creative they were, how they held the audience when play was one-sided. That's the true test of a sportscaster. How does the play-by-play man call the game when there is little excitement on the field or in the arena? This tape may run five or six minutes. Some teams lose more than they win.

How does the sportscaster hold the listener's interest when the crowd roar is low? Does his personality have appeal? That can override all else. Humor can also be a big plus. A good analyst has to be perceptive and point out things happening in the game that others may not have noticed. Comments have to add extra dimension to the telecast. They should be brief and accurate.

In your cover letter, write that you'll call the station in about a week or so to make sure the entry was received. If possible, also try to arrange an appointment for an interview if there seems to be interest. Don't be pushy—just mention the possibility. Nobody wants to sit around waiting for the phone to ring, so take the initiative by writing that you'll call.

In 2004 I was on a committee to select a new sports anchor and sports director for News 12 Long Island. I held both positions for eighteen years; but in my present contract I received permission from Pat Dolan, the news director and president of the News 12 Network, to give up my daily scoreboard routine in order to concentrate on covering major sports events, running their scholar-athlete program and presenting my on-camera "Point of View" sports editorials.

Under Pat's leadership, News 12 Long Island has had a remarkable record for its journalism production, earning numerous Emmy awards and nominations. The News 12 Network always fares well. Pat started out as a reporter and has the knack for selecting talented journalists to join his team. But if a story demands personal attention, particularly if lives are at stake, Pat will leave his office and join the news team himself.

Pat disdains personal publicity for himself; but when Haiti suffered a catastrophic loss of lives and property in the massive earthquake of 2010, Pat left his office for four days and flew to Haiti two or three times a day in his personal plane to bring medical supplies and food and assist in the emergency response effort. He's a boss who cares about people.

For my vacated position, we looked at over fifty submitted tapes from all over the country. Most possessed the same standard formula;

Kevin Maher, Bob, and Michael Coleman

many were good, but they didn't stand out. One had an extra edge. Michael Coleman, working at a small station in Texas, showed such natural rapport with his news anchors that he made a strong impression on us all. His light, humorous banter made the difference. That's what stood out.

Michael has excellent news sense and other strong qualities, and proved to be a fine choice; but the personable touch he displayed on his audition made him the winner. In 2010, Michael, who has a strong football background, accepted a sports anchor position in Kansas City, where he'll also be involved in NFL shows.

Bob, Ann Bernzweig, and Pat Dolan

Our new sports director, Kevin Maher, and anchor-reporter, Jamie Stuart, are both popular on-air personalities who received college experience at Syracuse University. We have friendly debates about how much talent is needed. Learning what to do is vital, they agree; but Jamie says, "It looks easy only when you do it well, and some people have that gift from the start." I agree with that but; as a former college professor as well as a current sportscaster, I know the art can also be taught.

People make friends with people who appeal to them. In business, people hire people who appeal to them. A four-minute tape and a five-minute in-person interview is sufficient time to make a strong impression.

Women have made amazing strides in sportscasting. They present themselves well and forcefully. They come to an interview prepared to win. Samantha Ryan, who went on to become a CBS Network sideline reporter for major sports events, came to me at News 12 Long Island seeking her first TV job. Her manner, her desire, and her enthusiasm impressed me. She exuded confidence and poise. I hired her as a reporter. Sam now continues nightly sportscasting on CBS-TV, New York, balancing family duties as well.

Tracy Wolfson followed Sam as a sideline football reporter for CBS. The short cover letter she sent me was so humorous, so creative, that I hired her, impressed by her creativity. A couple of paragraphs were enough to open the door. She stressed her sports knowledge, but it was her humor that struck a responsive chord. In 2010, Tracy was the sideline reporter for CBS's coverage of the NCAA Basketball Tournament.

Linda Cohn and Donna Fox were also on my team at News 12 Long Island. Linda had some major assignments around the country before she joined us and then went on to fame with ESPN. Donna was on air at News 12 before moving to the West Coast when her husband was stationed there in the service. He and her children became top priority. Donna has added book authorship to her talents.

Tina Cervasio, who took my sportscasting course at St. John's University, has a ready smile and an inquiring mind. Recruited from the New England Sports Network, she proves her versatility covering various sports events at Madison Square Garden.

An outstanding Hall of Fame basketball player, Nancy Lieberman took my sportscasting class at Pace University before joining ESPN and becoming a valuable addition to their sports team. She had an excellent understanding of the game, and it came through in her analysis. All of these women gained the experience they needed and then moved quickly to the big time. Nancy is a determined competitor who flew in from out of town just to take my course.

Dan Jiggetts, a former offensive lineman for Chicago Bears, came in from Chicago every weekend to become my student at Pace. His style, manner, and comments were all impressive. He's now starring on Chicago television.

All of these people went out of their way to get their jobs. They traveled to do so, made themselves known. That's the important lesson. They went after the jobs and got them.

I called the game at Madison Square Garden when Carol Blazejowski set a Garden scoring record, since broken, putting in 52 points for Montclair State. After graduation she made her TV debut with me as an analyst for women's college basketball and was outstanding. Her enthusiasm and knowledge were great assets. Her next big step was becoming the general manager of the New York Liberty, the Garden's WNBA team. A few years ago we were inducted together into the Garden's Walk of Fame.

When I began on TV in Washington as the city's first sports TV personality, there was no one with more experience. I needed hard-working enthusiastic people to work with me on a variety of TV shows. Experience was not a factor because no one had TV experience. My hirees were bright teenagers eager for a chance. We grew together.

Among my early hirees were two bright high schoolers. Phil Hochberg went on to become a prominent lawyer who served as counsel for numerous major league sports organizations. He was also the public address announcer for the Washington Redskins for many years. Dick Heller became an outstanding sports columnist for the *Washington Times* and an excellent baseball historian. Another enthusiastic teenager, Maury Povich, was my statistician and show producer before becoming a news anchor and a major attraction on TV with his own national show. All three continue as lifelong friends.

A young fellow just out of college, Ned Martin, called me one day. He told me he was working in Washington and was turning to me for advice as to how to become a sportscaster, so I invited him to my home to discuss what I could do. He told me that his present job was trying to get drug stores and supermarkets to carry paperback books, but what he really wanted to do was test himself in sportscasting.

I had him read for me. He sounded pleasant, low key, smooth—good enough to get a start somewhere. I recommended he try WINX radio in Washington, where I had once worked, and to tell them he could work on weekends, fill in on vacations, and be on call if a bigger position opened up. Ned got the job, then landed some minor league play-by-play at his next stop, where he also met Curt Gowdy. Ned kept in touch with me but we never had baseball openings. Curt did, however, and Ned became the number two man with the Red Sox. When Curt left, Ned took over and established himself as one of the finest sportscasters in the country. Quite aside from his ability, he put himself in position to be hired.

Ernie Harwell, Maury Povich, Bob, and Jack Guinan

Washington seemed to be a springboard to the top for other sportscasters as well. Jim Simpson, just starting out on radio in Hagerstown, Maryland, wrote to me seeking a TV job. I was impressed with Jim and used him to sub for me on some of my baseball pre-game TV shows when I was out of town. Later, when an anchor job opened in Washington, Jim took it and was on his way. A few years later he gave the scores and I gave the highlights on ABC's national football pre- and post-game TV shows. Jim continued at the top for many years on network events. A good-looking guy with a pleasant, easygoing manner, Jim turned down movie opportunities to stay in sports.

Warner Wolf came by to chat with me about sportscasting when he was just starting out in Washington. When his first big TV opportunity came—the chance to anchor a show in New York—Warner called me for guidance. I remember suggesting to him that given the choice between the early sports show or the later show, he should take the later one, as that's when the majority of scores and highlights are aired, with the night games ending. On air, Warner personified enthusiasm as his trademark. His catchphrase, "Let's go to the video tape," became familiar to New York viewers. Warner is particularly impressive delivering commercials. That's an art, too. In person, he's rather mild-mannered, but when that red light goes on, so does he.

Bill Malone, another Washington announcer, joined me at WPIX-TV in New York to do live commercials. He was one of the finest TV salesmen I'd ever seen. An auto racing enthusiast, this popular announcer died in an automobile accident far too young. He was a natural on the air, with a knack for delivering commercials in such an

Warner Wolf

appealing manner that customers bought the products. He, too, had movie star appeal.

I had a hard-working "A" student at St. John's, Bernadette McDonald, who worked diligently to learn the business side of sports. She's now vice president of broadcast operations for Major League Baseball.

All of these people had different qualities, but it was the drive to succeed that made them stand out.

Another of my St. John's students demonstrated at a young age which characteristics would serve him best. Carl Reuter enjoyed giving his opinions on sport issues—loud enough without a microphone to attract a crowd. These were delivered with the passion of a bleacherite. Carl worked for me at News 12 Long Island as a reporter, but then moved on to give sports opinion pieces on FOX-TV, New York, before returning to play-by-play on the new MSG Varsity network.

Mike Francesa was also a student of mine at St. John's. Mike's research and conscientiousness put him at the scholar's level. His early jobs came about because he made himself so knowledgeable about so many sports that he could provide valuable assistance to those who were at the microphones. His next step was to use the material for himself. Now at WFAN sports radio in New York, he does an amazing solo for five and a half hours a day, five days a week. His daily show is simulcast on cable's YES Network, and he also does a weekend show on NBC-TV.

By teaming Francesa with excitable Chris Russo on WFAN, producer Mark Chernoff developed a pairing that helped make sports radio talk a national industry. The duo would reply to listeners' questions with strong opinions, a practice that's now a staple product on stations throughout the country. In 2008, Russo left WFAN to go to Sirius XM satellite radio and become a soloist. Apart, Russo and Francesa continue to prosper. While the two were together, they held a powerful position on the airwaves.

Everyone who has been hired has made an impression on the hirer. People remember little things. Sounding cheerful on a phone call, the

Bob Wolff on court at Madison Square Garden

words one uses, the opinions one expresses, an enthusiastic manner, a happy personality, one's appearance, a strong handshake—they're all part of the portrait. Are you making your points in a modest fashion? The winning edge is one's appeal to the hirer.

When I was doing college basketball play-by-play at Madison Square Garden, I talked to players and coaches at practice and before games to pick up personal notes I could weave into the telecasts.

Whenever La Salle University was playing in a basketball tournament at the Garden, I always spent a few extra minutes with Bill Raftery, one of their stars. Bill always had a twinkle in his eye, a sharp sense of humor, and a joyful manner that made for lively talk. Quite simply, he was fun to be around.

"Bill," I said one day, "what do you plan to do after you graduate?" When Bill said he hadn't decided yet, I said, "Come work for me as my statistician on college and Knicks games. Pick up some dollars and learn the TV business."

Bill did both, becoming one of the nation's longest-running and best-liked analysts in the business. He has become a fixture on college basketball telecasts, including many of the most high-profile contests in the NCAA basketball tournament.

No résumé required, no audition necessary. I figured if he appealed to me, an average person, he'd appeal to the general public. I was right. Bill was hired because I enjoyed his company.

well their releases were written and then asked how many people read them. The answer was that they did get some space in the local papers, but not enough.

"How about radio?" I came back with.

"No, that's been a problem."

"Well," I said, "that's why I'm here. If you hire me, I'll guarantee to get your release material on the radio. In fact I will even rewrite it for the air and announce it myself."

"Can you guarantee it will be heard?"

"Absolutely."

"Then if we can meet your price, you've got a deal."

Now I had both a radio deal and a source of material—and two sources of income. Then came an unexpected occurrence. Playing baseball that freshman season, while caught in a rundown play between bases, my spikes got caught in the dirt. As I tumbled, I heard a sharp crack. I had broken my ankle. My leg was put in a long cast and my season was over.

WDNC was broadcasting the Duke games and others throughout the state. Folks at the station had heard my radio show, and I was asked to join their broadcast booth to comment on the baseball action. As I was already on the air doing well with my own program, moving into live sports action was an easy transition for me. My champion was WNDC's talented sports director, Woody Woodhouse, a Durham legend, who had taken to using me as a replacement on his sports show when he was out of town. I became a regular on the broadcasts. When the basketball season arrived, I was working a full schedule of night games throughout the state.

When I had been ushering at Quadrangle Pictures, I noted how few people attended the movies on certain nights. Wednesday nights especially seemed to need bolstering, so I came up with an intriguing idea.

"Here's the deal," I told the theater manager. "Just tell me your average attendance on Wednesday nights. All that money is yours. Now add this. Without costing you a cent, I will write, produce, and emcee a program along with a campus band and guest stars that will

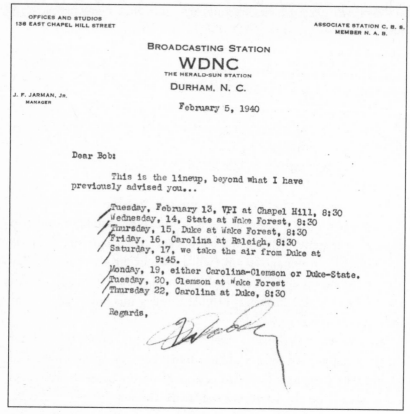

OFFICES AND STUDIOS
138 EAST CHAPEL HILL STREET

ASSOCIATE STATION C. B. S.
MEMBER N. A. B.

BROADCASTING STATION

WDNC

THE HERALD-SUN STATION

DURHAM, N. C.

J. F. JARMAN, Jr.
MANAGER

February 5, 1940

Dear Bob:

This is the lineup, beyond what I have previously advised you...

Tuesday, February 13, VPI at Chapel Hill, 8:30
Wednesday, 14, State at Wake Forest, 8:30
Thursday, 15, Duke at Wake Forest, 8:30
Friday, 16, Carolina at Raleigh, 8:30
Saturday, 17, we take the air from Duke at
    9:45.
Monday, 19, either Carolina-Clemson or Duke-State.
Tuesday, 20, Clemson at Wake Forest
Thursday 22, Carolina at Duke, 8:30

Regards,

Sportscasting schedule while at Duke

fill your theater every week. We'll split whatever money is taken in after you recoup your average Wednesday night attendance receipts. Let me repeat this," I said. "We split the new profits and it doesn't cost you a cent!" And so was born Bob Wolff's *Your Duke Parade*. It played to a capacity audience every week.

It's amazing how one step can lead to another. My next step was back to WDNC. I sold them the broadcast rights to *Your Duke Parade*.

Now for the music. I promised the two bands on campus I'd let them each appear on different dates. The number one band was Dutch MacMillan and the Duke Ambassadors. They performed on the debut show. The other band was Phil Messenkopf and his Blue Satans, a take-off on the

Your Duke Parade flyer

Duke Blue Devils name. They didn't get as many outside engagements as they would have liked, and came to me with a business proposition.

Phil wanted his band to be a regular feature on the show, which was now being heard throughout the state. Phil suggested that I front the

Bob emceeing Duke Parade show

band while he was playing the piano. I accepted and soon I was getting calls from state organizations for dance bookings or to emcee functions bringing some of my Duke acts as a stage show. Phil suggested paying me to front his band on a regular basis and also handle its bookings. I told Phil I'd consider this, but first I wanted to speak to Dutch, who was a good friend. I didn't want to intrude on his business.

I told Dutch I was proud of our association together but that I also wanted to give Phil some regular dates, too, if he didn't mind. Dutch said "absolutely." He then added, "Bob, just get me enough bookings so people know I'm still around. I'm so booked now that it's difficult to go to all my classes, too, so don't worry about the numbers."

Dutch played a clarinet while leading his band and in that big band era was on his way to real music stardom.

I wrote and emceed the *Duke Parade* shows and one night worked out a skit with Dutch that had unusual repercussions. One of my show's features was a quiz segment, in which I asked the audience questions for inexpensive gifts. It was designed more for laughs than prizes. I wrote some lines for Dutch in which he chided me for asking such easy quiz questions. "Do something tough," Dutch cried.

"Such as what?"

"Step up to the microphone and sing the next song," Dutch declared, "now that's tough."

"Okay, Dutch", I replied, "but you have to ask the quiz questions." He agreed.

I warbled a peppy rendition of "Hey, Look at Me Now," and the audience was vigorous in its applause.

The next day, Phil Messenkopf increased his offer to me. In addition to leading and booking, he said he'd like me to sing his band's scat rhythm songs.

"I heard you last night," Phil said, "and it's just what we need."

"Phil," I said, "I enjoy singing. I've done it for years, but I'll do this for you only if you assure me you're asking me because of my ability and not to increase your bookings with me." Phil said it would be an entertainment plus for his band, urged me to take the job, and I agreed to do so. I decided that the two bands would share dates and that pleased them as well. It was exhausting to be a full-time student and to have another career as well, especially with the traveling involved. But it was exciting and rewarding.

And, oh yes! As a band member, I got free meals too, plus my band fees. But did I handle the money and the numbers with all this income coming in? Absolutely not, I hired Bill Smith, an accounting major at Duke, and let him take that responsibility. I also signed other Duke students: Tom Fletcher as show announcer (he went on to a fine professional career using his voice), Bruno Zirato Jr. as my producer (next step for him was CBS-TV producing their network shows in

New York), and Harvey Pollock for publicity and promotion (next stop Hollywood, writing television shows).

At springtime the next year I yearned for baseball again and reported to Coach Coombs, who said he wanted to try me out at shortstop so he could fill a void there while adding more home run power in centerfield.

Coach's assistant, Bill Jessup, was assigned to hit me grounders. One hit a pebble or something, and the ball popped up toward my face. I got my right hand up as quickly as possible to ward off injury. I saved my head, but the little finger on my throwing hand was broken. It still remains swollen.

A bigger scare came a few days later, when I passed out on campus. When I went to the hospital to fix my finger, doctors there had given me a tetanus injection that contained horse serum. After this return to the hospital, I was told by the doctor to never allow that serum to be injected into me again. I understand that horse serum is no longer used in tetanus shots.

I began to think about the possibility of getting to the majors as a baseball broadcaster and was encouraged when I told Coach Coombs that I planned to stay behind the microphone. Coombs liked my decision. "Bob," he said, "you should make it to the majors that way. You're off to a great start and your voice will keep you in the game a lot longer than your arms and legs will." It worked out that way.

Another break was that the Durham papers owned the radio station. The *Durham Morning Herald* and *Durham Sun* gave extensive coverage to my programs. Hugo Germino, the sports editor, ran pictures of me interviewing sports stars and would quote my interviews. Shortly after that, WPTF in Raleigh, North Carolina, wrote to me asking if I had time to be their late night disc jockey. I was flattered, but my sleeping hours had already been cut drastically.

In addition to a prized diploma and a Phi Beta Kappa key, I also had a Duke scrapbook filled with pictures and stories of my professional radio work when I graduated. This was essential to my next big step.

When I graduated in 1942, I applied for a commission in the Naval Reserves as a supply officer and listed my experience at Duke as a show producer and host, as well as an "A" student. I received acceptance as an ensign, still needing to pass a physical and a training course at the Harvard Business School. Before I began Harvard, however, the Navy

Bob Wolff with Babe Ruth

War Bond Rally

PALMER AUDITORIUM

Saturday Evening, September 5, 1942

PROGRAM

MASTERS OF CEREMONIES

JOE LAURIE, JR.

ENSIGN ROBERT A. WOLFF, United States Navy

COAST GUARD ACADEMY BAND
Under direction of CHARLES W. MESSER

COAST GUARD ACADEMY BAND — "Any Bonds Today"

LEWIS B. DOANE, Mayor of New London

ARTHUR L. HJORTLAND, General Chairman of Sales of War Bonds
and Stamps

JOE LAURIE, JR.

MADGE EVANS

COBURN GOODWIN

CHARLES LAUGHTON

VIRGINIA GILMORE

ANN RUTHERFORD

INTERMISSION

BOND RAFFLE

"AMERICA" — Frederick Weld, leading

JIMMY ALEXANDER, Electricians' Mate 3/c, United States Navy

KALUA ISLANDERS

MARTIN BRANNER AND DON FRASER

JITTER BUGS

STAR-SPANGLED BANNER — Frederick Weld, leading

War Bond Rally 1942

sent me to the Naval Submarine Base at New London, Connecticut, to emcee a big war bond show.

The program featured one of Hollywood's greatest actors, Charles Laughton, as well as comedian Joe Laurie Jr., and a group of Hollywood screen beauties including Ann Rutherford and Virginia Gilmore. I guess my entertainment activities in college captured the Navy's attention. I felt so much at ease during the show that I sat on the steps leading to the stage while introducing the Hollywood stars, chatting with the audience, and I was thrilled to receive Laughton's praise after the show. He predicted a bright future for me after the war if I stayed in the entertainment field.

Admiral Nimitz

I never pursued a singing career, but used singing as a fun outlet. While overseas with the Navy in the Solomon Islands, I put together a band of SeaBee musicians and sang with them to entertain the troops.

Post-war, at Madison Square Garden, combining humor with lyrics, for years I composed and sang tributes to dogs on telecasts of the Westminster Kennel Club Dog Show. Famed organist Eddie Layton accompanied me, and sometimes I added my ukulele. There were no critics in this audience. No dogs ever spoke an unkind word about me.

Eddie suggested one year that we put out a dog show album, but I was concerned how many dogs would buy it, so that idea was left at the post.

Bob and the SeaBees

I did once sing and play the uke, though, before a crowd estimated at over 40,000 and a national TV audience. That came in 1995 at Cooperstown, New York, during my induction into the broadcast wing of the Baseball Hall of Fame. There was no clowning on this one. I sang "Take Me Out to the Ball Game"—enthusiastically.

That rendition was heard nationwide, but it was not my first national singing experience. While broadcasting the Washington Senators' games, I organized a group of players called the Singing Senators. All had musical talent. Our highlight was a long session on NBC-TV's morning show, hosted by Dave Garroway. I provided harmony and my uke, and added a professional accordionist,

Singing Senators Howie Devron accordionist, Truman Clevenger, Jim Lemon, Russ Kemmerer, Roy Sievers, Albie Pearson

Julio Moreno, Frank Shea, Bob Porterfield, Len Okrie

Howie Devron. Joining me on the NBC songfest were Roy Sievers, Jim Lemon, Russ Kemmerer, Truman "Tex" Clevenger, and our lead vocalist, Albie Pearson. All had excellent singing ability. On an earlier Singing Senators group, I was joined by Julio Moreno, Frank Shea, Bob Porterfield, Len Okrie and at times Milt Bolling, and Bob Usher. They, too, were well received.

Times were different then. Can you imagine trying to make that happen today? Asking players to join my singing group?

Incidentally, that uke, somewhat battered, like myself, still survives, and still appears at family parties and station outings.

Going to Duke was both fun and profitable for me. It also was a valuable learning experience. It certainly was a springboard to my future career on the airwaves.

The big lesson I learned in those days was that selling an idea in which you're included keeps you in charge and bypasses the process of applying for a job, where you no longer control your fate. Wrapping oneself in salable ideas was, and is, a faster way of working up the ladder.

Bob on uke and Stan Musial on harmonica

Putting the idea first is the system I try to use as often as possible. The singing and emceeing, plus thinking, in entertainment terms, have been valuable assets in sportscasting as well as personal pleasure. I felt ready to perform if the game were held up because of rain.

4: Emotion Is More Important Than Words

Myth: It's still the voice that counts.
Truth: Today it's emotion, complemented by words, that matters.

IT'S SAD TO relate, but in the communications field, words are not as important as emotion. As an English major at Duke, I worked hard to build up my vocabulary. I believed in using synonyms to avoid sameness and bring out the shadings and nuances which would bring a clearer picture to my calls.

Broadcasting baseball, I used to note on my scorecard that a base hit could be slammed, drilled, ripped, blasted, blooped, scorched, creamed, sliced, hooked, crushed, skied, blistered, lined—the list went on and on. Each verb added variety and increased clarity to the description; and, I figured, supplying better specific details might give me an extra edge in my calls. Eventually I discovered that on TV this added erudition did add a little zest to my comments, but others were surviving with repetitive words and phrases which had sufficient impact on the viewers. And on radio, some performed their own signature calls rather than specific descriptive ones:

1. Mel Allen—On home runs—regardless of depth or location—it was "Going, going, gone!" His cry of triumph. Devoid of details, but a most popular call.

What matters most is the tone of the sportscaster's voice. That brings the excitement. Familiar catch phrases are expected to bring a conditioned response as fans welcome the good news they covet. Of course, catch phrases lack reportorial details and overused may weaken the impact, but they do identify the play caller. Being recognized doesn't indicate approval or disapproval but does become a trademark. Word use is not necessary in achieving success as a sportscaster, either on the radio or TV. One has to know what's newsworthy; but particularly on television, a journalism background in English is not required. I don't enjoy admitting this. I'd prefer more emphasis on the verbal art but have long noted, particularly on TV, that the picture tells the story. The sportscaster's emotion and a few well-chosen words enhance the video. Here are a few other examples:

2. **Warner Wolf**, popular for years hosting sports segments on New York studio shows, never varied from two words—his staple products. A home run was preceded by "boom," and on a basketball shot that went in, Warner would say "swish." His voice level would rise with each call and his audience remained loyal. His clear exuberant tone made repetition a pleasant achievement. They don't teach that in journalism school.

3. The years go by and **Dick Vitale** still keeps chirping "Awesome, baby" to signify joy in a pass or an above-average shot. That's all that's needed. "Awesome, bay-bee!" Dick vibrates with emotion and energy—in person as well as on the air. Emotion makes him a winner.

4. **Marv Albert** uses even fewer letters. "Yes!" exults Marv on a made basket. No one can challenge that for brevity.

5. **Michael Kay** on Yankees TV uses two words for a Yankee homer, saying good bye to the disappearing baseball with "see ya."

6. **Dick Enberg** gets by with "Oh my!" **John Davidson**, when he broadcast hockey, "Oh baby."

7. For **Chris Berman**, every home run goes "Back, back, back, back."

8. On Yankees radio broadcasts, **John Sterling** intones as the decibels peak—"It is high—It is far—It is gone!" Whether the fielder leaps for

Chris Berman

it reaching over the fence or whether it soars in majestic flight to a higher resting place is second to the urgent declaration accompanying John's fervor. This Shakespearean rendition with the thunderous burst of triumph in his voice leaves no doubt that the ball has reached baseball heaven. Whether accepted as the greatest accolade or scoffed at as a complete affectation, it's John's own touch. John will even render this for fans on special occasions like a singer warbling his favorite song.

And if it's a game-winner, now referred to as a walk-off homer, John adds "And theeeeeeeeee Yankees WIN!" (Here his voice tremors but dramatically returns with orgasmic exultation bursting out with "Yankees Win" in this climactic moment, mating show business and sportscasting in a remarkable mix.) Is there a self-congratulatory twinkle in John's eyes for the performance, or is he overcome by the passion? Regardless, his call is remembered and replayed although it may not be taught in journalism school.

As a Yankee victory is sealed, John is poised for a closing declaration to bring down the house. "BALL GAME OVER, SERIES OVER," he says, adding with magical, unrestrained glee, "THEEEEEEEEE YANKEEEES WINNNN!" John may even repeat the last three words with greater fervor. An amazing performance. He's found a special niche in sportscasting with vocal hysterics.

I've known John for a long time. He's a holdover from the early radio days when his voice was the key to employment. TV changed that. John's bass-heavy voice was ideal for selling products then. Today TV calls involve higher range voices for rising excitement with more emphasis on content and style.

John was not known for word pictures in those early days but for strong opinions. Like others, he experimented with various sports terms including "bull's-eye" for a basketball shot that went in. This didn't find widespread appeal, so he searched for other words. With Yankee baseball and their ability to win, John found the right simple words to convey the good news to Yankee fans. John could use his stentorian tones to give these words even greater impact. Just add more emphasis and more volume.

His gimmick is pure show business, but, in a corny way, it's amusing and in a sea of sameness, commands attention. The old radio guys used to speak louder in daily conversation and emphasized each syllable to be noticed. John's calls are far more rooted in entertainment than journalism, but they help the Yankees sell tickets and draw listeners. When John's climactic verbal fervor and passion explodes over the airwaves, he's ecstatic. There will also be replays on most sports shows.

Some may laugh at John's method or at his exaggerated style. Journalistically, he's like the punt returner who kept dodging the tacklers all over the field before crossing the goal line. The coach later explains to him how he did everything wrong. "Yes, coach," he replies, "but how was I for distance?"

Here's the important lesson in electronic journalism: it's not the literary value of the words—it's the tone of the sportscaster's voice and the strong emotion, contrived or genuine that gives the impact to the call. John's act serves him well.

John is one of the very few sportscasters today who, in the old radio tradition, can be cited as having an "announcer's voice." It's low and distinctive, well-suited for soap operas as well. Most sportscasters have higher voices, giving them a better chance of letting it rise to a high pitch for the most exciting calls. John makes up for this with the urgency in his tone.

His calls would not win awards for descriptiveness, but delivered with emotion hit an appealing, responsive chord. Do they teach emotion in journalism classes?

And don't worry about your voice if you're just starting out. It's a myth that a beautiful voice is needed. Instead, it's the way you use it—the tone—that counts. One doesn't need a great voice to be a successful broadcaster. If it's distinctive, it's remembered. For an example, check out Chris Russo, formerly of WFAN in New York, now of SIRIUS XM Satellite Radio. Today it's not only how one uses his or her voice, but what the sportscaster has to say. In the long run, the top winners provide the most meaningful or entertaining content. Adding the proper presentation of content puts one in the top echelon.

Sounding pleasant, or excited, or musical, or authoritative—each is a viable option, and the sportscaster has the choice. Too many young broadcasters shriek calls that are more barbaric than informative. Strained voices get laughs, not jobs.

For years, broadcasting five or six hours every day, I developed a technique which I still practice. I sing my high notes—the exciting plays—they reproduce well electronically and the sound is more attractive. It's the tone that counts. Excitement is delivered at a higher pitch with more volume. Like a singer raising his voice, I glide up as the play develops, sustain the high note, then I glide down. Emphasizing each word also increases excitement. I never took a class or course to learn this. Like most others, I learned by listening to my tapes and finding out what worked. Speaking distinctly is vital, but sports talk should also sound natural, not announcer-ish.

I've been fortunate to have been at the mike for some memorable calls. I tried to mix emotion with the right words when I delivered them:

"It's a no-hitter, a perfect game for Don Larsen, Yogi Berra runs out there and leaps on Larsen, he's swarmed by his teammates, and listen to this crowd roar!" That was the story.

"Unitas gives to Ameche. The Colts are the world champions—Ameche scores!" Excitement and words complement the picture. Usually, I give the scorer first. But in this case, when I heard the playback, I was pleased that, by chance, I gave the headline first and the scorer second.

The Knicks two world championship seasons provided memorable calls. I echoed the emotion of the games. Natural emotion.

I try never to prepare climactic last lines in advance, though. I prefer to let the words just erupt naturally. Being natural is one's

Bob on the court at MSG

best weapon. The sound of the call, not the words, provides the impact.

Baseball has by far the most descriptive words to describe the action. Basketball is rather limited by the number of ways you can say a shot went in. Football provides variety with scoring coming via runs, passes or kicks, plus defensive opportunities with fumbles, interceptions, or safeties.

Hockey has the greatest problem. "He shoots, he scores" is all you hear. That doesn't give the sportscaster any variety. Anyone who comes up with a new way of calling a goal can become a pioneer. Of course, there's little time for the call. Howie Rose, calling a game-winning New York Rangers goal in overtime against the New Jersey Devils in Game 7 of the 1994 Eastern Conference finals, simply shouted the goal scorer's name, "Matteau, Matteau, Matteau" with such unrestrained glee that nothing else was needed. Electronic journalism.

My Larsen and Ameche calls, with their brevity, have been featured for many years on highlight records, but further proof that it's emo-

Bobby Thomson, Bob, and Ralph Branca

tion, not content, that counts, is demonstrated by the often-replayed Russ Hodges call of Bobby Thomson's famed 1951 home run.

"The Giants win the pennant, the Giants win the pennant, the Giants win the pennant, the Giants win the pennant!" Hodges roared. That's a pure emotion call, enhanced by hometown exultation. It's electronic journalism. The emotion makes the call—not the literary value of the words. Networks, playing across the nation, want more tempered excitement without the intrusion of rooting. That may be fairer, but it lacks the emotional impact of the local sportscaster.

So is modern sportscasting based on journalism and words, or do tone and emotion matter most?

It's a whole new mix, a new type of game, but the word use that once drew compliments now is complementary to the emotional tone and the new abbreviated word art.

5: A Wolff In Ship's Clothing

Myth: It's best to start in a small town or city.
Truth: You're a lot closer to the top if you start in a big city.

WHEN I GRADUATED from Duke in 1942, the big question was which one of my country's teams I wanted to join—the Army, Navy, Army Air Corps, or Marines.

Serving on a ship seemed most appealing to me, but what would an English major be qualified to do on one? I had rowed a boat in summer camp, done some water skiing, paddled a canoe, and supervised campers at the beach—hardly qualifying considerations.

I checked the positions within the Navy for which I might qualify and came across a department called Navy Supply. "That's tough to get into," a Duke guidance counselor told me. "Most naval officers are called line officers. Just a few supply officers are assigned to each ship, along with doctors, a dentist, and a chaplain, and the smaller boats may not have any." I considered my business capabilities for supply.

At Duke, I battled to get all As in my classes, but was most concerned about my grade in economics. This was an introductory course dealing with topics such as the law of supply and demand. Having earned a good living on campus with my radio and show enterprises, I gambled on taking this course.

The class met at 8:00 AM, and this scared me because only five absences were permitted without losing points from my grade. I was broadcasting Duke or other college basketball games at night at various college sites, and my studying began around midnight. Getting up early was a chore, and I believe my grade was settled one morning when only my athletic ability got me into class on time. The professor always locked the door at 8:05 and the race was on. There was only one way to beat his deadline. With the class on the ground floor, I leaped up on the window ledge, came tumbling through the open window, sending papers and books flying, and meekly muttered, "Sorry about that" as the class roared.

But the professor wasn't smiling. I apologized to him after the class, but knew that I would have to get all As in my other courses to continue my Phi Beta Kappa pursuit. Fortunately, I earned the key after my junior year. I realized quickly, though, that economics would not be a strength and I had been foolish to sign up for it.

But a supply officer must deal with supplies. I felt things like commissary supplies, ship's store supplies, clothing supplies, and perhaps war supplies did not require an accounting degree, and I'd be fairly safe counting how much came in and how much went out.

I thought the Navy might be impressed by all my business dealings at Duke, so I listed those on my application to become a Navy supply officer, along with my experience broadcasting, emceeing, and singing as a professional. I put the form in the mail.

In a matter of weeks I received the big news. I had been accepted as a probationary officer candidate pending my passing a physical and courses at the Harvard Business School. If I passed, I'd be an ensign in the Supply Corps and assigned to duty.

Soon after arriving at Harvard I discovered that my classmates were either accountants or lawyers or thriving young business executives— all well-versed in accounting procedures. Then I observed that supply officers had to be skilled in two categories to pass the Harvard course: how to disburse funds (they were in charge of the payroll) and how to deal with supply problems.

5: A WOLFF IN SHIP'S CLOTHING

I had never dealt with a checkbook before—at Duke I hired an accountant for that. I had neither the knack nor desire to personally handle money, but a lot of that was driven by fear. What would the penalty be if I messed up the Navy payroll? Was ignorance an excuse? I worked my tail off to understand the monetary side of supply that my colleagues already knew, while contemplating the dire results if I failed, which included potential court-martial if I botched the financial records of my shipmates. It could add up to disgrace.

I had made friends with many of my new classmates and the faculty as well—I led early morning calisthenics in the field house—but I needed tutoring in accounting, and I found the right man in Don Watts, a tall track star from UCLA. We were seated in the classroom alphabetically and Don saw my plight and told me he'd help.

To say I needed help is putting it mildly. We had the weekends off, and Don volunteered to remain at school one weekend in order to teach me enough to earn passing grades. How fortunate I was. That was a great sacrifice of his free time. Don worked with me hour after hour until I felt confident that I had learned enough to survive.

"Don," I said, "as a little reward, I'm going to get you a date with the most beautiful girl in New York." Don just smiled at my boast and told me his reward was in watching me learn enough to get through.

I knew no girls in New York City—regardless of size or shape—but I did have one possible contact. I had dated a girl from Alabama who told me she had a sister who worked in New York for a major radio star at that time—Ralph Edwards.

Edwards's program, *Truth or Consequences*, was a long-time network favorite—a quiz show in which winners who determined whether a statement was true earned prizes, and losers had to perform zany stunts as a consequence. The show had a beauty soap sponsor, and although this was only radio—there was no TV yet—models were used to read endorsements of the sponsor's facial product, attesting that it was the reason for their beautiful skin and fine complexion.

After a little reminiscing over the telephone with Edwards's secretary, I explained the predicament I was in and asked if she knew any models who wanted to sacrifice their time for the betterment of two men in the U.S. Navy and go out on a date with Don and myself the coming Saturday night. I refused to call it a patriotic gesture.

The call came back, and it was all set. I thanked the secretary profusely and told her where and when we'd meet the girls, and wrote down the models' names and phone numbers. The two girls were knockouts—Cindy Mathieson and Barbara Salisbury.

On Sunday afternoon, while Don and I were on the way back to Cambridge, his date Cindy was crowned the Press Photographers' Woman of the Year with her picture in all the papers.

On Monday morning, when the word of our dates had spread all over the Harvard campus, there was a line of young Navy officers-to-be all wanting to double-date with me. Don Watts viewed me as Superman. I amazed myself with my luck. And somehow, I passed the final exam.

The biggest breaks were still to come, though. After graduation, I was assigned to Camp Peary in Virginia, as a supply officer with the 11th Special SeaBees Battalion. Assigned with me was a brilliant, personable ensign—Bud Skopil. We'd be a two-man team. One of us would serve as the disbursing officer, taking care of all the money, and the other would handle the supplies. I was fortunate when Bud agreed to do the disbursing. If he hadn't made that decision, I shudder to think of the consequences. Without Bud and Don Watts, my life could have taken a completely different turn.

The big news at Camp Peary was the arrival of a large group of Navy nurses. What a glamorous sight it was when they came into the mess hall. As I looked around, my eyes spotted a beautiful brunette—Jane Louise Hoy—and I was instantly spellbound. Maybe she felt—even from afar—the intensity of my gaze, for she looked back and our eyes met. At that moment I knew that she was the one.

I called on Jane in a visiting parlor at the Nurses Quarters—and became a steady visitor.

In high school and at Duke, dating was always a big game to me. It was like being on stage, attempting to be witty and charming, knowing that my date was trying to do the same. All the time we were assessing each other's strengths and weaknesses, before moving on to somebody else. These surface relationships rarely touched on any topics of substantial value, but with Jane it was different. There was no pretending involved. I felt at peace in her company—just being with her. I was in love. I had found the girl I wanted to marry.

But in a few weeks I'd be heading overseas. Would Jane wait for my return? How long would that be? Would she find someone else while I was away? And then there was the dreadful thought—would I come back?

Jane told me she'd wait, and I was on my way to the Solomon Islands in the Pacific. One of the islands was named Banika, and it would be our battalion's mission to erect a base on this heavily-wooded terrain that would include a landing strip from which our planes would launch further attacks in the war zone. Supplies were needed to build the runway, the base, a commissary, a ship's store, medical facilities, and more—all to be accomplished quickly in tropical heat and ever-present rain. When we arrived, all one could see was a small beach and a forest of trees, plus a large dumping ground with boxes and boxes of supplies, including packaged foods and, somewhere in the mud, requisitions to be filled and reports to be sent to the Supply Department in Washington.

The SeaBees (whose name is a play on CB, short for construction battalion) were remarkable people to work with. Through their construction talents, they made a home out of the jungle.

There were beautiful, magnificently-colored shells on the beach called "cat's eyes" which a SeaBee craftsman would incorporate into highly prized bracelets. When ships came into the harbor, I'd take some of these bracelets and trade them to the well-dressed supply officers on ships for fresh food—meats, milk, butter, vegetables—all they could spare. They took pity on the ragamuffins sweltering on the island. No requisitions were made for these transactions. Our 11th Special paper forms were buried in mud under hundreds of crates we were still sorting out. Life at the time was primitive to say the least.

Solomon Islands Navy assignment

Then suddenly a realization hit me—and hit me hard. All of us taking the indoctrination courses at Harvard had learned how to cope on ships or sitting in buildings in big city supply duty. Nothing had been taught about how to set up, and survive on, advanced bases under the most basic living conditions. New classes were underway at Harvard and the problem still existed.

I believed that dealing with advanced base problems should be recognized in the Navy supply regulations and in the training handbooks, movies, and classrooms. I had our battalion photographer take before-and-after photos of how our camp was being built and wrote an accompanying book detailing new supply procedures mandatory for these advanced base conditions. My battalion commander, Commander Banforth, a former Merchant Marine, would not okay my sending this back to the Department of the Navy, though. "The Navy tells us what to do—we don't tell them," he said.

"Commander," I said, "I can understand your opinion, but this book will go to the Supply Corps—that's whom I report to—just like your doctors and dentists report to the Medical Corps. It's the Supply Corps who should read this—and that's whom I work for."

The commander relented under those circumstances and that's where I sent it.

I knew nobody in the Supply Corps in Washington and nobody there knew me. I had no idea if anybody would read it—maybe it would just be filed or thrown away. Or perhaps someone would ask who this impudent young fellow thinks he is, trying to change the existing regulations?

Two weeks later, I received two letters. Together, they formed the turning point in my life.

One was a letter of commendation for my book. The other, which I carried with me for years, was an airmail order to return to Washington on the first available transportation. I'd be placed in charge of revising Navy supply regulations to include advanced base procedures. My handbook would be published for Navy use. I'd be writing new training material and instructional movies, while continuing assistance related to advanced base supply.

Navy Supply Commander Hugh Haynsworth had read my book; and wanted me to work in his department in Washington. One of the finest gentlemen I've ever met provided the lucky break that changed my life.

Jane was still waiting. Like me, she was now a Navy lieutenant. And she was waiting in Washington, working at the nearby Bethesda Naval Hospital in Maryland after service at the White House. We were married at the Navy Hospital Chapel.

Washington also proved to be the right place to make it to the major leagues. I became the first television sportscaster in the nation's capital in 1946, and the NBA's (then known as the Basketball Association of America) first team telecaster with Washington for the '46-'47 season.

Bob and Jane's wedding photo

The coach was Red Auerbach. Then I became the Washington Senators' first TV play-by-play announcer in 1947. Washington became the launching pad for all the excitement still to come. Overseas or in the States, I'm a firm believer that location is important. And there I was at the right place and the right time.

My marriage, my family, my career—no greater capital gain than that.

A harrowing experience came in the early days in Washington. I was selected to be the host of a nationwide recruiting series for the United States Marine Corps. We would record forty shows, and the Marine Corps Band would be featured with their music. Each program would be a half-hour long. I would introduce the numbers, read their Marine Corps commercials on each show, and supply a recorded interview with a current sports star. My first guest was Bob Feller of the Cleveland Indians.

We would do four shows, one morning every week. I would stand at a mike facing the musicians, about seventy of them, and the Marine Corps would supply the script, including the commercials

I asked the producer an innocent question before my first show. "If I stumble on a word in the commercial, I'm assuming we'll just do it again, right?" I asked. His answer jarred me.

"No, we're pressing the master disc," the producer said. "If you make a mistake, we'll have to do the entire show all over again."

"You mean the musicians will have to play again all their music on the record—every number?"

"Yes, that's right."

Bob Feller

"Why can't you keep all their music and just put in my second-try commercial?"

"Sorry, can't be done."

The musicians were ready to begin. Major William F. Santelmann, the bandleader, was poised to get the show underway. I had no further recourse.

I did all the shows without a stumble, a bobble, a poor read, a wrong inflection, a deviation from the script—all the shows except one. The pressure kept mounting on each program, realizing that one mistake by me would mean every member of that band would suffer. They'd have to perform every number in the program again with no assurance that I'd be perfect on the second try.

With one commercial to go in the fourth show, the pressure finally got to me. My mouth was dry, my heart was thumping, my forehead was wet with sweat. If there were a finish line, I would have collapsed at the tape. My shirt was drenched. One more commercial was all I needed. I'll never forget the word that did me in—Chapultepec.

I was reading at a brisk pace when I encountered this four-syllable word, the site of another Marine victory, and I emphasized the wrong syllable. It should be "Sha-PULL-te-pec" not "Sha-PULL-TEP-ec". As I said it, I watched the instruments being held by the Marine musicians turn into bayonets—they were now forced to record the entire show over again.

No apology would be sufficient. I asked if we couldn't change the locale to another Marine triumph site and was told, "Not without official clearance and that would take too long."

I practiced the correct pronunciation—and nailed it the second time.

This still remains vivid in my mind—one mispronounced word uttered so long ago. Technology would make this so easy to fix today. So much for the "good old days."

In the long run, though, the technology is there to assist. The sportscaster supplies the words.

6: The Evolution Of Broadcast Partners

Myth: Early broadcast teams were hired as on-air partners.
Truth: Early partnerships were difficult as announcers didn't interact on the air.

T HERE WERE VERY few viewers in the early days of television. Sets were expensive, the picture needed constant adjustment, TV salaries were low, and there wasn't much belief that this new invention would succeed.

It took a few years until the newspapers carried TV show listings. "Test pattern" wasn't an intriguing title, and the big radio stars were staying put. It wasn't until the major radio networks started putting their top stars on television that the medium took off as essential entertainment.

My basic income had come from radio, but I was intrigued by TV's possibilities. I had a full schedule of TV games, plus pre and post-game TV and radio shows and network programs as well.

I've never had more fun. I had complete creative freedom to plan, experiment, test, and produce any show that might attract an audience. At age 26, I was the oldest guy around. No one, no executive—and there were very few—had more experience.

I hired bright, young, energetic guys and girls, high schoolers and collegians—they all contributed—and each show became a wonderful adventure. We were our own audience and we applauded each other. For the most part we were the viewers.

I added a sports program—*The Washington Nationals Show*—using players and the coaches or manager as guests. This show was particularly exciting because I discovered and used a whole batch of films of old-time stars including Walter Johnson. The ball club loved this program because it helped them sell tickets.

The Senators was the original team nickname in 1901. It then became the Nationals as well in 1905. Both names were used. The short version "Nats" could be used for either name. I called my singing group the "Singing Senators" but used both names. We had a local sponsor one year, Senate Beer. You know which nickname they favored. Then we had the National Brewing Company. They preferred Nationals. The team in Washington now is known as the Nationals, but the Senators' tag still has popular appeal because it's unique to Washington.

The sportscasters were the commercial spokesmen on camera; and to safeguard against any problems with their products, the National Brewing Company asked me to practice my beer pouring during my weeks with the team in spring training. They wanted a perfect head on the pour—a beer that could hold its head high in any company. Their product was National Bohemian Beer and their symbol was Mr. Boh.

Each morning, I'd grab a cold bottle out of the refrigerator and demonstrate good form as I held the glass upright and let fly. Tilting the glass would be cheating. In talking about this wonderful, refreshing brew, I had to be looking right at the camera, not watching my pour. This took delicate timing. Too strong a pour would cause the beer to flow over the glass. A weaker pour would mean a flat head.

My confidence grew with each pour. I fact, I became equally proficient with both my right and left hands. I was an ambidextrous beer pourer.

Washington Nationals Show

Opening Day arrived and I was ready—the starting pourer. Out came the first commercial pitch—over the glass, over my clothes, over my scorecard, perhaps over my career. At the post-game meeting, after talk about my nerves—or Opening Day jitters—my young assistant, Joe DiMona, who later became both a lawyer and an author, asked the key question: "Where did the beer come from?"

"From the press box," a cameraman said. "It's stored there." Joe dramatically rendered his decision at our post-mortem meeting.

"Gentlemen," he said, "Bob's pours in spring training were done every day with beer chilled at just the right temperature. The warm beer he was handed today just gushed over and out—as all warm beers do. The solution is to put a small refrigerator in the TV booth and Bob will give you perfect pours." Another happy ending, made even better by a rare Washington win.

• • •

Before TV opened up sportscasting opportunities with the hiring of separate crews for TV and radio, a natural conflict had developed in radio sportscasting, particularly with baseball games, when broadcast teams were put together. This was particularly true at the major league level where the standard policy was to hire two announcers. One was considered "the voice" of the team, while the other had fewer innings to call and no designated title. The two did not banter with each other. The second man was essentially a relief announcer who enabled the lead man to stand up and stretch.

A budget was drawn up and the lead announcer, usually an older veteran, received the larger salary. The two men, neither an analyst, sometimes had different styles. The top man usually broadcast the first and last three innings and the second announcer the middle three. Experience seemed more important to the hirers at the time than the abilities of the broadcasters.

The public, with letters and phone calls, would give their opinions as to which sportscaster they preferred. Advertisers would do the same. Newspaper columnists would weigh in also. The senior announcer would be called on to emcee major team appearances and was sought more often for interviews and guest shots on other shows. In some cases, rivalries developed between the announcers. The second man could hope that, when an opening occurred in some other city, he'd be interviewed for the number one slot. If the two had spoken together as partners on the air, they might have been considered a team instead of separate voices.

6: THE EVOLUTION OF BROADCAST PARTNERS

Some of the well-established announcers, wanting to ensure their status, had clauses written into their contracts that gave them the right to help choose their second man. Invariably, they selected excellent play-by-play men who would be content with a secondary status and salary scale. Many remained as longtime back-ups, well-respected for their abilities, but rarely in the spotlight.

There was no standard way to call the games. Some broadcasters were slow-paced and laid back while others announced at high voltage. There was no "right" method. The older guys were stylists, well accepted in their areas. Younger fellows were closer in style to the top network men, infusing more excitement into their calls. All sportscasters are known for their style. Examples are plentiful. Al Trautwig for versatility, Bob Ley for preparation, Mike Breen for naturalness, Chris Berman for enthusiasm, Walt Frazier for word use, Jim Nantz for poise, Keith Olbermann for passion and Bob Costas for authority.

In St. Louis, Harry Caray was a strong voice. At the microphone, this rabid "bleacherite" would show his emotional reaction at the same time of his call. Harry was completely involved in the game. He was disconsolate after a Cardinal error. "How could he throw that ball away?" he'd scream. "Makes big money and throws the ball away? How can that happen?"

The insignificance of a play wouldn't matter—to Harry every pitch was life and death. He'd shout "ball one" with gusto, as if his life depended on it, and kept this pace up for the entire game. A radiant personality, Harry would lead the fans in singing, "Take Me Out to the Ball Game" for the seventh inning stretch, loud and close enough to the tune. He drank with fans at his restaurant in town and was a major factor in selling game tickets. Harry entertained. St. Louis produced a lot of good baseball broadcasters, but none more memorable than Harry, whose son Skip was a long-time favorite broadcasting Atlanta games, followed by grandson Chip, also popular on Atlanta on Braves' broadcasts.

The Cleveland Indians had two outstanding sportscasters. Both had charm as well as talent. Bob Neal had a twinkle in his eye, a smooth-speaking style and a great rhythm to his calls. Jimmy Dudley had a ready smile and excellent pacing. Both men had big followings.

They could speak to their listeners, but not to each other. I never asked why. I liked both men.

When I called the World Series in 1956, 1958, and 1961, I was one of the two radio announcers and we split the innings, each doing solos on half the game. There was no bantering.

I worked with Bob Neal, a fine play-caller, during the 1956 World Series. In 1958, I partnered with Earl Gillespie. Earl had a warm personality, was always smiling, and was skilled at verbal description. In 1961 I teamed with former pitching great Waite Hoyt, a favorite in Cincinnati for his baseball stories and a play-by-play style that no one else used. Every other sportscaster I've heard call games used the present tense: "Jones winds, here's the pitch, Smith swings, there's a fly ball going out to left field, caught by Green for the out." Waite used the

Larry Doby

past tense: "Jones's pitch was swung at and missed." "Smith has flied out to left." That's more accurate, but not as lively.

The advent of analysts, however, made for greater harmony in the baseball booths. The lead announcer would do the play-by-play. The analyst, usually a former player, would have a separate role—analysis, opinions, commentary on replays—and bantering with the play-caller. That added the touch that had been missing from earlier broadcasts—fun. These partners in the booth were enjoying the games together. Because the analyst now had a separate function in the booth, the rivalry ended. Some networks even began to add a third announcer for commentary.

In New York City today, Howie Rose and Wayne Hagin enjoy each other's company on Mets radio broadcasts. Howie is the senior Mets radio man, but the banter adds to their partnership on the radio.

The Yankees have their radio voice, John Sterling, with his distinctive manner and his stylized approach, paired with Suzyn Waldman, the first female announcer in Major League Baseball. Suzyn, earlier in her career, also did play-by-play, but solidified her hold in the booth as an analyst with Sterling doing all the play-by-play calls. Suzyn worked to learn the finer points of the game and her comments are accepted as authoritative. Like Howie and Wayne, John and Suzyn have loyal followers. There are fewer teams still with two play-by-play announcers on radio and no analysts, but those who remain speak back and forth unlike their early predecessors.

With both TV and radio now, each club requires two full-time play-by-play announcers. And every team has one or more analysts, usually a former big league player, manager, or coach. The Yankees use a group of them for different channels and shows, but it's a harmonious operation as is the Mets. Each broadcaster gets a fair turn on air.

With so many sportscasters, though, and with pictures so important on TV, it's difficult to build one's reputation as the early sportscasters did, especially those with national voices. In the constant battle to build audiences, early hirers began to discover that losing teams needed more than eloquent describers to hold listeners. Former players might sacrifice sound, or grammar, or better word use, but might add certain insights and their names might bring additional appeal.

Once the door was opened, the avalanche began. The early sportscasters could have unearthed a lot of material by speaking to pitchers, catchers, managers, coaches, hitters and fielders and passed along this "inside information," but that didn't happen too often. Some took the initiative and worked on their content, while others watched as many players developed into fine sportscasters.

Now the number one men do all or most of the play-by-play and the second men are not competitors. Instead, they're partners adding analysis, opinion, and banter to the show. Some also do a few innings of play-by-play, mainly on TV. Most of the old second men stayed on radio, but for others, new jobs would open.

Today, with so many baseball broadcasters emulating the national style, local personalities with their unique ways of appealing to their audiences

Suszyn Waldman

remain fond memories of the past. Most of the present sportscasters keep their tones at a more exciting level than many casual old-timers.

When I arrived in Washington, Arch McDonald was a radio fixture at the microphone. He had a genial Southern manner, a low distinctive voice, a slow, comfortable-to-listen-to style, and an easy-going manner which reminded me of his popular nationally-recognized friend, Arthur Godfrey.

In those early radio days, each region with a big league team had a voice that defined how games were to be called. The national style was heard only on the World Series, but it set the standard.

Arch's slow rhythm made good use of pauses. He'd leave the mike to get a swig of water at the cooler, have a few words with someone en route, and return to say "ball one." No one asked Arch to hurry. Pauses became the norm. That was his style and it was accepted as such, completely natural. It seemed well-suited to a team that wasn't moving upward in the standings, a relaxed method that worked well for Arch for many years. Call it easy listening.

There was no need for Washington to hire a public address announcer. On line-up changes, pinch-hitters, and pitching changes, Arch would shift over to the P.A. mike, turn that on, and perform double duty while the radio audience waited.

I would do the entire game on TV along with the pre- and post-game shows. Eventually when the same sponsor took over both TV and radio, I'd do a few innings on radio and Arch would move to TV. We never bantered together on the air. That was the system in those days. It would have been fun to work with Arch on the same show, but it didn't happen that way.

Arch did spend 1939 in New York working beside newcomer Mel Allen, but it takes time to convert a city to a different style and Arch returned to Washington. Chuck Thompson, an esteemed baseball and football broadcaster in Baltimore, eventually succeeded Arch. Chuck had broadcast both football's Colts and baseball's Orioles. Our third man, Bailey Goss, the commercial spokesman for the sponsor, National Bohemian Beer, had a great personality and was a terrific salesman.

Arch MacDonald

Chuck had great pipes and a sense of humor. He was an excellent play-caller, and I loved the fun of rain delays, when we'd trade lines. What I remember also was Chuck's thoughtfulness. One day in Washington, when he was on-air setting the stage for the broadcast, Chuck was handed a paper, scanned it quickly and noted that Washington had just made a major trade. In olden days, the announcer would have read it. This time Chuck handed the paper to me and said on the air, "This bulletin has just come in—a major trade for the Senators. It's only fitting that the voice of the team, Bob Wolff, brings you the news."

That gesture really moved me. Frankly, I didn't care about doing the reading, but the fact that Chuck thought I would meant he understood what a partnership is about. Incidentally, Arch, Chuck, and I share a brotherhood. We're all in the broadcast wing of the Baseball Hall of Fame. And speaking of honors, what a wonderful honor I had in Washington on June 6, 2009. Stan Kasten, the Nationals' president, unveiled a plaque to hang on the home team's TV booth, naming it the "Bob Wolff Suite." It was a beautiful ceremony, and the Nationals won the game.

All the cities in the early radio days had their sportscasting characters. There was Rosey Rowswell in Pittsburgh yelling, "There it goes, Aunt Minnie," for each home run as one heard the sound of a window shattering on his radio calls. His canned recording always worked on time.

Bob Prince was a colorful personality who also had a big following in Pittsburgh. With a low, gravelly voice, Bob added an off-beat humorous touch to a struggling team, even diving from his hotel room window into a swimming pool one day when things got too dull. Bob was different enough to land some network events.

In Minnesota, when the Senators moved there and became the Twins, Ray Scott, a top-notch talent with a terse, effective, clipped manner of speaking partnered with me on TV and radio. But it was our third man, Halsey Hall, a former sportswriter, who stood out,

Bob Wolff Suite

BOB WOLFF'S COMPLETE GUIDE TO SPORTSCASTING

drawing unusual attention. Halsey was known throughout Minnesota for mentioning weddings and births. He knew families, backgrounds, dates, and fans lined up to meet Halsey, tell him their stories, get on-air mentions, and go home happy. Halsey chose his air spots well, hitting the most dramatic times. When the bases were loaded and the game was at fever pitch, Halsey would burst in with a quick birthday congratulations to fifty-year-old Sarah Hornswoggle in Duluth, a wonderful fan, and then get back to the game.

Halsey was at his best with a cigar in his mouth, which he rarely removed, even for birthday greetings. Halsey was a trouper, though. He detested flying and made provisions for that by getting to the airport early and preparing himself at the bar. When we'd get to the plane, someone would shout, "Where's Halsey?" He'd be tracked down and hoisted onto the plane, where he'd sleep peacefully until we arrived at the next city.

Halsey never auditioned for the job. He didn't have to, because he was loved.

7: Watching The Parade Go By

Myth: It's important to speak fewer words on TV.
Truth: The number of words is not vital. It's using words that complement the picture, not which describe what the viewer can see.

I **'VE DONE A** lot of hiring during the years and doubt that mine is the conventional method, but it certainly works for me. If a candidate appeals to me as a person—if he or she is bright, confident, enthusiastic, fun to talk to—if he or she is a member of the human race, that's all I need to make my decision. I'm not concerned about age, gender, pigmentation, or years of experience. Hiring isn't a science—it's a feeling. If I'm thinking of a person for on-air work, and if that candidate has appeal to me, I believe the public will relate to him or her the same way. When I taught broadcasting in the classroom, it took me only one or two classes to determine which students had potential. They were usually the questioners taking notes, the ones who'd come up after class to ask for further clarification of a point discussed, the ones who'd sit within easy listening distance and, in general, exhibit a sincere interest in the subject. A student who comes to class without a notebook or pen does not make a good impression. If a student missed a class, I wanted to hear a good reason. A big problem in grading is determining which counts the most: the effort of the student or the final test score? The bright kid usually has the edge, but many youngsters have talents which cannot be measured by academic grades.

When World War II came to an end in 1945, I still had a few months to serve in the Navy, but the time had come for me to see if I could make a good impression on radio hirers in the nation's capital. I took my scrapbook from Duke University, filled with pictures and stories of my work on CBS Radio beginning in 1939 while still in college, and started to make the rounds of Washington stations that seemed to have an interest in sports programming. I was still in my lieutenant's uniform, but had received clearance to work after closing afternoon hours and to tell prospective employers I could join them immediately, if hired, although I'd still be in uniform until officially discharged.

The first two stations I called on listened to what I had done and read further proof in my scrapbook. Both were interested in hiring me, and I was in the enviable position of asking how they would like to use me. One station, WOL, told me that their sportscaster, Russ Hodges, was leaving Washington to work in New York and that I could take over his assignments. The other station, WINX, the *Washington Post* station, told me they had great interest in doing the Washington Senators broadcasts and planned on buying those rights. I'd do the games, they said, but meanwhile I could begin a nightly fifteen-minute sports show and do play-by-play of college and high school games. The *Post*, they said, would also run ads and stories to announce that I was joining them. Having the *Post's* backing was a major step forward, and I agreed to join them.

I worked with Bill Gold, the *Post's* news director, one of the most talented men I've ever met and one of my closest friends. The *Post* gave me terrific promotion, with continual ads about my nightly show, and I helped with investigative pieces that made their sports pages.

I kept waiting to hear about their acquiring the Washington baseball games, but when news finally came, it wasn't what I expected.

The *Post* told me they had decided to take a different approach. They aimed to become a classical music station with operatic offerings like WQXR, the *New York Times* station in New York. The *Post* would stay in my corner—my sports shows would continue—but I could look elsewhere for baseball play-by-play.

I had heard about a new invention called television. Things always seem to happen for a reason, and looking into the television picture was a prime example.

Les Arries Sr. had a small office, a dream of the future, and an opening for the first sportscaster in Washington's television history when I approached him in 1946 and signed a contract that year to work for him. The station was WTTG, part of the DuMont Television Network. There were very few believers in TV at the time and even fewer with TV sets. There was only primitive programming, and movies viewed TV as a future rival. Sets were too costly, the picture kept jumping around, and with no more than a couple of hundred viewers, sponsor interest was low.

But the station had college sports, then pro football, basketball and hockey, plus a few old westerns—and was ready to accept new ideas. which was right down my alley.

My first show was a quiz featuring a panel of sports celebrities. The clues were voices from my radio recordings used to identify a star guest, and then the guest would appear in person. Sometimes we'd use pictures as clues, drawn by Zang Auerbach, the talented brother of legendary Boston Celtics coach Red Auerbach.

Next came *Wolff at the Door*, which featured a studio audience. This show was comprised of quiz questions with prizes, songs I'd sing (and play on my uke), and sometimes a guest singer, in addition to interviews with celebrities. Then came a big sale, to a sponsor, of another idea: *Bob Wolff's Sports Clinic*—a weekly program about sports strategy with sports films and guest stars. The show was also televised to New York, becoming the first network-sponsored sports TV show. Barney Kraft, president of the Southern Venetian Blind Company, called me on the phone, told me he wanted to be the sponsor, and

1946 Wolff signs on as telecaster for DuMont TV

became a pioneer, too. Each program was introduced with writing on blinds, opening them to reveal the show's title, then the sponsor. I discovered some films of old-time Washington stars like pitching great Walter Johnson for a weekly Washington Nationals Show. The ball club was delighted that it helped sell tickets. I was excited to find that the pitcher called "the fastest ever," even by Bob Feller, used his long arms and a sidearm delivery. He'd throw inside but never used his great velocity to intimidate batters.

My parents would watch my flickering image in the basement of Gimbel's department store in New York where TV sets were on display. I could not afford to purchase one, but my wife would take a bus to the TV station in the Harrington Hotel and sit with the oper-

Wolff at the Door, **early TV show**

ating engineers to watch the show. I had a bigger audience standing in the street, where the sound was piped out while the on-sale TV set in the appliance store showed the video behind the glass window. I believe I received something like $25 a show for those early programs.

To enhance their network value, I'd run a few blocks to the Capitol Theater, which booked vaudeville acts as a supplement to their movie fare. I enticed stars of that day to make their TV debut with me, for experience and to add to their résumés. For most, it was a disappointing experience. Jack E. Leonard, a fast-talking comedian, sweltered under the intense heat of the early TV lights and bolted from the set, shouting, "Put another log on the fire." I never saw him again. Donna Mason, an in-demand singer at that time, perspired so profusely that her mascara ran into her eyes and she almost fell over a few chairs while groping for an exit. Lanny Ross, a singer from Yale whose rendition of the "Whiffenpoof Song" was an integral part of his act, apparently became nauseous from the heat, clasped his handkerchief over his mouth, and raced to the men's room. I never saw him again, either.

While I sat at a desk overseeing this operation, sweat not only ran off my forehead and down my cheeks, it splattered and collected in a pool on my desk. In getting up, my pants always stuck to the chair, and produced an unseemly noise when I arose. I was never sure how much of my pants I had left behind as a souvenir. Within a few years another

Harry Truman

millionaire had been made—the person who figured out how to keep the lights just as bright while reducing their heat at the same time.

My stature grew in the TV field, however, due to my reputation for versatility. In 1949, the presidential inauguration was saluted with the first televised Inaugural Parade. Floats representing each state would travel down Pennsylvania Avenue, accompanied by a multitude of bands, and then turn to go by President Truman and his party in the reviewing stand.

Being a commentator for the first televised presidential inauguration was considered a major assignment and the networks decided to pool their top announcers to cover the parade properly. Each network would take a specific area along the parade route.

In the early TV days, there were no news departments. Each network had a nightly news program and that was about it. There was no staff of reporters and no hook-ups around the country. News was reported by some talented journalists, but it was considered an extra service, not a moneymaker.

For the inaugural telecast, NBC-TV selected Ben Grauer, a widely respected voice. CBS-TV chose a seasoned veteran, Doug Edwards. I was the DuMont TV selection. I later found out why. "We know Bob can ad-lib with the best of them," the DuMont general manager said. "He's our best ad-lib person. He knows Washington, is a good interviewer, has good presence, he'll do well." And frankly that's what calling a ball game is—ad-libbing for three or more hours every day. There's no script.

The moment I got the assignment I was thinking of a plan of attack. As a young veteran of television, no broadcaster had more experience in the field than I had, and I knew it was the picture that counted. Content was the key to complement the picture. I found out where the floats were being made—in the large airplane hangars at the National Airport—and that's where I went every day for a week. Every float had a state theme and showed a demonstration of a state's products or buildings or achievements, which had to be explained. I was prepared to deliver a meaningful narration about what the viewers were watching.

My colleagues from the networks had prepared as they would for radio—to read notes about past inaugurals and presidents, and offer casual observations about the beautiful floats going by.

As the broadcast progressed, more and more the TV director came back to my specific notes about each float. Interspersed were a few of my interviews on camera. I wound up handling the bulk of the air-time, knowing that my preparation was the key to extensive exposure.

My seat was in the open bleachers. The day was chilly and overcast. There were no toilet facilities in sight. My one luxury was that Bill Gold, the *Washington Post* columnist, WINX radio news director and on-air commentator, sat beside me as an act of friendship. Bill was a true expert on the city and its politicians, a journalist with a passion for the story and accuracy. Bill was my insurance if I needed assistance, particularly with identification.

Four years later, I was asked again to do the presidential inauguration—Bill Gold was again beside me. This time, though, I was the lead anchor for the Mutual Broadcasting System, sitting in a newly constructed communications area directly across from President Eisenhower as the floats came by his reviewing stand.

The biggest excitement occurred when a cowboy, twirling his lasso, stood up on his float and, when the president rose to applaud him, let fly with his spinning rope. His lasso circled Eisenhower's upper body, pinning his arms to his sides. Secret Servicemen rushed to untangle the president, who seemed no worse for the experience, but watching that helpless moment was a quick reminder of everyone's vulnerability. I don't anticipate that we'll see that stunt again.

The *Washington Post* sold WINX to Dolly and Billy Banks. They were smart radio operators, but their finances were a far cry from the *Post* operation. Money-saving became a high priority. One of the first announcements was there would be no more personal calls allowed on the telephones. A pay phone would be installed. If an emergency arose and one had to use a company phone, ten cents or more should be left with the engineer on duty. The daily struggle over whether a phone call to a news source was personal or business proved a constant irritant.

One day, my guest was Jim Tatum, the head football coach at the University of Maryland. Just before the show Jim said, he'd like to call his wife to let her know so she could listen in. I told Jim to go to the control room to make the call and tell the engineer he was my guest, while I went into the studio to set up.

The engineer in the control room came up to me after Jim had left and said the coach had left a dime for the station.

"How did he know about the charge?" I asked.

"I told Jim if this was a personal call, he'd have to leave a dime to pay for it. Jim explained that he was going on the air and asked, 'Wouldn't that qualify as a business call?' The engineer said, 'Sorry Jim, it's not my rule, it's the station's policy.'"

The station got the dime, but they lost out on the big money—I joined WWDC and brought the show and sponsor with me. It turned out to be a propitious move. The station aggressively went after sports events and was very promotion conscious. Their general manager, Ben Strouse, was a go-getter and their creative publicity chief, Irv Lichtenstein, was a heavy promoter of my activities which kept expanding with early network TV shows, Madison Square Garden events, and football bowl games. Regardless of my location, I always kept my fifteen-minute radio show going in Washington. I'd comment via telephone from wherever I was and station announcer Bob Will would give scores and the day's sports highlights. Fortunately, the show kept its high rating and its sponsors. I wanted to keep my voice alive in Washington and I liked the people who worked there. When the Senators moved to Minnesota in 1961, I moved with them to do play-by-play of the team, rechristened the Minnesota Twins, but I continued my show via phone to Washington. It was a wonderful relationship for me.

8: There's No Farm System In Sportscasting

Myth: If you're good, they'll find you.
Truth: If you're hungry, go find food. Don't expect room service.

A S A CLASS, today's sportscasters enjoy good-guy status. They're courteous, enthusiastic, have upbeat personalities, and possess personal appeal. They stay around for a long time because they wear well.

The number keeps growing. With a few exceptions, all TV stations and networks—commercial, cable, or satellite—employ sportscasters, both men and women. There's been an explosion in the number of sports covered. There are play-by-players, analysts, studio anchors, reporters, and talk-show hosts at different levels of pay and exposure. The Internet covers sports as well. With fewer newspapers, the electronic world has kept increasing. This is a far cry from the early days of TV and radio sports, but then or now, one has to go after the jobs.

In early radio, there were just a few big names—all giants in the business. The big events to cover were the World Series in baseball, the Rose Bowl in football, and the college football *Game of the Week;* championship fights on radio were also major. The fellows who did these events fought like presidential nominees to hold their spots, and the in-fighting was just as bloody as current political attack ads designed to denigrate opponents. In the battle for audience and popularity, no holds were barred. Phone lines were cut to keep competing stations off the air and name-calling and rumors and innuendos of salacious behavior were constant.

There was no second place. One was either the star or out of the picture.

Two people determined who got the top assignments—the sports director of the major networks and the advertising director of the sponsor. One had to court these people while keeping track of how one's colleagues were doing with them—I had a scouting report of colleagues' activities which was more meaningful than my notes on any ball club. One sports director did some of his hiring at the pub he frequented after the working day. Eager sportscasting candidates who made sure the hirer would get home safely were in line for an air-time reward.

In those days the on-air kingpins were Bill Stern on NBC, Ted Husing on CBS, Harry Wismer on ABC, and Al Helfer and myself on Mutual. I was Al's young sidekick. Mel Allen was the big man on baseball. Radio was the king, but TV was on the rise as a medium for regional sports. I was doing Washington Redskins games on a Southern ABC-TV group of stations while Harry was on the Redskins large radio network.

Boxing had Don Dunphy on radio and Jimmy Powers on TV. Don was a gentleman, modest, a family guy. He made strong, blow-by-blow boxing calls, his voice rising with the action. Jimmy, a New York *Daily News* sports columnist, didn't speak much and let the TV picture tell the story. He would give the round, mention the color of each fighter's trunks, and let viewers watch. On camera, he displayed a friendly smile. The only big sponsor underwriting the World Series, boxing, college football, and other major sports events was the Gillette Safety Razor Company, whose advertising director was Craig Smith.

I competed for all the major events as a television pioneer and a young radio veteran, a freelancer not tied to exclusivity with any one

Al Helfer

organization. I could move among the various networks and do either TV or radio. I'd win many assignments, but when I lost, I'd concede that the fellow who beat me out must have been a great personal salesman with some behind-the-scenes maneuvers that topped mine. Talent was never the issue. Name value was vital then as it is now. Exposure was the path to increasing one's name, and that meant winning the big jobs. I listened to all my competitors very closely and found that Harry Wismer had an excellent, upbeat tone, good pacing, and was a top-notch football announcer. What else did he bring?

When he greeted me at a Washington Touchdown Club dinner, his first words were, "You're doing a great job." The compliment lost its meaning when I discovered he greeted everyone at the dinner the same way.

Harry loved New York, but on every network game he talked about the great work of the Washington Touchdown Club and the fine

George Preston Marshall and Harry Wismer

fellows, by name, who ran it. It was a constant refrain as was his gushing of thanks at season's end when once again he was named the club's Sportscaster of the Year.

Harry was a great salesman. He found that flattery was a big asset. And what better way to use the Redskins games he broadcast on the radio along with his Saturday college schedule than to mention those wonderful people who sponsored his shows and those with whom he hoped to do future business. Working through his checklist for verbal pats on the back, Harry would end plays by noting, "And he's tackled right there on the forty-yard line in front of Ted Andrews, who's doing a great job at Smith and Burns Advertising." Harry showed remarkable dexterity in spotting all these top executives at convenient spots in the stadium. He avoided any media repercussions by extolling on air each writer's merit. Everybody laughed at good old Harry's tactics, except for a few who took exception. It seems that some of those that Harry had mentioned were at the game were nowhere near the

Washington Touchdown Club Dinner
Dinner chairman; Bob Wolff; Joe Ives, Associated Press; Jim Thorpe; Leon
Hart, Notre Dame; Otto Graham, Cleveland Browns; Kyle Rote, SMU;
and Ray Krouse, Maryland

stadium and their surprised wives were beginning to suspect that their
husbands' business trips needed further explanation.

"But dear," the wife would say, "Harry said you were right there at
the game. He spotted you at the forty-yard line."

In time, the references began to lessen—as did the awards.

Harry played his greatest game of one-upsmanship when we both
were in contention to do the telecast of an Army-Navy football game.
I had a lot going for me. I was already broadcasting Navy games, had
done Army football as well, was seen on network TV sports events as
play-by-play caller and anchor, was a fixture on Washington baseball,
Redskins football, and had done network bowl games every year. I
did not emphasize my Navy service as reporters stress impartiality. We
were close to hearing who would get the assignment when I tuned in
to Harry's broadcast of a Maryland football game.

"What a pleasure to have such great citizens, such terrific men as my guests in the broadcast booth today," Harry said. He then proceeded to name a top admiral in the Navy, an outstanding general in the Army, business executives from the Army and Navy athletic departments, and the president of the ad agency whose major sponsors were on the coveted game. Under my breath, I congratulated Harry and accepted an assignment on another network game. Those were the so-called "good old days."

Harry was broadcasting a football game one year, and I assume he agreed to also broadcast the finals of the college basketball tournament which was part of the festive week, as sort of a throw-in. The basketball game was tied at the end of regulation, which meant a five-minute overtime. I guess Harry was new to college hoops because he gave the tie as the final score. Then when someone tipped him off that they'd play a five-minute overtime, Harry was quick to praise the tournament officials for making such a wise decision in letting the game continue to determine a winner. The mistake didn't seem to faze Harry at all. He kept the excitement going and seemed genuinely pleased with the extra airtime. It was an extra opportunity to salute the committee for proceeding with this "new ruling."

Eventually Harry became more salesman and entrepreneur than announcer. His preparation suffered and he eventually gave up the announcing. He brought together investors and with bank support became the club owner of the AFL's New York Titans (now the New York Jets). The Titans didn't draw well, but Harry gave out such inflated attendance figures that laughter at his exaggerations overrode sympathy for his plight.

Talent-wise, however, I always felt and still believe that Harry's football tones made him a deserved network star before his preparation began to falter. In those days, his tactics were viewed by some as part of the selling process. He could have won awards the old-fashioned way.

In those days, network football announcers—there were so few of them—were treated like royalty. It was a big event when a network announcer arrived in a college town. To earn such treatment, one needed to make an impression on the hirers—that's where the assignments came from. That's where the battle was fought. The selection committee included the network's sports director, the major sponsor's advertising chief, and the influential people running the bowl game.

Becoming known to the people in power demanded subtlety in one's approach. Occasional letters, postcards, clippings, and goodwill phone calls were standard follow-ups to reiterate one's interest in a continuing association. Being too pushy could hurt, but still seemed to be a characteristic of many of the early sportscasting stars. One rarely hears that a present-day sportscaster is "temperamental." But "winning is what counts" seemed to be the philosophy of the business then, and upstaging one's partner on the airwaves became a common practice.

In local baseball, one announcer might be the selection of the sponsor, while the other was chosen by the ball club. The station would also have its say. Behind the scenes, the battle for which announcer would get the most innings was always going on. Both prestige and money were at stake.

Today, the economics of the game have changed that. A single powerful sponsor is no longer possible. TV and radio rights have risen so much that it takes multiple advertisers to put on an event. The local stations and the networks now hold the power, not the sponsors. The ball clubs also have a say in keeping their favorite broadcasters in the mix.

During the 1950s and '60s, the Gillette Safety Razor Company was the number one sponsor of network sports. They controlled the sponsorship of the World Series and the Rose Bowl, the two biggest events in sports. The National Football League had a championship but no Super Bowl (until 1967), the National Hockey League was still a regional attraction in those days, and the National Basketball Association was just beginning to receive more national recognition.

Broadcasting the World Series to me was like advancing to the number one spot behind the microphone. I had plenty of network credentials—the college and pro football TV *Game of the Week*, assignments on all the major networks, TV and radio play-by-play of the Washington Senators, and the baseball Game of the Day on Mutual—but I hadn't yet broadcast the World Series. I figured that was my fault. The Gillette executives didn't know me, perhaps had never heard me. Their advertising director was Craig Smith.

I called Craig on the telephone one day to introduce myself and told him I'd love to have lunch with him on the Senators' next visit to Boston to play the Red Sox. Craig agreed, set the date, and also brought with him Al Leonard, Gillette's public relations executive. It was a delightful experience. While trying to be as modest as possible, I wove in details of my work ethic, achievements, humorous baseball stories, opinions, and strategic observations while making sure to inquire more about Craig and Al and the Gillette Company. At the end of the relaxed two-hour luncheon, I felt I had just made an impact with a lively audition.

"So what's your next ambition?" asked Craig.

"My big ambition is to be a World Series broadcaster," I answered.

"Well, here's how they're selected, Bob," Craig said. "One announcer comes from the winning American League team, one from the National, one from either the TV or radio network carrying the games, and the fourth selection will be ours."

"Craig, I don't believe that the Senators will win a pennant in my lifetime so I'm eliminated there," I said. "I've made great strides with the TV and radio networks but they've got many favorites there as well. How does one make the Gillette roster?"

"We're aware of your work, Bob, and you'll certainly be in contention," Craig said. "Just a little something more can make it possible. Stay in touch with us."

That "little something" proved to be the baseball All-Star Game in Washington in 1956. Gillette wanted to use a Washington announcer, and I was Gillette's selection.

The broadcast went so well, and the listener reaction was so good that Gillette told me I had made their announcing team for their future events. Later that same year, 1956, I was at the mike for the World Series, which included Don Larsen's perfect game. That Gillette association continued to blossom. I continued to call many of their major sponsored events, including three World Series, two Rose Bowls, and two Sugar Bowls, but eventually sponsor power faded as rights money rose. It took multiple sponsors to put on a game, and networks regained control of announcer selections as they do to this

Maxon Inc. *Advertising*

12 E. 53RD STREET · NEW YORK · 22

October 16, 1961

Mr. Robert Wolff
3063 Harrison St. N. W.
Washington 15, D. C.

Dear Bob:

We have been inundated with favorable comments on your work in the World Series broadcasts. Your thorough preparation, skillful exposition and baseball know how have never been brought to better use than in the last few days.

From the commercial standpoint you did a splendid selling job for our World Series Encyclopedia.

You may not realize that you have now broadcast more World Series games in the past seven years than any announcer save for Mel Allen and Vince Scully whose choices were made automatic by their connections with championship teams. Since neither the Minnesota Twins nor their predecessors in Washington can be classified as champions, it is evident that you have compiled this record strictly on your own abilities.

May I add my own sincere congratulations for a job well done.

Best wishes.

Cordially,

Joel P. Nixon

JPN/c

Gillette letter from Joel Nixon, Maxon Advertising

day. To continue to do major national events, I joined ABC-TV and then later switched to NBC-TV as their lead play-by-player.

Patience is a great asset, but in sportscasting, unlike baseball, there's no farm system and no scouts. Those who rise usually have to make an extra effort to get noticed.

Howard Cosell, I believe, became the best-known sportscaster of his time, but not the most liked. He believed he should have earned more respect, but Howard delighted in being boorish. He always pushed himself to the front. In a room full of interviewers, each waiting to pose a question, Howard would not only jump in first—he felt no remorse in making an insensitive observation or asking an indelicate question. After one boxing match, Howard asked a battered, swollen-eyed fighter barely able to speak through puffed lips, "How can you consider asking for a rematch after your disgraceful exhibition in the ring? Will you consider retirement?" Howard prided himself on his sensitivity, but his shock questions didn't show it.

One day, just before an NBA press conference was to begin, Howard shouted across the room to a friend, NBA Commissioner Walter Kennedy, "Walter, I'm getting sick of defending you against all your prejudices!" Walter just smiled and said, "I guess Howard has arrived."

Howard would justify his approach by stating, "I'm just telling it like it is."

When we were both at ABC-TV, I was hosting their scoreboard shows, while Howard was reporting and commentating. Only rarely did he use his act on me. One day, he asked me how I could keep saying nice things about the Washington Senators.

"Well, Howard," I replied, "I like to look at the bright side. I'd rather laugh with them than at them."

That was about it. I think he liked my smiling reaction to his statement that, "The public just doesn't understand me." I'd laugh and say, "Too well." For whatever reason, he held his punches with me. I felt that Howard had invented the role he was playing and knew I shared the secret.

His haughty demeanor brought him laughs when guesting on the major shows. Those who served as his targets weren't laughing, though. Eventually, he seemed to tire of playing himself and told me it was time to deal with brighter people—he was considering running for public office. "Do you think our country is ready for that?" I'd say. We'd both laugh and keep walking.

A close friend of Jackie Robinson, known for his friendly jousting with Muhammad Ali and his concern for minorities, Howard became quite upset when he was denounced as a racist for referring to a shifty running back as a "little monkey" during a *Monday Night Football* broadcast.

"Whites always call little acrobatic youngsters playing on bars in the playground 'little monkeys,'" Howard proclaimed afterward. "It's a flattering term. They admire their dexterity."

Howard expected support for his statement, based on his record in matters of race and his subsequent explanation. The problem was he now needed support from those in the media he had ridiculed, and he didn't receive what he had hoped for. The polls were more negative then positive, and Howard's jibes were no longer designed for laughs. Some of his "tell it like it is" tactics were being directed at his colleagues, to the dismay of those at the network who had hired them. There was no laughter coming from his backers. Howard then put his opinions in a book, creating the impression that he had grown bitter. His support had eroded.

Howard Cosell particularly enjoyed overwhelming athletes as an interviewer, and wasn't shy about asking indelicate questions. He particularly enjoyed overwhelming athletes who could not understand his more-than-two-syllable-words. His look, his tone of voice, and his demeanor all showed his distain. His irreverence was either laughed at or feared—but was always well-known.

One night when I was telecasting a game before a capacity crowd at Madison Square Garden, a sudden roar erupted, and I quickly looked around to see what happened. My statistics man whispered to me, "Howard Cosell just arrived." I doubt that any other sportscaster would create such attention.

Howard Cosell, Bill Whitehouse

Howard became an almost comic figure, playing himself. He not only was a regular with Frank Gifford and Don Meredith on *Monday Night Football*, but he also appeared on numerous situation comedies where just the name "Cosell" drew laughs.

Cosell worked without notes and when emceeing luncheons would zing the headliners on the dais with biting remarks that had the audience roaring. If I happened to be an invited guest, I was always baffled by his soft approach to me. I figured either he felt I was unworthy of being harpooned or else he wanted to hold me as an audience as we returned together to the ABC studios where we both were working. I usually listened to his sound-offs with a smile.

I always wanted to tell Howard that he was a sesquipedalian, given to using big words, to see if he knew what I meant, but never got around to it. He was certainly the most famous and infamous sportscaster of his time.

Eventually, the time came for Howard to mellow with age, but the mellowing never happened. How much was act and how much was a perverse nature, we'll never know. He had a completely different approach, however, to the fun and games business, and provided further proof that acting negative, whether natural or contrived, can be a powerful force in receiving attention.

Howard might have saved his image by becoming a more light-hearted elder statesman, but this didn't happen.

He had an amazing ride while it lasted. He invented himself and eventually pulled the plug on his own creation. He did get sportscasters to begin asking more investigative questions, a trend which has continued to this day.

. . .

As a young guy starting out, trying to make friends in influential circles, I began to get first impressions of many stars which belied their on-air personalities.

The legendary voice of the Brooklyn Dodgers, Red Barber, was loved and revered as an all-time great. In a low-key, professional manner, Red stayed in control, setting the pace for his broadcasts by using his soft Southern drawl and picturesque terms to charm his listeners. Red was also strong-willed in his beliefs, and didn't mind straying from the role of enhancer if his views were different than those of his public.

Red would have been better served if his public financial battle with Gillette about his price to broadcast the World Series had been fought behind closed doors instead of in the newspapers. Red would have benefitted if an agent had handled the negotiation as well. I don't remember the exact figure that Red was then receiving for each Series broadcast—it was something like $250 per game—but I do remember that, as a young guy just starting out, I knew that the honor of being selected to broadcast the World Series would automatically raise one's pay level in the future. Just the fun of being selected would have satisfied me. Getting paid any amount would be a bonus. This was the nation's top sportscasting assignment at that time. The public shows little sympathy for sportscasters seeking more pay for what's considered a "fun job."

Doing the World Series for Gillette, I never asked what my fee would be, nor did I ever care. I did know I'd get paid per game and therefore rooted for a long series. Two of the three World Series I broadcast went to seven games. I never rooted for a competing team. Instead, I rooted for the best broadcast I could do and a full series.

In an unexpected surprise at Christmas time, Gillette also sent me a Christmas bonus check, which I considered a liberal gift for my Series work. I found the company to be more than fair.

I had a friend in the radio business who had a long-time association with Red Barber, and he said it might be good business to meet Red in New York and spend some time with him. Back then I was televising the Washington Senators, doing nightly shows in the nation's capital, and appearing on network TV and radio shows. I thought it would be thrilling to meet with Red. I had heard him from time to time, admired his low-key, academic approach and his homey style and knew that he was a powerful figure in the sportscasting business. We set a date and made the meeting early enough in the day so I could fly back in the afternoon in time for my evening broadcasts.

When I arrived, I was greeted by Barber's secretary who told me that Red was tied up for the moment, but would be with me shortly. After an hour or so of waiting, I inquired again and was told he'd be available in just a short while. Lunch hour came and went. Just as I was set to leave for the airport, Red whisked by on his way out the door.

"Sorry, kid, I've been busy," he said. "Give me a call. We'll try again."

That was my only conversation with Red Barber, although I did continue to hear his work on World Series and network shows. He was easy to listen to.

One of the reasons the early sportscasters wanted to work as soloists is that their pacing, repeated day by day, became part of their individual charm. If paired with a sportscaster with a different style—one more exciting, more upbeat—there was always the chance that the new guy's approach might attract fans as well.

In later years, Red switched over to become one of the Yankee broadcasters. Some listeners, used to the other Yankee broadcasters who had a more animated style in their calls, thought that Red was too laid back, perhaps less interested than he was during his Brooklyn days. Crowds had fallen off at Yankee Stadium, and Red believed he was just being honest in showing and commenting on the empty seats, but this was the last thing that management wanted to emphasize or see in Red's broadcast. It wasn't too long before one of those empty seats was Red's. The problem was not honesty—it was discretion. Red continued on public radio, where his popularity remained intact.

My dad had a friend who knew Bill Stern well. Bill had the greatest voice of any sportscaster I've known. He also knew the importance of the crowd's roar on football broadcasts. When turning the dial on Saturday afternoon college football games, the NBC game always sounded the most exciting. That was not by chance. Bill had the mikes strategically placed to pick up the crowd noise and kept the volume high.

One day, my dad called to tell me that his friend had arranged a get-together with Bill Stern, and I was delighted that Bill was looking forward to meeting me. When I arrived, I was ushered right in. Bill couldn't have been more gracious. At that time my career was just starting at Duke University. I was doing college sports events on CBS radio while going to school and was proud of my early advancement on the air.

At the end of a long conversation, Bill told me to keep in touch. If there were any Duke games on his schedule, he said, he might consider using me as a spotter. When I told Bill that I'd like to keep moving up in the sportscasting field, Bill suddenly turned very serious. "Forget that stuff, kid," he said. "Use your education to do something beneficial. Be your own boss, make some money—you don't want to get into this cutthroat business. The odds of making it to the top are too great. That's my advice to you. Forget about it."

Being a young kid, this stuff just rolled off my back—the rantings of a disillusioned man who apparently had some tough times along the way. It certainly had no effect on my aspirations, but I thanked him and left.

When I told my dad of our conversation and Dad told his friend, they both were visibly angered. I told them I enjoyed the experience and my enthusiasm to remain a sportscaster had not diminished.

At that time Bill did a weekly show of sports stories of supposedly true events that were so ludicrous people laughed at them. He'd say:

"And so that first baseman went out late in the day to take extra fielding practice. He wanted to smooth out the ground where the bad hop hit a pebble and had bounced away from him. As he raked the diamond, he found not one, but more pebbles which were sparkling. First base proved to be a gold mine. That first baseman is now a millionaire and in fact owns his own ball club."

Eventually, the network was forced to issue a disclaimer stating that "Some of Mr. Stern's stories are based on hearsay."

One story that wasn't used is this. A few years after Bill advised me against a career in sportscasting, he would end every college football game by saying, "And now stay tuned for Bob Wolff and the 'Camel Scoreboard Show.'"

For the rest of his life, he would begin every new conversation with me by stating his remorse about the advice he gave me. I'd say, "Bill, forget it. If I hadn't been lucky, it would have been great advice."

A few years after that Bill left NBC to move to ABC, where I was united with him in the radio booth as his color man and game analyst. That's my Bill Stern story and it's a true one.

One year Leo Durocher, the former manager of the Giants and Dodgers, was my color analyst on NBC-TV's *Game of the Week*. By this time, Leo had become a Hollywood celebrity. He had married actress Laraine Day, was a fixture in the Dodgers' clubhouse, and was always good for a mention in the gossip columns.

Leo made a strong impression from the first day we met in our TV booth. Impeccably dressed, his first impression was on my hands—one handshake and the fragrance of his lotion remained until the next day. Leo's first words gave me a good indication of what he thought of my baseball background. "Kid," he said, "I want to help you all I can. On each pitch, look at me. I'll hold up one finger if it's a fastball, two if it's a curve."

I had never managed a major league team, but I had a good baseball background myself which now included calling games for the national

Game of the Day. I told Leo how much I appreciated his offer, but that I believe I had mastered that knack. I said I'd call on him for other information when it was needed.

There was no doubting Leo's presence. He was loud and declarative.

Ted Husing was also a fastidious dresser. A "dandy" was the term in those days for those who dressed to the hilt for everyday occasions. An outstanding network sportscaster, Ted was heard coast-to-coast on major football games. His distinguishing characteristic when one turned on the radio was his deep, sonorous, booming voice.

A "radio voice" was a great asset in those days. Voices were deceptive. "Crooners" were in fashion in the music world. Their romantic mike tones conveyed aural images that often were shattered by seeing them in person. Most of these songsters learned the secret of singing close to the mike to make a weak voice sound forceful. Commercial announcers who could stimulate sales through their warm readings were big moneymakers.

Husing spoke a bit more slowly and deliberately than his competitors, emphasizing each syllable as if it were to be preserved forever. His approach to word use seemed to be more elegant than bleacherite. This resulted in unusual extremes. When broadcasting boxing, he would avoid anything as realistic as mentioning blood. Instead, Ted might say, "There's a powerful punch to the nose, and now there's claret pouring forth from the pugilist's nostrils."

Most of his listeners had no idea what claret was, but understood it couldn't be good.

As with most sportscasters, Husing kept his popularity for a long time until he was beset by a severe medical problem. His eyesight was failing, which is a tough blow for a sportscaster who specialized in calling football games.

In those days, big football games were often covered by more than one network and sometimes local stations as well. Once, I was broadcasting an Army game from one booth while Ted was doing the same in another close by. At halftime, I left my booth to get a drink of water, passed Ted's booth and saw that his spotting board was covered by a large black cloth. On my return to my booth, I noticed the cloth was off and there was a large cluster of names and numbers with lights by each one. Ted's close friend, James Dolan, was standing by ready to touch the light showing the name and number of the runner, then the tackler.

Husing, courageously, was calling the game that way. I didn't linger to watch whether Jimmy would write down a figure for yards gained or if Ted still had enough vision to see this, but I knew I had witnessed a major feat of perseverance. I'd heard that the show must go on and I had seen a great example.

In today's world, a small electronic device in front of the play-by-player can post the correct player's number and provide immediate on-screen information such as his name, height, weight, age, and any other needed statistics. Under difficult circumstances, Husing may have been the first to explore and utilize an electronic method. Husing soon thereafter switched his broadcasting career to the studio, where he spun records, made comments, and his tones remained golden. His slow, deliberate sportscasting style, aided by his experiment with lights, set a pace that might at a later time have worked with TV, but he proved on radio to be a sportscaster who made the most of his voice—and his fortitude—to still produce a winning effort.

Another of my part-time partners surprised me. There's nobody in baseball history known more as a showman than Bill Veeck. Popular, creative, loved by fans, Veeck enjoyed nothing more than a spirited baseball conversation. On the airwaves, though, working with me on the TV *Game of the Week*, he spoke so softly I was always concerned that I was overriding him. Bill was flamboyant, but in a low-key way.

Marv Albert is a most exciting broadcaster. Marv perfected a rapid-fire style that was terse and right to the point and which emphasized specific words others might consider secondary rather than long sentences. I've always been an admirer of his work.

When Marv started out, however, he was already well-versed in the eager-to-win tactics which were then the normal course of sportscasting action. I was doing the TV calls of Knicks and college basketball games at Madison Square Garden at the time. I also filled the Knicks halftime show with my analysis and a few on-camera comments from my statistician—former Knicks captain Sonny Hertzberg, a celebrity guest.

A small teenager spoke to me one night before a Knicks game. He looked like he was thirteen or fourteen. He told me he was the Knicks ball boy, but I had never noticed him. Then he told me he was ready to take over the halftime show.

"What do you have in mind?" I asked, trying to be pleasant, but surprised by his offer.

"I'm the head of the Jim Baechtold Fan Club—a large organization," he said, "and we'd like to honor him on camera for his contributions to the team. I'll take care of the program for you." Baechtold was a little-used reserve, hardly a halftime story, and here was a teenager, without experience, telling me he would run this event on camera.

I asked the youngster his name, and he told me it was Marv Aufrichtig, which was a little unwieldy for show business. I told him that if we ever did a halftime show on fan clubs, I might consider it, but just honoring one club would bring calls to do the same for other players as well, and I'd prefer not to do that series at this time. I told him my halftime had already been planned, but that I'd keep his suggestion in mind.

I admired young Marv's drive, and his creative approach to getting airtime. In the years to come I also became aware of his outstanding talent, a great style with impact. Marv built a large young audience, and deservedly so, with his radio calls of Knicks games. One night when I was on TV and Marv was on radio in Detroit, the TV cameras were across the floor from the scorer's table and the team benches. We'd show them every time the action moved back and forth. Just before the game began, the radio crew taped a huge sign in front of the scorer's table which our cameras couldn't miss: FOR THE BEST DESCRIPTION OF THE GAME, LISTEN TO MARV ALBERT ON THE RADIO.

Not only did I find the gamesmanship amusing, I also couldn't quarrel with the statement. I had learned in my early TV days that radio descriptions were always more descriptive and delivered with more sustained excitement than the abreviated captioning supplied on TV, where the picture was better than a thousand words. The sign also noted the station and its spot on the dial.

Frankly, though, the reasons so many of my TV calls, including the Knicks championship years, are still used on TV specials is because in the last minute of a close basketball game, or game-turning play in football, or last big out in baseball, I delivered a radio description at an emotional pitch and closed my call with all the excitement a great finish deserved. I knew that when the final score was given, the director would tell me to let the picture take over, showing the ecstacy or the agony. That's a tip I pass on to all sportscasters. The extra words can help make the game even more memorable. There aren't that many chances to close with a flourish. This is one way to do it. But stay calm. Urgency does not need vocal hysterics. Work with the picture.

In the early days, this was routine behavior. Gamesmanship, practiced on the field and in broadcasting as well, was tolerated as a clever way to win without breaking any rules. Pranks were routine business among friends and considered childish but harmless.

I admire Marv's work as the most exciting radio basketball sportscaster I've heard and accepted his little gambit as an amusing bit of gamesmanship.

Spike Lee

9: The Power Of Laughter

Myth: Everyone enjoys a good laugh in the TV business.
Truth: Everyone except sponsors, if the laugh is on them.

THE ABILITY TO laugh well—with a genuine musical laugh, not a forced one—is a great asset in television or radio. It's fun to be around a person who laughs, and partners who do so naturally are tough to find.

Ed McMahon became famous laughing at Johnny Carson's jokes and ad libs. He was the ideal straight man. Most people on the air fancy themselves as witty and humorous, and when they get off a good line they expect a laugh from their partners.

When I came up with a surefire idea for an easy-to-sell TV show in my early years on DuMont, I sold the show to a sponsor—Valley Forge Beer—and hired a young newspaper guy from the *Washington Daily News*, Eddie Cook, who was bright, energetic, and laughed with gusto at my wisecracks. That built my confidence and I noted its entertainment value. Eddie became the straight man—my audience.

When I told the owner of the brewery—Mrs. Corita Sandler—the show I had in mind, it was an immediate sale. In my heart, I knew it couldn't miss. I told Mrs. Sandler we would build a studio set that resembled the tap room in a tavern. There would be tables around me with people sitting there quietly talking, drinking and being served Valley Forge Beer.

I would be center stage at a table right in front of the camera with a microphone hidden in a table decoration. I'd be talking sports on this nightly fifteen-minute sports show with a glass of Valley Forge beer in front of me which I would drink intermittently throughout the show. I'd be speaking to the camera and to my right hand man, Eddie Cook, about the day's sports events. Eddie would ask me for my views on the daily happenings, and the repartee would bring out the fun of the game. Eddie's robust laugh would be a plus, and his enthusiastic guzzling of the beer would be a great commercial asset.

In addition to the public, a few of our station's employees would sit at tables. I'd also mix in some celebrity guests, who would sit at a miked table. During the show, I'd leave my table to join these guests for a chat before going back to my spot.

Behind me would be the show's greatest attraction—the bar, with a large Valley Forge sign behind it. The WTTG handyman would become an early TV star. He'd dress like a bartender, pour the beer, serve it at the tables, and take care of refilling the glasses.

I told Mrs. Sandler this show would be fifteen minutes each night of pure commercialism with a little sports thrown in—an original program designed for her beer.

Eddie's job would be more than just laughter and asking questions. He loved beer and after every long swallow, he'd extol its merits. "Boy, that's great beer!" And I'd smile and say, "You're right, Ed. It just hits the spot." Valley Forge sponsored the show, and it was an immediate hit.

The show became so popular that fans pleaded for tickets. Station employees vied to be seen at the tables and guest stars lined up to join us. Fans wrote and called in hoping to sit on the set.

One day, Mrs. Sandler herself called me and said her son would be home from college for a vacation break. He loved our show and the way we praised his mom's brew, and he wanted to attend a program.

I said, "Absolutely, no tickets needed. As my guest and friend, we'll have a table for him and I'll chat with him after the program. Have him come up to me and identify himself. His name will be at the door for whenever he can make it."

He arrived one evening. I wasn't aware of his presence and he was ushered to a table. What I forgot was that Eddie had a devilish sense of humor and that night he demonstrated this to the fullest.

The son enthusiastically rushed up to his hero, Eddie Cook, right after the show to congratulate him on how well he expressed his love for the beer.

"Thanks," said Eddie, not knowing who this stranger was. "I appreciate the compliment, but frankly I can't stand that slop. I'm pleased, though, that you like my act. That's nice to hear."

It wasn't nice for the kid's mother to hear. Mrs. Sandler had me on the phone the next day, and it mattered little that I explained what a kidder Eddie was.

I knew that show had nothing left but foam. The beer was going down the drain. Our bartender returned to being a handyman, his TV career over. Eddie Cook returned to the newspaper. Valley Forge stayed with me but only as a radio sponsor, and it wasn't long before Federal regulations came in prohibiting our drinking beer on camera. But if beer drinking on camera ever returns, there's a can't-miss show idea. Just notify your cast in advance of our obligation to the sponsor.

• • •

Being in Washington, and being adventuresome in what I put on the air, the Federal Communications Commission kept a friendly eye on what I was up to.

In those early TV years, the sportscasters also sold products. They were the commercial spokesmen. Eventually, commercials were put on film (and later, tape or disc) and, fortunately, professional commercial announcers were then hired to pitch the products. In those first TV years, though, sportscasters served as spokesmen for beer and

Sponsors enjoy being mentioned

tobacco companies. If the company purchased sports rights, they sometimes used their commercial announcers to do play-by-play of games, whether they knew the sport or not.

In New York, cigarette commercial announcer Andre Baruch used his mellow tones to sell smokes while doing his best to also describe Brooklyn Dodgers baseball games. He had a short season.

I went through a succession of beer and cigarette sponsors in Washington, and in each case I had to survive their concern that I had been the spokesman for a competitor. The ball club had to fight for me, explaining to the sponsor that the baseball contract would be dependent on my calling their games. This finally brought me to accept the title "Voice of the Washington Senators." For years I had resisted this billing, feeling it was unfair to colleagues who also did a few innings on games while I shifted from TV to do a little time on the radio side. Certainly they had a voice in the games and took pride in that. I decided to accept the club's decision when they explained to me that being their "voice" would protect us both if they gained a new beer or cigarette sponsor. The designation made it so I was no longer the voice of any sponsor, but instead the voice of the ball club.

One season, in a prankish way, I went a little too far in my playfulness, or at least far enough for the Federal Communications Commission to make an experiment a one-time only affair. I agreed with their ruling, not because of what happened, but because of what might happen in the future.

My post-game TV sponsor was a local appliance chain, George's TV and Radio. On the show I interviewed the star of the game and went over other scores and highlights. On occasion, I'd bring in other celebrities to be my on-camera guests.

Bill Veeck was then the owner of the St. Louis Browns. It was tough for Veeck to compete with the wealthier and more talented St. Louis Cardinals, so Bill worked to bring in colorful players, some with excellent talent, and create publicity with unusual stunts. One gimmick which caught my eye was when Veeck hired a hypnotist to instill in his players a vision of winning that would inspire confidence and produce more victories. The hypnotist was a sports psychologist, Dr. David Tracy.

What a great stunt, I thought. I placed a call to the doctor and asked him to be my guest when the Browns came to Washington. Dr. Tracy agreed. When he arrived I asked if, in addition to describing his mission with the Browns, he would also hypnotize my viewers into going out the next morning and purchasing an RCA television which my appliance sponsor was now featuring. Dr. Tracy said he'd be delighted to do so. In fact, it became material for his upcoming book. On that big night, after our baseball talk in the booth, Dr. Tracy went full screen with a head shot facing the camera, exhibiting a chain around his neck. In a low, sonorous voice, he moved a little pendant on the chain back and forth while exhorting our viewers to go to a George's store in the morning and purchase an RCA TV set. It was a masterful performance—a TV first—using hypnosis in an attempt to sell a product.

I checked the stores in the morning and they did report a slight upsurge in sales. That was a daily occurrence though, as TV sales were on the rise. Then I received a call from the FCC, asking me to explain what had happened.

"Did you hear any complaints?" I asked.

"Well, no complaints, but four or five people called to tell us you had put them to sleep."

"I get that complaint every night," I explained. "It's the late hour and it's my show. It's a bit dull unfortunately—it does put some people to sleep. I'll have to pick up the pace. Thanks for the critique, though. I promise to make it livelier."

To my knowledge, that was the last use of hypnosis on TV. As for the Browns, they still didn't win, even with hypnosis. But they did seem happier losing.

That story made the Washington papers, but earlier I had been on the front pages through no effort of my own. There was a narrow runway leading to my TV booth. When we were on air, we'd pull shut a full-length cloth screen to shut us off from the press box as a notice that we were on air. One night, Howie Williams, then the Senators' PR director, who also did some part-time baseball broadcasting for us, was my post-game guest. Howie came in, sat down, and I turned to the camera to speak briefly about the game and then introduce my guest. I asked Howie my first question while facing the camera and then turned to look at him for his response.

Howie was having a difficult time answering. The screen was open and there were two hands around his throat, strangling him on camera. I never read about that possibility in a communications course, but action was vital. "An unexpected guest," I blurted out, trying to pry off the fingers so Howie could breathe. The nearest cameraman jumped in quickly to assist, and soon our narrow booth was crammed with fighting bodies. It was like one of those old Western brawls we had seen on TV. We could see security men rushing to our aid and hear police whistles screeching.

The station picture went to black. A studio sign came up telling viewers to stay tuned. The drama ended with the intruder being hand-cuffed by police, dragged from the scene, and put into a police car. TV viewers saw him being escorted away.

An officer told us the stranger had kept muttering that he had a message to deliver on the guest microphone. We only noted that the intruder was not acting normally, and in a dangerous way. We never did find out why. What we do know is that the intrusion was covered by the press, and the TV program resumed with our sponsor—an appliance dealer—presenting the police department with a brand new TV set for their heroic work in coming to our aid.

The Sporting News
THE BASE BALL PAPER OF THE WORLD
REG. U. S. PAT. OFF.

Wolff's 'Fan in Stand' Turns Out to Be Nixon

Interview Broadcast at Nat Twin-Bill

WASHINGTON, D. C.

Sportscaster Bob Wolff, who broadcasts the Senators' games over WWDC, scored a real diamond "first" on Memorial Day.

He aired an exclusive interview on baseball with Vice-President Richard Nixon between the first and second games of the double-header between the Nats and Yankees.

Wolff dropped a microphone into the vice-president's box at Griffith Stadium and chatted with Nixon as "just another fan at the ball park."

The interview marked the first time Nixon had been interviewed impromptu from the park, although he has attended numerous Washington games.

Among the many highlights revealed in the interview were that Nixon is a Washington rooter and that the double-header was the first game seen by his daughter.

Proceeding in a light vein, Wolff did not introduce the vice-president by "name or occupation" when he first put him on the air. Until the "kicker" came in at the conclusion of the broadcast, Nixon was just another "well traveled" fan enjoying a game in the nation's capital.

Excerpts from the interview follow:

WOLFF—Have you had a chance to see many other games this season?

NIXON—Well, I came out opening day and saw the President throw the ball out. Washington lost, but it was a pretty good game. However, I've been watching most of the games on television—and have seen you too, Bob. I saw the game on television which started this winning streak.

WOLFF—I see you brought your daughter with you today.

NIXON—Yes, and she has never seen a baseball game before except on TV. This has been a lucky day for her. She has a baseball autographed by Lavagetto.

'Traveled Abroad in Last Few Years'

WOLFF—I think it's wonderful that you can be here today. Have you done much traveling around the country?

NIXON—Yes, I have been in most of the 48 states at one time or another and have also traveled abroad in the last few years.

WOLFF—Then you have had a chance to see quite a bit of baseball.

NIXON—Well, not as much as I like, but I have seen it quite a bit on TV.

WOLFF—Did you have a chance to do any playing of sports yourself?

NIXON—Well, I'll tell you. I guess the reason why I like it so much is because I went out for the team and never made it, so I like to watch others who can do it.

WOLFF—How long have you been here in the nation's capital?

NIXON—Off and on I have been here about ten years.

WOLFF—Then you're practically a native here now.

NIXON—Yes, I'm practically a Washingtonian by this time.

WOLFF—What sort of work to you do?

NIXON—I work for the government. My boss is President Eisenhower.

WOLFF—And what is your job, sir?

NIXON—Well, I'm the vice-president.

WOLFF—Ladies and gentlemen, our guest has been the Vice-President of the United States, Richard Nixon, and what a thrill and privilege and pleasure to have you on, sir.

NIXON—Bob, it's been a lot of fun and I hope that the fact that we came to this game means good luck for the Senators.

Veep as 'Man in Grandstand'

VICE-PRESIDENT RICHARD NIXON proved to be a regular guy when he submitted to an "anonymous" interview with Bob Wolff (right) between games of the Memorial Day double header in Washington. Wolff interviewed Nixon, accompanied by daughter, Pat, 11, as just another "man in the grandstand" and didn't reveal the vice-president's name until it was over. Nixon showed a surprising knowledge of baseball. The Vice President remained until the finish of the two games.

WWDC "SCORES" ANOTHER "HIT"

Folks get together over WWDC Radio

The post-game show never attained that kind of excitement level again. The next season a new sponsor appeared on the screen, and it wasn't until I interviewed a man-in-the-stands named Richard Nixon that we made front page news again.

But there were two other trying moments. The advertising agency of a later sponsor, Gunther's Beer, planned a creative way for the brewer to salute all the towns on the networks carrying the Washington games. They had cards printed extolling highlights of each town, including libraries, recreation areas, specific build-ings, historical spots, and anything else the local folks would take pride in.

It was a good idea except for one problem: where to insert these mentions in the broadcast. The ad agency preferred a dramatic spot in the game, when the largest audience was listening. With men on base, and the game reaching a climax, I was given a card to read by the agency person in the booth. I quickly scanned the card, handed it back to the hovering ad rep, and whispered to him, "Let me dis-cuss this with you at the first break in the action. I've got a problem with it."

The ad man commanded, "Read it now." When I put it down and called the game action, he stormed out of the booth.

The next morning came a call for an emergency meeting at the agency's headquarters. I was told that what I had done was treasonous, that my job was at stake, that they were outraged. Finally, one said, "Can you explain this intolerable behavior?"

"Gentlemen," I said, "I can understand your feelings. What I did was to protect you, to protect all of us. This promo was to salute Washington and one of its greatest treasures, and my concern was the wording. Let me read it to you." I took out the card, which I had held, and read what was written on it: "Today, I want to tell you about the biggest erection in Washington."

I paused as all of those in the room burst into unrestrained laughter. "Our listeners would have had the same reaction," I said. "We would all have been laughed at. Fortunately, I was able to save us from that.

I'm sure there are better ways and times to describe the Washington monument." The meeting broke up shortly thereafter.

I continue to believe that the national pastime shall mean baseball although the manufacturers of Viagra may disagree.

Later, there was the "drinking on camera" problem again. Another beer, Old Georgetown, had come on the scene and drinking on camera—every half inning—was part of the sportscaster's job. The sponsor had the entire game, which made me fear for my survival.

I felt squeamish telling the sponsor that drinking his beer was a problem, particularly on doubleheader days. I planted a seed, though. How about a designated beer drinker? The idea took hold, and the perfect choice was Johnny Batchelder—a Washington on-air personality, an excellent commercial announcer, and a softball buddy of mine—who loved beer and drank it with a continual smile. He had great stamina, too, though he did need a little propping up during doubleheaders or in extra innings.

"John," I said, "I have a great idea if you're getting woozy. I'll bring a bucket to our booth, and if you have to, tell the folks how great the beer is, take a swig, then hold it in the back of your mouth and spit it out when the red light goes off."

The ploy worked, until one fateful day. As John later explained, "Somehow I thought it did go off. Maybe it was the sun on the camera." It must have been a shock to the sponsor and to the viewers to see John declaring how great the beer was and then watching a stream of suds heading from his mouth towards its new resting place. Old Georgetown, our sponsor, wasn't laughing. And soon thereafter, beer drinking on camera hit the bucket for good.

Today, all that is a memory. Beer drinking is not done on camera. Most commercials are now pre-taped with commercial announcers or actors doing the selling, not the sportscasters. Cigarette commercials are no longer permitted. Sportscasters still do commercials on radio, but rarely on TV, yet do promos for other shows. Advertisers still have power, but networks have now regained dominance. The battle for survival has changed now that there are different hirers to please.

10: Changes In Runs, Hits, And Eras

Myth: It's difficult to change one's image.
Truth: Images keep changing; some by design, some designed by others.

IN THE EARLY days, tabloid warfare carried over to the men on the microphone. Seven newspapers in New York City alone battled for survival. Gossip columnists were major celebrities. Radio sportscasters fought for the few major assignments. Broadway columnist Walter Winchell was also a national radio star with the power to make or break careers with his pronouncements. Television was still in its early stages and top-level sportscasters waged campaigns to hold their dominance with the fervor of old-time politicians. Aggressiveness was considered a prized trait.

Today, there are more sportscasting jobs than ever, yet fewer top power positions. Sportscasters now work together, assist each other and remain friendly while still competing for preferred jobs. Since the radio-only days, television opened up numerous jobs for sports anchors, sports reporters, play-by-play men, and sports analysts. Cable and satellite added to that. Now print is fading and the electronic world has taken over.

Radio and TV added analysts and talk-show personalities and many work in both media.

Networks still have their sportscasting stars, but most employ them for weekend sports shows or special events. There are many more sports to cover—many more major league teams and ESPN and regional sports networks open up more opportunities for young talent. Booth camaraderie is a major consideration for employers who want sportscasters who keep sharing the excitement of fun and games. Networks want to present their viewers with happy faces, and for the most part they do.

Yes, there has been some blood-letting in these difficult economic times. High-priced sportscasters and sports writers, regardless of the quality of their work, are being laid off due to dwindling advertising revenue or declining ratings or circulation figures. Salary slashing is being done unceremoniously, sometimes softened with a going-away package, but little chance of future employment. This is a harsh reminder that sportscasting and sports writing, too, are business enterprises. As practical necessities become more vital than cultural embellishments, artistic enhancement is feeling the pinch. Some are finding new homes on the Internet. In the early years, new sportscasters received terrific publicity. Today most arrive with no fanfare and others that leave do so quietly and quickly. News 12 Long Island is a notable exception. Those who spend time there and then leave are saluted with thank-you ceremonies which are fun and sentimental.

The sportscasting greats of the past laid the foundation for the present. Some are still active and in demand. Many have undergone major personality changes which have added career longevity. Yes, it is possible to change one's image.

Tennis great John McEnroe, though a perennial champion, made unsavory headlines with his boorish behavior, screaming at umpires and line judges. John somehow felt he never got the calls. Now a middle-aged and under-control tennis commentator, John has transformed himself into a mellow, charming gentleman with merriment, not anger, in his eyes. He's a perceptive broadcast analyst. His brother Patrick, a former captain of the United States Davis Cup team, is a fine commentator as well.

Tennis star Serena Williams had built a positive public image with her brilliant play, her professionalism, and the winning style she shared with her talented sister, Venus, but her actions in one match caused unwelcome headlines. Serena has many national sponsors who back her with financial support and benefit from the association. She signed a book contract as well, based on her popularity and good image. Then in a matter of seconds, Serena exploded in a profane outburst on the court, threatening the line judge who called a crucial foot fault against her on match point, ending her semi-final match at the nationally televised 2009 US Open. The national TV broadcast of her distasteful display tainted her image instantly. Serena showed no remorse in her statement the next day as the tide of disapproval grew stronger. But two days after the incident, she posted an apology on her website—addressed to the line judge, her opponent (and eventual champion) Kim Clijsters, the USTA, and tennis fans.

We live in a forgiving society and Serena recovered. With the apology, her sponsors and book publisher were able to breathe easier. Image restoration takes time, effort, and atonement in some unselfish manner. It also demands the desire to go all out to do so.

No personal image exploded more than that of Tiger Woods. His multiple infidelities devastated his marriage and his sponsorships. His skills as a golfer draw acclaim, but the strain on his image will be difficult to eradicate.

The public rarely gets to know the athlete or the entertainer outside of what they view on TV or read about them in the press. Same is true of sportscasters. That's why a TV incident is so important. It receives such widespread exposure that it overrides any daily activities which may merit applause, but rarely receive it. Sportscasters seem to be held at a higher standard than movie stars who are constantly in the gossip pages. Sportscasters concentrate more on conveying news than making it.

Some safe bets for athletes are to always congratulate the winner, never alibi a loss, admit mistakes without blaming others, apologize if necessary, and do all of these things without being prodded to do so, in a sincere tone. As everybody makes errors or mistakes sometimes, the public understands. The memory of an unpleasant incident may remain, but forgiveness is a possibility. There's almost always a chance to atone in some way depending on how serious the transgression was. Words will never be enough if a career or a life is involved.

One small tip for athletes being interviewed. The sportscaster will use your first name, yet most interviewees do not respond by using the interviewer's first name. Don't know or don't care? It sounds friendlier if they know and use the first name, but don't guess. It would be disastrous if a wrong name were used, so don't gamble.

A most dramatic complete image change was made by boxer George Foreman. Early in his career, Foreman was known to be surly and non-communicative. He maintained a continually menacing expression, a keep-away-from-me attitude, and shied away from interviews. He transformed himself into a witty, smiling, obliging interviewee who was constantly in demand for a fun-filled mike session. I'd watch George go down a line of thirty reporters at a big fight and give each three or four minutes of can't-miss material. He emerged not only as a network commentator, an amusing analyst, but as a multi-millionaire with his George Foreman barbecue grill. Was his sudden personality change due to a spiritual awakening or was it a wise business decision? Whatever, it was a remarkable and most beneficial turnaround of his life.

In Washington and later in New York, Richard Nixon was my guest on sports shows and watched my work on TV. He was a keen observer of sport techniques, an excellent evaluator of talent, and delighted in selecting his all-time baseball team.

In our conversations, Nixon was a relentless questioner, trying always to gain knowledge, to answer questions with specific facts, not generalities. He'd ask me about batting averages, pitching records, who had the best curve ball, the fastest fastball, and then sprinkle this new-found knowledge into his on-air answers, amazing fans with his current knowledge of the game.

A Duke Law School graduate, Nixon always sought that winning edge. In 1960, in his famous debate against John F. Kennedy,

I believed Nixon's intense preparation would give him an advantage. But Kennedy countered Nixon by coming to the debate equally prepared and certainly more relaxed and personable.

Nixon had a heavy beard and perspired a lot. To counter the dark beard problem, he applied white, clownlike makeup. The trick here is to put on ruddy makeup to take away the shadow and exhibit a healthy glow. That was the Kennedy appearance. Nixon looked pale and haggard, and his perspiration was particularly evident over his upper lip. There was no question about his knowledge, but Kennedy's performance and look made him the winner of this crucial debate and, subsequently, the election.

In the early 1960s, Nixon resumed his law practice in New York. He went to a New York Rangers game with me at Madison Square Garden and again was relentless in seeking knowledge about the hockey rules and players. To run for office again, he had to reinvent his personality to appeal to the voters. He assembled a staff to make that happen in order to win the 1968 presidential election. His paid commercials showed him smiling, laughing and enjoying life. That new personality was vital to his winning the election against Hubert Humphrey.

Richard Nixon

His winning at any cost did him in. The Watergate scandal ended him with his resignation early in his second term. Out of office, he worked diligently to reform his image again, using his quick mind to assist others, serving as an elder statesman. My last interview with him was at Shea Stadium at a Mets' game.

On Christmas Day 1986, the Knicks and Celtics were playing at Madison Square Garden. Marv was on the radio, and I was sitting at courtside with a TV assignment after the game for News 12 Long Island which I had joined in November. The producer of the Knicks' radio broadcast that afternoon tapped me on the shoulder. "This game is running late," he said. "Marv has to be back at NBC to do his nightly sports show and has to leave. Can you finish the game for him if it goes into overtime?"

It was the Knicks against the Celtics—a great rivalry. I knew all the players well. Further preparation wasn't needed. And with time running out, the Knicks, who had been trailing by as many as 25 points, were making an incredible comeback. "Let's go to the booth," I said, delighted to help out.

Red Auerbach and Bob Cousy

The Knicks came back to tie the game. I moved into Marv's vacated spot and John Andariese said, "And now to be with you for the overtime play-by-play, here's Bob Wolff."

That remains one of the greatest Knick victories I've witnessed and the only one I've broadcast as a closer. The Knicks won in double overtime, Marv got to his show on time, and once again, I happened to be in the right place at the right time. So I guess we did work on the same broadcast, but not side by side.

Marv and I worked with many of the same Garden partners during the years—Cal Ramsey, Richie Guerin, Bucky Waters, John Andariese—all talented men.

And I not only filled in for Marv, home or away, when I had available dates, I also did the same for his brothers—Steve and Al. Their talented family includes one of my new group favorites—Kenny. He's versatile in many sports, and one of FOX-TV's top talents.

Bucky Waters, basketball analyst

PART TWO
Doing The job

11: The Importance Of Words

MY INNER DEMAND for perfection has been both a plus and a minus for me over the years. On the plus side, I would never put my books down when studying until I felt convinced I could answer every possible quiz question. But I anguished if I made a mistake, unwilling to accept that, after such intense preparation, this could ever occur.

When broadcasting football games, I knew both squads' numbers so well that, years later, I could still rattle them off, even after a week of going from baseball to basketball (college and pro) to football (college and pro) to hockey. Somehow I never mixed up numbers. The added task was uniform colors, learning both numbers and colors.

Championship games, I knew, would have replays on highlight tapes and films. My concentration could not have been greater. I went through World Series games and other championships plus bowl games without a bobble. This all put a strain on my mind and body, I'm sure, but it was worth it so I could rest easy, knowing I had lived up to my expectations.

Meanwhile, I watched the devaluation of words on the airwaves, in advertising, in print, and in public speaking. I'd hear a news anchor, while speaking of a tragedy, say, "And this organization takes credit for the brutal slaying of these young people." It took years before news directors would figure out there's no "credit" in this; the word is "responsibility." Sportscasters still say, "Jones is credited with the error." Sorry, there's no credit there, either. He's "charged" with the error.

There are hundreds of examples. "It's him," is incorrect. It's "he." "He only has two hits" is also incorrect. It should be, "He has only two hits," changing the misplaced "only."

The problem is so few people care—neither the hirers nor the public—or else this might be improved. Sportscasters are not graded on their word use or grammar. I strive to be on top of the word game, but I believe it's more for personal pride.

After all, sports talk is full of inconsistencies. Popular jargon with repeated use becomes acceptable. All play-by-play description is a split-second after the action—"Jones flies out to left field" not "flew."

Words should be important to sportscasters in speaking on TV and radio, in expressing their views, and in writing their material. More important than sportscasting alone, words should be vital to all communicators, but reading, writing, and speaking courses run well behind business, science, and computer arts in college and high school curriculum. Test results throughout the country confirm that verbal scores are well below those in mathematics. Math and science are now being emphasized more than reading or writing.

For thirty-three years as moderator of the Con Edison Scholar-Athlete Awards in Westchester County, New York, and twenty-three years doing the same for News 12 television in Nassau and Suffolk Counties on Long Island, I have watched what has happened to the SAT scores, which are still vital to being eligible for our awards. There are three phases to these nationally administered exams—perfect scores are 800 for Verbal, 800 for Math, and 800 for Writing. To qualify as a News 12 Scholar-Athlete, one has to receive a minimum total score of 1950, plus be outstanding in athletics, leadership, and school and community service. Each year there are fewer eligible candidates because poor verbal scores keep students from reaching the minimum total. Newspapers fold, book stores close, and computer verbiage becomes more and more abbreviated as young people Twitter away. Top-salaried writers are dropped. Undisciplined bloggers have a way to sound off, with or without facts or fact checking.

SATs, in my opinion, measure only one aspect of learning—academic potential—the ability to understand lectures, grasp significant points, and comprehend textbooks. Due to college admissions criteria, youngsters work feverishly to do well on SAT tests to enhance their enrollment chances at the colleges of their choice. The SATs have more reliability than school grades do. High schools hype scores by posting weighted grades, making a mockery of true academic potential. Unweighted high school grades have more validity.

But rarely will one see SAT scores, or high school or college grades posted in a business office or a doctor's or dentist's office, or anywhere else, because employers' main concern is what one can do to help them, not how one did in school. If one is a performer on air, a sports anchor or reporter—or a sports director or producer—one demonstrates ability in a broadcast, a tape, DVD, or film, or a volume of achievement. Actions are what count.

SAT scores certainly demonstrate potential, but they don't necessarily correlate with success. A smart quarterback may have poor verbal skills, a quick-witted comedian may never have finished high school, a talented actor may read lines well but not be able to compose his own, and high test scores may have little to do with being a great artist, or business executive, or surgeon, or sportscaster. Presidents have had great variance in test scores. A person may be brilliant in one aptitude, but below par in another. Bodies are different, just like minds. Some people have dexterity with their hands, but not their feet. The ACT test, which measures ability in subjects, is making inroads on the SATs. SATs don't measure the most valued traits of many successful sportscasters—personality, wit, voice, conscientiousness, preparation, judgment, personal appeal, and character.

In the early years, there was continual monitoring of radio speech. Mistakes and grammar were corrected so they didn't occur again.

Today, they are rarely noticed. They can still effect hiring, however, if the hirer cares.

I believe that Bob Lorenz on the YES Network has excellent ability to host shows. He has a pleasant manner and a fine personality. He's bright, well-researched, ready for big assignments and can also do play-by-play. His partner is Jack Curry.

Recently, Bob signed off a post-game show by saying twice, "for Jack and I." I kept wondering why some friend didn't tip him off to make it "Jack and me," which is the proper use and so easy to fix.

My teachers, my mother, my colleagues were always ready to let me know of a personal miscue and I was so appreciative. With Bob's potential, this same grooming assistance given to players by a manager, coaches, agents or colleagues is a great plus in growth.

At an early age, when strengths are detected, youngsters should be encouraged to work on them, but for different reasons. Liberal arts courses, which are now plummeting in attendance, are basic cultural courses in reading and writing—courses that bring pleasure to lives. Scientific and vocational courses can result in job opportunities, and that makes them vital. Taking liberal arts and science courses is an ideal solution.

The problem with relying on school grades is that schools have different standards of teaching, grading, and enrollment. Many grades are distorted. A 4.0 grade point average looks perfect until a follow-up phone call reveals that it's 4.0 out of 5.0.

The biggest problem is not the schools, however. Teachers need more assistance from the parents, particularly in the early learning years at home. Without early reading help from parents, kids start school working to catch up. And many teachers have not learned how to communicate their knowledge to their students. That's a separate skill.

Here's a suggestion for young scholar-athletes looking at colleges and considering the communications field. Whether you want to be on camera or behind the scenes, check out what the college offers in practical skills—employment skills. Most colleges offer a multitude of courses involving history or theory, but for a sportscasting job you should include some practical experience working on shows.

Syracuse leads the way in producing sportscasters. Fordham does well, too. Hofstra, Emerson, and St. John's are Eastern schools that provide practical experience. Northwestern has that reputation in the Midwest, UCLA and USC on the West Coast. Missouri does a good job. Oddly, many Ivy League schools do not have communications departments. One doesn't have to be a great scholar to be a terrific director or producer, comedian or technician, or performer, but one has to have a show business knack, a style, an appeal that standardized test scores can't reveal. The fundamental requirement is knowing what an important story is and how to get it on the air or in print with maximum impact. No one does this better on TV than CBS's *60 Minutes*. They pursue stories with meaning. The majority of TV shows are concerned solely with audience size. That's what the business is based on.

Particularly in tough economic times, employers want to know what you can do for them, not what they have to teach you.

For years, one out of every ten applicants would qualify for consideration for our weekly scholar-athlete award. Now only one out of thirty qualifies, and the main reason is that verbal scores have dropped so dramatically. On average, they're now more than 100 points below math scores.

The Internet is now the major source for information, and unsupervised blogs are not subject to tests for accuracy, judgment or good taste.

For many years, the boys held an edge in winning the awards. Now in Westchester and Long Island, the girls outnumber the boys with better grades and more activities. Football has shown the greatest drop-off in grades. Girls now outnumber boys in college acceptances as well.

There are a few exceptions, of course. Youngsters who come from two-parent homes tend to be exposed to books and reading at an early age, but too many growing up without this advantage have a difficult time in coping with schoolwork. Perhaps the overall de-emphasis on reading and concern for words is reflected in what little regard this art is held in sportscasting, in advertising, in movie scripts, and in popular music. Old-fashioned journalistic standards have given way to the more freewheeling ways of electronic journalism.

One other note. Don't judge a college or university course by the number of degrees or books the professor has earned or written. Those accomplishments prove they're learned people, but they don't mean they're good teachers. The ability to hold students' attention, to convey thoughts—to inspire—is a rare art seen too seldom in classrooms. Remember, teachers don't take a course in this; it's just hoped they make each class a true learning experience and not just a dull monologue. A great teacher can make a lasting impression.

And remember, playing sports and the fun of just competing—win or lose—teach character traits not stressed in classrooms. Teamwork, assisting other members of the group, coping with the ups and downs of winning and losing, how to stay fit physically as well as mentally and the fun of sharing a common goal all add to more enjoyable lives. For a lucky few there are athletic scholarships, even pro contracts. Other possibilities are coaching, managing, scouting, sports administration, sports agenting, sports writing or sportscasting. Learning the different sports may give one a future outlet as a fan—perhaps even a listener or a viewer. One doesn't have to play sports to enjoy them.

12: Content Makes The Difference

IF YOUR SPORTS show is the same as all the others you may remain employed; but without being distinctive, what's your selling point? This is where creativity is important. Content can make the difference. It's the proper mating of words and pictures. Just like music and lyrics.

I've watched newcomers come and go in New York, many of them with gimmicks that worked somewhere else. Those that stay remain for a reason. Russ Salzberg worked hard to cover major press conferences in person after arriving in New York City and then made sure to ask tough questions. That brought him a following. Russ has become more declarative in expressing his views over the years. Bruce Beck also gets out of the office to cover stories in person. It's called hustling.

Pete Franklin, who built a large radio following in Cleveland, delighted in making sarcastic comments. His aim was to shock. It was a different approach, but didn't wear well in New York and Pete left town. A clever person, Pete gambled on an act that was unlike his kinder personality. In my one appearance on his show, he couldn't have been nicer.

Bill Mazer, an early NBC radio sportscaster in New York, has a beautiful deep voice and an amazing memory for sport facts and events. On Channel 5 in New York for many years, he was one of the first talk-radio hosts. The NBC Network signed Bill and me as a team for a pioneering national sports-talk show. Unfortunately they couldn't clear enough stations to attract a prospective sponsor, and it wasn't until some years later that national sports-talk radio was tried again. Bill eventually did a talk show on a variety of topics on WVOX, New York.

Former New York Jet John Dockery gained an early reputation as a tough sideline reporter. Jim Gray later did the same. Chris Myers made this his specialty. Now, with talk radio, some sportscasters are even more challenging. Many males on the sidelines have given way to more diplomatic and more attractive female reporters. These sideline reporters, male or female, are on air so briefly there's rarely time to probe anything of a substantial nature. With coaches on the way to the locker rooms, this is hardly the time for long discussions. It does give the interviewer a quick bit of on-camera exposure, though.

Every station looks to hire talent with distinctive personalities. Most who win jobs have verve. They're upbeat, excited, and place an emphasis on being newsworthy. Those with strong personalities have the best chance for success.

Jerry Seinfeld became a millionaire doing a show about "nothing." His "nothings" were the small foibles of today's society and relation-ships, relevant to most lives, in a fast-paced half-hour show with four or five storylines in each program weaving into a laugh-filled con-clusion. "Nothing" is made clever with skilled writing and acting to make it so. Everyday situations strike a responsive chord and trying to solve them can provide the groundwork for laughter. Frills are not needed. The *Seinfeld* sets were a one-room apartment and a booth in a restaurant. *All in the Family* used one living room set; *The Odd Couple* did the same. These were memorable shows that became all-time win-ners. They were creative, well-written programs.

For years, Andy Rooney has done commentaries drawing smiles on topics such as all the lost keys in his desk or the small print listing the ingredients in food products. He pokes fun at ordinary occurrences. It looks easy—but if so, why aren't there more performers who do this?

Andy's style fits for his content. He's Mr. Everyman trying to cope while trying to find something in his stuffed desk drawer.

It takes a lot of creative writing to come up with a short essay each week that is meaningful, humorous, and newsworthy. This is made more difficult because video is not always available to illustrate a viewpoint.

I'm aware of this as I do my 'Points of View' segment every week for News 12. They're all different, but I can't claim they're all prize winners. I try for humor, but intersperse some serious topics that I feel strongly about. I always feel better when I exercise this privilege of rendering an opinion which may help others.

Strong writing is the key to all the legendary programs. Well-crafted humor is a wonderful asset and tough to find. Few sportscasters have the chance to show off their writing ability. Studio sports shows are crammed with scores and highlights—leaving little time for clever writing. Today, sports-talk shows escape the pattern of similarity.

TV has gone through a parade of popular genres—westerns, mysteries, detective stories, beauty pageants, award programs, talent shows, game shows, talk shows, judge shows, and reality programs—that featured a raft of similar shows. Today, the top-rated shows are competitive new programs such as survival shows and talent shows featuring aspiring singers, dancers, and variety acts. Beauty contests like Miss America no longer have the impact they once had. The competitive part of talent shows—who will win—adds the extra dimension of emotion with rooting audiences that bring ratings. With cheering studio audiences, the emcees use the high tones of sportscasters at major sports events. This is entertainment with emotional appeal. The audiences are more involved with the contestants, skilled or otherwise. Emotion provides the extra appeal—just like it is with sports.

Good writing can still be a great asset in rising to the top. Poor writing can send one on their way down. Clever sportscasters can use humor and wise opinions to stand out from the crowd. That's enough to make the difference. There are just a few sports analysts on evening TV sports shows these days. Good content still provides the winning edge.

12: CONTENT MAKES THE DIFFERENCE

For many years, Jack Whitaker was noted for his essays on major sports events. Bob Costas does this effectively as well. Mike Francesa delivers his opinions in a no-nonsense manner. Few sportscasters are given the opportunity or the time to present researched, well-thought-out viewpoints. Therefore, most report what others have said. I've been presenting opinion pieces for more than thirty years. By delivering opinions, I've received Emmy nominations, and awards. The satisfaction, though, is in expressing one's views. I've been given that privilege on SportsChannel, Channel Nine, Madison Square Garden Network, News 12 Long Island, and News 12 Westchester. These pieces are more meaningful than reciting scores and highlights. However, scores and results, if wrapped with comments, can stand out in a telecast.

Remember, if ninety-nine percent of the sportscasters are giving scores, this is a great opportunity to be different in a meaningful manner. And if you can make your point with humor, that has even more impact. Radio sports-talk shows have opened up the doors for more opinions—from hosts, guests, and callers.

Being part of the crowd is important, particularly to young sports followers. Fashion designers sell individualism to keep up with the latest trends. Using celebrities to pave the way, soon all the individualists wear the same garb. Jeans manufacturers made their product the uniform of the day. The new true individualists then become those who haven't joined the pack.

Hats disappeared for men, neckties are no longer required—and sports attire is in. Men's hairstyles and beards reflect Hollywood tastes. Sunglasses, with or without sun, have become a fashion statement. Marketers of sports merchandise keep doing well. Ball clubs want you to wear their uniforms, or shirts or caps. And they've added income with frequent uniform changes.

Keeping up with what management wants and what the public approves of is part of a sportscaster's job. I still wear shirt, tie, and coat when I go on camera, and most network guys still do the same. But this doesn't mean it will remain that way. In the office, dress is more informal. In a selling business, advertisers and stations pay heed to today's styles in fashion and in speech. Performers are well aware of this.

Many older sportscasters use young-age enhancements—hairpieces, contact lenses, makeup, and, I suspect, surgery in a few cases. I wear glasses for reading on camera, but first checked that this was okay with my news director. Most older performers wear contacts. On location, it's strictly ad-lib without glasses. My hair is still my own, although there's less of it than there used to be. Hairspray keeps it in place. I use a light makeup in the studio to cover my beard shadow if I haven't shaved for many hours. Powder also helps.

More important than makeup, though, is good lighting. Well-placed lighting directly on one's face can eliminate wrinkles, while poor overhead lighting can add unflattering years to one's appearance. On location, in booths at ballparks, lights are also used if one is in a darker place, especially at night. Makeup is optional, but light is always needed. Some powder is usually sufficient, put on with a soft brush. It helps to take a look at oneself in the monitor to check out one's best lighting—before the show, not after.

There are two aspects of sameness I won't tolerate. One is the smoking habit. Smoke dries up my throat and makes me cough. All my allergies start acting up. There's no smoking when I'm on the air. In the early days of television when cigarette and cigar companies were major sponsors, they insisted I take lessons in how to smoke their products and look comfortable doing so. There was no discussion. The sponsors ruled. I complied when I was on camera, but during the broadcast, the area around me was smoke free.

The second lack of tolerance on my part is with swearing. I do not allow curse words to be used around me. I never use them; and I don't want to gamble that one of my assistants will, in some emotional moment, let them slip over the airwaves. I also have an aversion to their lack of originality. Swearers use the same old tired words—the shock is gone. What's left is poor taste. I guess some people use gross words for effect, or because they have a stunted vocabulary, but I have zero tolerance for them. To me, swearing is unprofessional conduct.

One year while teaching at Pace University, tired of hearing obscene language, I assigned my class to come up with some brand new, original, never-before-heard swear words with their own assemblage of letters to be used whenever their passions were aroused in class. The experiment brought us a lot of laughs that year.

The popular term for a game-ending, game-winning hit or home run has now become "walk-off." It's the "in" word for sportscasters. Now I ask you: what sounds more exciting to shout if you're an announcer? "There's the game-winner!" or "There's the walk-off homer!" Walking is such a leisurely activity. What's exciting about walking off in an emotionally climactic moment?

There's no rule that says one has to speak like the so-called in crowd. Holding on to one's individualism is an edge in itself. It's not mandatory that you act "cool."

Public relations professionals thrive on the proper choice of words. Sportscasters do, too.

No salesman will try to sell you "death insurance." "Life insurance" has a better chance.

When I broadcast some bowling shows at Madison Square Garden, I was told never to use the phrase, popular at that time, "bowling alley." An alley, they said, had the feel of a dark street with muggings. Our broadcasts should come from a "bowling center."

When I broadcast the Minnesota Twins during their first year, 1961, their new home was Metropolitan Stadium in Bloomington—halfway between Minneapolis and St. Paul, the twin cities. The ground-rules for announcers were explicit. The team was called the "Twins." Neither city should be given preference. There were to be equal mentions of both cities. If I mentioned Minneapolis first one time, it had to be St. Paul the second time. I was reminded, "Never say 'here in Minneapolis' and 'over in St. Paul.'" If I ever mentioned a former St. Paul minor league star, I was to give equal time to one from Minneapolis. The ball club wanted to sell tickets in both cities, and the advertisers wanted to sell products in them as well.

Ford Frick, the baseball commissioner at the time, gave his "welcome to the majors" speech before Opening Day at a packed luncheon in a Minneapolis hotel. The hotel site was determined by a coin flip. Frick's first words almost disrupted the big event. "I want to congratulate you folks in Minneapolis for the great job you've done," he said. The booing was so loud, the commissioner stopped, stunned, and turned to his assistant. "What happened?" he asked. The aide quickly whispered, "Plug St. Paul."

The commissioner had not been briefed beforehand. He came back strong, though. "But this would not have been possible without the full support and creativity from the good folks in the city of St. Paul, renowned for their baseball background, and their willingness to make this a wonderful partnership—brothers—Twins—in every way."

Applause and cheers resounded.

Don't hesitate to check the pronunciation of a guest's name with the guest before the show begins, either. If the name is tricky, have the guest pronounce it before you begin the show. This is an important part of your checklist. Don't ask someone else. Go to the person involved.

Words are important. "Garbage men" would prefer to put "sanitation engineers" on their résumés.

I learned many lessons emceeing dinners, banquets, and ceremonies. I tried to avoid mentioning celebrities in the audience, particularly those in the media—press, radio, or TV. People who typically get mentioned expect it and think nothing of it; those not mentioned, either by design or oversight, have long memories as do their wives and families. They feel insulted by the lack of recognition, as do the stations or papers they work for. You can forget a mention of your forthcoming TV show. I try to avoid mentioning people who are not on the dais; and if they have to be mentioned, it's vital to not only pronounce their names correctly but also get their titles right. Signing off at a season's end can also be hazardous. In thanking people, the one you forget will not forget and may "forget" to mention you for a future assignment. Steer clear of long "thank you" good-byes. On TV, let the credits roll on screen, not from your lips. The people I mention in this book are those I personally had the most contact with—some are stars, some are not. There's no best in this business. It's impossible to define.

With dais introductions, watch out for the use of adjectives. At a luncheon in which I was introducing ten noted ladies in attendance, I knew immediately that I had taken the wrong road when I introduced the first lady, the wife of an important executive, as "the talented Jane Doe."

I knew immediately the trouble I had put myself in. I had nine more women to introduce, which meant I either I had to come up with nine more adjectives or not use any at all, causing all nine to wonder why I had singled out just one as "talented."

It was a losing situation, but a good lesson.

Sportscasting is always a learning experience, however. Styles and techniques keep changing. It's vital to stay fresh; stay current or the parade will pass you by. Yesterday's act may not hold up. Repetition can become boring.

Every time I vote on sportscasters for possible inclusion in the broadcasters' wing of the Baseball Hall of Fame (the Ford Frick Award) I have to remind myself I'm judging them on the style of that time, not the techniques of today. In the early days, the sportscaster just gave the facts. Today, that's just part of it. The enhancements he or she provides are an equally important part of the job.

My early baseball broadcasts, for example, were based on describing the game with few embellishments. Today, identification, vocal presentation, and compelling content all are vital parts of a broadcaster's repertoire. Ad-libbing, in some cases in those early days, was more filling time than giving newsworthy material.

Today, the garnishments include observations, opinions, strategy, stories, statistics, banter with colleagues—sometimes humor—a broader range of entertainment. It adds up to audience appeal. Fortunately, I made the switch to content early in my career. I was aided by a team with a losing record. To hold an audience, I had

With Ralph Kiner at the Hall of Fame Induction

to change the tune. I wasn't going to dwell on records, statistics, or the score of the game—particularly in Washington. If I just gave the score, 10–2, Senators fans knew which team was losing. I came to each game with material designed to hold the audience—to be used if the game needed something more.

Many old-timers have changed techniques to bring the public what it wants to hear. Sometimes having the right partner makes a vital difference. Pat Summerall, a former New York Giants place-kicker, entered the broadcasting booth bringing a low pleasant voice, a youthful collegiate look, and an amiability to fit in with others. It was a positive image. Pat was particularly good at low-key play calling—on tennis and golf in particular—but high-pitched excitement calls were not part of his more reserved personality. Basketball and football demand a more emotional technique to accompany the roar of the crowd.

CBS teamed Pat with John Madden, who gave the analysis of football games with an easy-to-follow, strong, declarative manner that kept viewers from straying from his booming voice. It became the perfect combination with this great oddity—Madden, the color man, the analyst, became the shouter, the role always taken by the play-by-play man, and the play-by-player, Pat Summerall, took on the calmer demeanor and speaking style of the analyst. Either by chance or design, it worked. Together they became the top football broadcast team on the airwaves.

Brent Musburger, like almost all sportscasters who speak well, may have a word or two which are distinctively his style. For years, he's announced the "Chevrolet Player of the Game" at a game's conclusion. Brent speaks like many bleacherites making it "Chev-a-lay" skipping by the "ro" sound as in "Chev-ro-lay." It has acceptance as popular usage, although the "r" is used in commercials. Brent stayed with his pronunciation.

Brent started out his sportscasting career with such dramatic over-play that he seemed to be over-selling the game. Deciding a change was needed, he came back with a completely different approach. This time he used a more natural and very pleasant sound, but was so meek, he provided no vocal enhancement. Brent then resurfaced with an appealing middle-ground level, emphasizing content in well-modulated tones. Brent chose the right games to keep his spot on top network games.

For both the 2011 Rose Bowl and the NCAA college football championship games, Brent apparently decided to concentrate on his strength—his low register, old-fashioned announcer's voice. In order to keep his voice at the same low level, he refrained from vocal excitement and controlled any desire to raise his voice along with the crowd roar.

This dispassionate call, particularly in the championship game, might have seemed too laid back, but from an overall TV standpoint, it was a comfortable viewing experience. And that's because "Herbie" as Brent refers to his colleague Kirk Herbstreit, became an analyst noise-maker, adding vigor and vocal excitement to the method used successfully by John Madden and Pat Summerall, with Pat the subdued play-caller and John the exuberant analyst.

Many football sportscasters call Notre Dame "Noter Dame" instead of correctly pronouncing it "No-tra Dom." Years ago somebody would have cared. Nowadays, not even the sponsor or the university would suggest otherwise. Popular usage gradually became the criterion. I did many "Notra Dame" calls on numerous national football games and some basketball games, too, but received calls and letters regarding "Notre" and "Dom." "Notre" is the French pronunciation, as is "Dom." I called the PR department at the school to find out their preference. They said most people say "Notra Dame", which they like, but they accept "Noter Dame" as well. They added "Fighting Irish" is okay too.

Listening to my own tapes, I discovered poor speaking habits I developed that needed correction. I'd use the word "certainly" as a rhythm word in my speech pattern, as in "he's certainly up for this game." "Certainly" required elimination. "Of course" is another throw-in which I had to throw out. "Of course, you know what I mean" had to be eliminated. Worst of all are "you know" and "and, err." All of these are used to keep the rhythm of a sentence going—but all are unprofessional. Listening to one's tapes is important to note how one's speaking. Shorter sentences are a quick cure to eliminate "and, errs" and the like, which are usually employed as a bridge to the next thought. "You know" is part of a speech rhythm. Become conscious of this habit and it can be eliminated, never to return. It's important to break this habit before job-seeking. It can mar one's chances for employment. When sportscasting, I go up at the end of every sentence in order to hold the audience's attention for my next sentence. For example: "The Yankees are playing the TIGERS. On the mound for New York is TOM JONES. For Detroit It's SAM SMITH." It makes it more exciting that way. Try it. If you go down at the end of a sentence, so will the viewers attention

I've found that once you become a professional, it's up to you to police your own work. Few dare to suggest or correct. Most don't want to offend you, others don't care, and many don't notice. I listened to all my tapes and worked for purer speech. Don't ramble, get right to the point, speak distinctly, emphasize the key points, hold the audience's attention—this is what top performers strive to do.

Occasionally, changes can't be made. Jim Carvellas, a top-notch basketball announcer for many years, had a low, distinctive, gravelly voice and a slow, deliberate style of calling games. A charming guy, his outgoing personality added to his appeal. Jim had an unusual speaking quirk. When he was covering the Knicks, Rory Sparrow was on the team, and Jim kept pronouncing his last name "Speer-oh."

Jim was not aware of this, but apparently someone had mentioned it to him, and one day he asked me if this were true. "Yes," I said, "but it can be corrected. Here's how to say 'Sparrow' correctly like 'arrow' instead of 'ear-oh': just open your mouth real wide. You're saying 'Speer-oh' with your mouth almost closed and your lips pursed."

Jim practiced this and it made all the difference—but confessed he couldn't hear it.

The next game, he was back to "Speer-ho" again.

"What should I do, Bob?"

"Jim, first of all, don't worry about it. I don't think anybody is objecting. But you're in luck. Rory has an unusual first name—just call him 'Rory' and everybody will know whom you're talking about."

That worked.

Television and radio are businesses, though; and quite aside from word use or grammar that is rarely noticed, standards of ethical conduct have continued to erode. Promos include coarse language, provocative sex scenes, violence, and degenerate conduct as audience grabbers. News shows go from one negative story to the next. The more salacious, the greater the appeal. Sports shows which appeal to families have been violated by the crudest of TV commercials. All this is justified by networks proclaiming "that's what people want to see" or "it's freedom of expression." Too many players have made headlines with steroids, assault, alcohol, drunk driving, guns, and other tawdry charges. Skill models in sports are not necessarily role models, as Charles Barkley has suggested.

Few talk about the responsibility of the media to upgrade their presentations or the importance of good taste. Nor do they admit an utter disregard for the family audience. The line for acceptable sports talk keeps getting lower.

Is anyone battling for the people?

In New York City, three TV sports columnists are serving as watch guards for the public. Phil Mushnick at the *New York Post*, Richard Sandomir of the *New York Times,* and Bob Raissman of the New York *Daily News*. Their concern is quality (word use, content, message) and good taste (high standards)—in short, responsible journalism. Outside the city, Neil Best of *Newsday* and Len Shapiro of the *Washington Post* also work to keep quality high. I know there are many others across the country who also keep the same vigil and exercise similar influence in their areas.

They're the conscience of the sportscasting business; they fill out the report cards for programs and individuals. They have the courage to render judgments—critical or approving—and have the power to stimulate change for the better. Their concern is quality. Remember, audience size does not equate with quality although, occasionally, one can produce both. Audience size, however, equates with profit.

13: Thinking Big Can Bring Big Bucks

I'VE FOUND THAT breaks come from within. Personal motivation to do something is either there or it isn't. Having a creative compulsion to do something different is a great starting point.

I practiced sports as a young kid, in high school and in college, hour after hour, because I wanted to get better and had fun practicing. No one pushed me to do so. I had the urge. I was the same with music: learning an instrument, putting on shows, learning harmony, getting booked on radio shows. My parents never pushed me. Becoming a professional broadcaster at Duke, singing with a band, and producing a campus variety show had nothing to do with the curriculum there. I just went out and did it.

A good idea—one that gets the right audience and attracts sponsors—and a radio (or, in later years, a TV) station will help to make it happen. If you can be program creator, salesman, writer, producer, and performer, you've hit the jackpot. In the early 1960s, I accomplished this on a national TV network, NBC.

At the time, Major League Baseball was not using its present drafting system. The teams all scouted top prospects and then competed to sign them. Bonuses were a big weapon, but so were individual sales pitches. A scout who saw a terrific prospect almost moved in with the parents of the player. The scout was there, game after game, at birth-day parties, family celebrations, graduations—guarding his talented prize, hoping that out of loyalty, he would be the one chosen when the bidding began.

I was doing the play-by-play on NBC-TV's *Game of the Week* with one of my all-time favorites, witty Joe Garagiola, as the analyst. Actually, we did two games a week—one Saturday and one Sunday. Harry Coyle was our director.

One of the most sought-after young baseball players in the nation at the time was Rick Reichardt, who was soon to be graduating from the University of Wisconsin. A hard-hitting, personable All-American outfielder with a large devoted family in Stevens Point, Wisconsin, Rick was being wooed by all the baseball powers.

Who would sign him and how would they entice him? Rick was about to make the rounds to hear the various pitches, along with his advisor, now part of the free-agent business. Rick's parents also accom-panied him on many trips along with the Los Angeles Angels scout, Nick Kamzic, who had joined the traveling team.

Carl Lindemann had recently replaced a TV sports legend, Tom Gallery, as sports director at NBC. I made an appointment with Carl, whom I now reported to as the network's TV play-by-play man.

"Carl," I said, "I want to do a most unusual sports show for the net-work—something that's never been done before outside of a play-by-play event. I want to show on TV an intriguing story in progress without knowing its conclusion at the start. NBC-TV will not only cover the story—we'll be there for the climax of this sports drama as well.

"This is not the usual documentary that takes place after the event," I continued. "This is live on tape coverage of a story still taking place. The climax will be live—a sports TV first. The story is about Rick Reichardt, perhaps the number one baseball prospect in the USA. In the next two weeks he'll have been wooed by the Yankees, the Los Angeles Angels, Kansas City, maybe others—and we'll sit in on what methods they're using to win him over.

"The clubs are using celebrities, athletes, movie stars, entertain-ers, everything they can to show Rick a good time even before the

In the TV booth for baseball's *Game of the Week*

money offer. Each club will have a sales pitch—the World Series possibility, the caliber of their team, the length of the fences from home plate and the fence height, the city itself—and we'll be eavesdropping as the courtship continues. Then, on our program, we'll broadcast the live announcement of the winner."

"Bob, what do you want out of this?" Carl said.

"Carl, obviously, I'm the show's creator," I said. "That has to be recognized. I also will be the program's producer, the writer, and the host-announcer. I want billing for those four categories and want to be paid for each. I also need to start immediately and need a cameraman to be with me from now to conclusion. On the weekends, however, I'll still be doing the baseball play-by-play for you. The deadline for a decision will be in two weeks. I'll work with the winning club to make the formal announcement live on an NBC Sports Special. That's covering a story as no one has covered it before—you'll be praised for this creativity along with your sports department—and I'm ready to begin right now."

Carl thought it was a terrific idea. He and I agreed on the billing and the four fees, but Carl asked for one concession. "Bob," he said, "I have a great producer, Jack Shugrue. He knows all the technical stuff, the editing, the mood music, and the like. Let him be the producer and you'll be the associate producer. He'll help get you in on time, and you'll also get that production fee."

That seemed like a fine idea to me. I agreed, and Jack showed exceptional talent.

It was going to be an exciting race against time to make it happen, so I started the next morning. I was on my way to Stevens Point with a cameraman to meet with Rick and his parents. His dad was a prominent doctor and both parents were most hospitable. They were proud of Rick's accomplishments, but concerned about which city he'd choose. Rick had an agent, but mom and dad's main concern was their son's happiness, not the size of his bonus.

I filmed an interview with the parents and filmed Rick playing basketball in the driveway with a hoop on his garage. His brother and sisters were delighted to offer on-air comments about their big brother.

Rick was flying to Los Angeles to hear the Angels' pitch, and the cameraman and I made reservations on the same flight. We filmed on the plane to get sound from Rick to add to the realism of the show, and also filmed the Angels' scout. In Los Angeles we hit the jackpot. Angels' executive Roland Hemond had arranged a welcoming party of executives and celebrities at the airport, followed by a big party complete with Hollywood stars and starlets. Rick was a single fellow with movie star looks, and at the party he was the center of attention. Our camera took it all in—and recorded personal comments from the stars as well. We didn't have to ask them. The camera did the attracting. Actor Lee Marvin was particularly elegant in trying to sell Rick on the wonderful life in California.

To add to the drama, I called Charlie Finley, the insurance tycoon who owned the Kansas City Athletics. Charlie established himself as an outspoken owner who would go all out to win, sometimes using show business ingenuity in lieu of bank reserves. I told Charlie that I was calling from Los Angeles where Rick was the new idol of the Hollywood set.

"Are you trying to get Rick, also?" I inquired.

"You bet I am," Finley said. "I've spoken to his parents. Rick's a young kid with family values. He's a Wisconsin kid. He should be in a nice family environment while playing ball—not a wild city like Los Angeles or New York."

"What do you plan to do, Charlie?" I said.

"I've got an offer ready he can't refuse," he said. "I'm going to let him live with us. I've got plenty of room. I'll be flying into Kansas

City to meet him tomorrow for dinner. And I'm bringing my wife with me to show our personal interest. We believe in family first."

The emotion was building. And then I discovered that Rick, prior to my getting involved, had already paid his first visit to New York. There he had been wined and dined by the Yankees and taken on a tour of night spots along with visits to Broadway's biggest shows. I spoke to the Yankees and they exuded confidence. A Yankee executive confided, "Rick's also met some of our players, visited Yankee Stadium with us and expressed great interest in our offer."

"Okay," I said, "here's the deal. If Rick agrees to sign with the Yankees, just give me your word that you'll keep it quiet until we broadcast the press announcement and ceremony nationally on NBC-TV. We'll do this from a hotel like the Waldorf-Astoria, with media invited, and show the entire Reichardt filmed program up to the announcement part. Then we'll go live to introduce Rick, the Yankee brass, players, and the rest to conclude the show. The hotel is better than the Stadium. If we held it at the Stadium, the secret would be out. Everyone will know you've signed him. At the hotel, all we'll announce is the preview of an NBC Baseball special with a most newsworthy ending. It will be a great coup for you and a fantastic program for us."

The Yankees agreed to our plan and were excited about our coverage.

In Kansas City, we filmed Finley's arrival, then taped the As' dinner pitch which emphasized the personal care they'd bestow on Rick. He'd be taken in just like a family member.

Rick and his agent were at the same hotel, ready to fly back to Stevens Point the next day. As a precaution, I had befriended the night desk clerk and asked him to let me know immediately if anything different was happening with the star of my show. Around midnight, I received a phone call. "Rick and his agent have just checked out!"

"Checked out? At this hour? Where's he going?"

"I did overhear them tell the bellman to pick up all the baggage quickly in the room and make sure it was put in the taxi with them. There was mention of a Los Angeles flight. I guess that's it."

There went my New York ending, but not the show's ending. I called NBC-TV in Los Angeles, made sure they'd film Rick's arrival and then cover the press conference which I correctly assumed would follow soon after.

"Make sure the NBC-TV reporter asks Rick if all the beautiful young girls in Hollywood played any part in his decision—and did he expect any marriage proposals after his bonus was announced? And pick up the laughter."

While Rick was smiling and answering "yes" to those questions in a shy fashion—the reaction I anticipated— I was on a plane to Stevens Point to interview Mom and Dad about Rick's decision.

Rick and his agent hadn't gotten much sleep the previous night. First they traveled to Stevens Point to have a past-midnight emotional conference with Rick's parents, explaining their decision to accept the Angels' offer. Then they left for an early morning flight to the West Coast. The parents did not accompany them. When I arrived at their home, the mood was somber. No laughter there.

They, too, had little sleep.

Rick's father summed up what happened. "I guess Rick and the agent thought it out together and thought it was the right thing to do," he said. "It was their decision."

There were no smiles, no celebration. No talk about money. Just parental concern about a lifestyle that differed greatly from the one they had provided their son while he was growing up. I felt a sadness for them that still lingers with me. I recorded this adventure, but the unexpected had occurred.

There was a new ending to the show—but I must admit William Shakespeare got there first. "All that glitters is not gold."

The show was a success, and in retrospect, the new ending had more meaning. Rick Reichardt had a creditable major league career, playing eleven seasons, but never attaining superstardom. His career batting average was .261 and his highest home run total for a single season was 21.

14: Fulfilling A Need

I F YOU'RE JUST starting out looking for an on-camera job in sports television, there are countless ways to create one.

Convince the programming director of any station that you have a program idea for the station. It's even better if you've already discussed this with a possible sponsor and drawn some interest. Basically your idea can fill a vital need that no one else is doing for them. Try for a meeting in person and state the show has sponsor possibilities and explain the audience it would attract.

Choose any of the following for a weekly program. A coach's show, a weekly review of current sports books, magazines and movies, a discussion show of sports issues, a sports technique show demonstrating better ways to win, a sports humor show, a weekly visit to the home of a sports star, a where-are-they-now show about past sports stars, a sports quiz show, a sports business show, a sports law show—all of which you'll organize, produce, and announce. Don't forget advice shows, scouting shows, how-to-play-better-ball shows, inside information shows—sell the idea and you're the one to do it.

The key is that you're not asking for a TV job. Those are tough to get without a résumé. Instead, you're bringing the station something of value. A program and you're part of it.

There are a lot of talented men and women who make a living in TV by creating their own jobs.

Sports Illustrated, in its booming early years before TV and replay took the place of still pictures, hired a personable go-getter named Keith Morris, who used a great weapon—his personality—to bring the magazine great exposure.

I was being seen and heard nationally, regionally, and locally televising all the major sports at the time, and Keith was always calling me to plug a story in the magazine. Keith became a close friend. No one had a more upbeat personality, or laughed more—or worked harder. He was not only my friend—he rapidly became a personal friend of every athlete on every sport team in New York, on visiting teams, along with writers and other broadcasters. Everybody knew Keith.

Keith made his friendships a thriving business for *Sports Illustrated.* Here's how:

When these athletes came to New York with their teams, Keith made sure some were his guests at lunch or dinner or a Broadway show. *Sports Illustrated* picked up the tab. Guests included those who played on the New York teams—Keith was their New York host.

Keith would interview all of them on film without charge, friends glad to oblige, and send these interviews to TV sportscasters throughout the country to be played on all the local shows. All he asked for in return was a mention of *Sports Illustrated.* A logo on the microphone— and a banner in the background would add to *Sports Illustrated*'s exposure. All the stars of the day were now available through their friend Keith and *SI.* The athletes were delighted to do the shows as a favor to Keith, and sportscasters across the nation were getting celebrity interviews without cost.

In addition to entertainment when they came to the city, Keith added the pro stars to his Speakers Bureau. They received large speaking fees and, even more, appeared in well-paid commercials for *Sports Illustrated* advertisers.

Keith Morris single-handedly got continual national publicity for the magazine—all based on his thousand friendships. He made friendship an art and a business.

One day when I was preparing my TV notes for the NBC *Game of the Week* in Detroit, I needed some background information about a player profiled in a previous *SI* edition whom I'd be talking about in the game. This was in the days before computers made answers readily available.

I called Keith to find out, and he told me he'd have an answer in the morning. I asked Keith to call me before eleven at my hotel because I'd be leaving after that time to go to the ballpark to call the game.

At 10:30 AM there was a knock at my hotel door. I opened the door and there was Keith, roaring with laughter at my surprise to see him. He had flown out from New York in the early morning with the material I needed. I believe his main satisfaction was watching my reaction, but the chances are he would also spend time there promoting *Sports Illustrated*.

Keith was an avid hockey fan. So was Joel Nixon, one of the finest TV producers I've ever known and one of my all-time favorites as a person. Once, when I was broadcasting a New York Rangers game in Montreal, both made the trip with me just for the fun of it and joined me in the TV booth—assisting with notes, spotting, compiling statistics, and handling any other chores that developed. I enjoyed their company, and Keith also had a chance to visit with the Canadian announcers, combining business with pleasure. Wherever Keith went, that was his business office.

I did come up with a radio scheme that served Keith and myself very well. For years I had a nightly fifteen-minute radio sports show in Washington, along with my nightly TV show and game broadcasts of the ball games plus pre- and post-game shows. I suggested to Keith that he might want to incorporate some of my daily interviews into the *Sports Illustrated* show he was sending around the country. Keith liked the idea.

I said, "Keith, after I give you my interviews, feel free to edit out any timely references because with mailing time for your shows you don't want them to sound dated."

Then, I came up with a better suggestion. "Keith," I said, "we can put on a national show and it will cost *SI* only a small telephone bill. Once a week, let's have a conference call with reporters in the major cities, particularly places where news is breaking. We can also use timely interviews if we want.

"You'll be the New York reporter. I'll be the host from Washington and the conference call can be taped in every city on the line with us for their use, too. It will be our personal network show."

"Let's do it," said Keith.

And it was that easy. We did it. The show's name was *Calling All Stars.*

Keith was a true star in the public relations field. He died some years ago and was never replaced by *Sports Illustrated.* That's understandable. Nobody could replace him—as a force or as a person.

It was rewarding artistically and financially to control one's destiny in the broadcast field. At this point, I was creating my shows, writing them, producing them, and hosting them. But I relied on a station or network to air them, sell them, and pay me for my services.

Then it dawned on me. Own the shows and control the finances. Later, sell the shows to the station or network and let them make a profit with their advertising sales. If I owned the material, I could sell the shows to more than one outlet. The greater the number, the greater my profit.

So I formed my own company, Bob Wolff Productions Inc., and did just that. My TV interview shows in Washington—*Dugout Chatter, Tenth Inning, Inside Pitch, Locker Room Lowdown*—and my variety show, *Wolff at the Door,* were all owned, produced, and hosted by me. I hired the cameraman, worked with a film lab, did the selling, and controlled the finances. I was simultaneously doing local and network play-by-play—250 games a year—so it was non-stop work, but it was the wise way to go.

My venture got off to a flying start. In 1954, I began televising Madison Square Garden events for WPIX-TV in New York. I commuted to New York from Washington.

The station's manager was Lev Pope, one of the most-respected men in the TV business. His station also carried the New York Yankees

```
RADIO STATION WWDC AM AND FM
1627 K Street, Northwest
Washington 6, D.C.
STerling 3-3800
From: Irv Lichtenstein
                                FOR RELEASE UPON RECEIPT

SPORTSCASTER BOB WOLFF SIGNED TO TELECAST MADISON SQUARE GARDEN EVENTS
IN NEW YORK AREA; TO CONTINUE WWDC SPORTS SHOWS AND REDSKIN TV GAMES

     Sportscaster Bob Wolff has been signed by TV Station WPIX, New
York City, as one of four announcers to telecast 69 sports events from
Madison Square Garden during the 1954-55 season.
     The sports telecasts will be aired over WPIX, the New York Daily
News station, and a sports network set-up for the Madison Square Garden
events.
     The first telecast will be an ice hockey game Wednesday, October
20th.  Included in the 69 sports events from the Garden will be three
telecasts of the National Horse Show, two telecasts of the Westminster
Kennel Club show, 15 professional New York Rangers hockey games, 23
professional New York Knickerbocker basketball games, 18 New York college
basketball games plus championship playoff games in hockey and pro basket
ball.
     The sportscasters who will work the Garden events are Jimmy Powers,
Bud Palmer, Kevin Kennedy and Wolff.
     From October 20th to January 1st, Wolff will be working three nights
a week (Tues, Wed. & Sat.) from Madison Square Garden.  After January
1st until the middle of March, his schedule in New York will increase
to four times a week (Tues, Wed, Thurs. & Sat.).
     All of the Garden telecasts will be in addition to his nightly
sports commentary over Radio Station WWDC, Washington (6:00 to 6:15
p.m., Mon. thru Sat.) and his Washington Redskins pro football game
telecasts over the ABC-TV network.
     Arrangements have been made for Wolff to fly to New York City,
after his 6:00 p.m. sports broadcasts over WWDC Radio, in time for the
Madison Square Garden events.
```

Signs on with WPIX

games. I told Lev that my company could provide an ideal pre- or post-game Yankees show for his station featuring interviews with all the top baseball stars of the day including shots of them in action discussing their techniques, all produced by my company with me as host. Lev knew my abilities as I was doing all the Knicks, Rangers, college basketball games, and other Garden events for him all winter.

Lev asked for a pilot film. I put together interviews with Ted Williams and Mickey Mantle (I owned the interviews and all the players received my thanks and a small gift and as friends were delighted to do it). And Lev arranged a meeting with the agency for Colgate-Palmolive. They bought the show moments after they watched the screening. It became the Yankees pre-game show.

Working against the clock with the baseball season approaching, I quickly sold the series to the Boston Red Sox as their pre-game show and to the Kansas City A's as well. In Kansas City, I also hired their topflight announcer—Merle Harmon—to film a local opening for each program. Some years later, when I was doing ABC's studio pre- and post-game shows for college and pro football, the network needed another sportscaster to do the West Coast version of the show. I suggested Merle, whom I liked as a person as well as a talent. He got the job and kept moving up the sports ladder to become one of the nation's top play-by-play men.

When the indoor season was over at Madison Square Garden, and before the American Football League was formed, I put together a football package for Lev Pope which he also bought for WPIX. The Tri-State area had some great semi-pro teams comprised of former college stars, NFL veterans, and some excellent athletes who had good-paying jobs that didn't leave them much practice time but were available on game days. These teams competed in the Atlantic Professional League, playing under lights in nice stadiums and drawing five to ten thousand fans a game. All of the players had starred somewhere along the way. Some hoped to be discovered by the NFL, while others just had a passion for the game.

The teams were comparable in talent and the games were exciting. The players looked like pros—they were the same size, dressed in natty uniforms, played well, and had great vocal support from their community fans.

I put together a league *Game of the Week* package, had a meeting with the league officials, and told them I'd pay the league (the money coming from WPIX) so much for each game for the league to divide as they saw fit.

The station would supply all the technical side—producer, director, cameramen, and the rest. I'd be paid for creating the TV package, for my

In the TV booth for the football *Game of the Week*

expenses in putting the schedule together, and also get a fee as executive producer and play-by-play man. A separate fee would go to the analyst I hired, Frank Tripucka, a former star quarterback at Notre Dame and in the pros. My fees and the amount for the league were based on Lev's belief on what the ratings would be. Advertisers equated ratings with people hearing about their product. We also agreed that there would be a bonus coming if we topped the ratings prediction.

We had no problem bringing in sponsors. This was not a big money venture; but football was on the rise for the viewing public and we were satisfying the need, and with limited competition, ratings held up well. A few calls to sponsors of my other shows also brought them aboard. The project lasted until the NFL was joined by the American Football League, and we could no longer be the only guys in town doing more football games. We had done very well with this project. I closed up shop and I was on the way to other ventures. We had learned that community support for the teams and exciting play could attract an audience. It was also evident that, as the pros advanced in popularity, in the New York area college programs started to decline.

Getting exposure is a big part of the sports and entertainment business. This again is a creative exercise. Publicity people are a great help personally, but only if they have something to talk about or write about, and they're not affordable until one reaches a higher plateau on the income scale. If possible, give the PR people newsworthy quotes from your venture and let them feed them to selected writers via phone calls or e-mail. With a physical mailing, the material is no longer fresh on arrival.

Another way to keep exposure going is by writing. The biggest stars still use this gimmick. Any book they write will get them on talk shows all around the country—TV and radio. That euphoria doesn't last long, but its a fun venture.

I've always used writing as a supplement to my broadcasting work. When the Washington Senators were on a forty-station radio network, I wrote a weekly column for use in all the towns and cities carrying the games. The local editors heard me every day on the air, so it was easy to have them say yes to a print version.

In Washington, I added a new twist. My columns appeared in the *Washington Post* and at times in the competing *Washington Star* as sponsored columns by one of my baseball sponsors with a little commercial blurb mixed in among the items. The sponsors paid me, and the newspapers in Washington placed them as ads and profited from the ad money.

When I moved to New York, I wrote articles published by *Sports Illustrated* and the *New York Times* and then began writing humorous and serious TV commentaries which continue to this day. In the early days, Norman Ross and Rob Kirshner put them on Channel 5 in New York, then Executive Producer Phil Harmon at Madison Square Garden used them as "One on the Smile." Succeeding producers at the Garden kept the streak going for over thirty more years, and for the last twenty-plus years the "Bob Wolff Point of View" has had a weekly spot on News12 Long Island. Expressing one's opinion on TV is a rewarding experience, particularly when one's suggestions provide benefits to others.

I met a lot of guys and gals who have such remarkable tenacity they have hustled themselves to top positions in the sports world. They have created their own niches in the broadcasting field by combining plenty of hard work along with their talent. Bill Shannon, a long-time friend and journalist who, sadly, died in a fire in 2010, was a big figure in the sports statistics business and as a sideline, a paid official scorer at New York Yankees games. Howie Karpin, a sportscaster on radio, also is an official scorer for the Yankees, also a part of the stadium sports scene.

Ed Randall is truly a man-on-the-go. He comes up with sportscasting jobs on the networks, the local stations, and through his baseball friendships, puts together his Talking Baseball interview shows on TV and radio with an amazing variety of baseball guests. The program airs in the summer on WFAN, New York. Ed is gracious, always well-prepared, gentlemanly, and appealing. It's always an upbeat experience to hear him.

Ann Ligouri does golf and tennis for WFAN and does TV interview shows with the stars. She's a well-known and respected figure in the sports media.

Mike Mancuso is a veteran—and a good one—at giving updates of current sports events to New York stations as well as others around the country. Bob Trainor, a talented freelance reporter, is a regular at the games, well-respected by his colleagues. Bill Stimers is also on hand to supply statistical knowledge at Mets and Yankee games. Ed Lucas, a famous blind sportscaster, is also a regular. Ed was married at home plate at the old Yankee Stadium.

Sports television personalities in New York like Scott Clark and Sal Marchiano are cheerful guys who made going to the ballparks more fun and Russ Salzberg is always on the prowl for a good news story. Unfortunately, Sal and another excellent veteran, Len Berman, despite their high quality work, were caught in salary purges in today's economy. For years, these personalities have been an important part of the New York sports scene. Scott decided to retire at the end of 2010, deciding he just wanted to get off the daily deadline business. I'll miss his always cheerful nature. They are excellent people whose work I always enjoyed.

. . .

Our youngest son, Rick, has carved out a unique role for himself on the airwaves and in print. Rick is a Harvard graduate, magna cum laude, drafted by the Detroit Tigers who moved into the sports writing and broadcasting business while still in uniform by writing a book about his experiences in the minor leagues. After his playing days, Rick was a coach for the Cleveland Indians, then Mercy College, and now is a publishing executive with Grand Central Publishing. An author of eighteen books, mainly on the subject of sports parenting, Rick also hosts a weekly radio show on WFAN

Rick also teamed with his son, John (also drafted as a baseball player out of Harvard) for a father-son book entitled *Harvard Boys.*

Broadcasting college and pro games can be a most emotional experience, but I've found nothing more exciting than watching our children excel in sports and in their careers. Watching our kids play well at different levels was a gratifying experience that I treasure. Rick's older brother, Bob, like Rick, was a three-sport headliner at Edgemont High School in Scarsdale, New York. After starring as a pitcher in high school and American Legion ball, he went to Princeton where his pinpoint control and his assortment of breaking pitches kept him undefeated for all four years against all opposition from New York and New Jersey, including baseball powerhouses St. John's and Seton Hall.

Pro scouts were always at Bob's games, marveling how he could succeed without registering big numbers on the radar gun. Low-scoring complete games were the result of his guile and location, but the general feeling of scouts discussing his future was that velocity might be mandatory to move up the pro ladder, a problem that all-time Yankee great Hall of Famer Whitey Ford might have faced if he were being scouted today. Ford relied on a great curve ball, terrific control, his pitching knowledge, and the absence of radar guns then. Jamie Moyer is another family favorite.

Bob was faced with a career decision. In order to pursue his desire to attend medical school, he would have to give up summer baseball

Whitey Ford

to take the required courses. Bob decided on a medical career, and concluded an outstanding senior year pitching for Princeton. He completed medical school at Boston University, first in his class in pediatrics. He began his private practice in Westchester County, New York, in 2006, before accepting a position teaching at Harvard University and practicing at Boston's Children's Hospital. For the past three years, *Boston* magazine has named him the city's top pediatric neurologist.

Rick and Bob's sister, Margy Clark, was a talented athlete well before women's sports received their present recognition. She was also a cheerleader and bat girl at her brothers' games, with a knowledge of sports and speaking ability that could have made her a sportscasting star. Like my wife, Jane, Margy became a nurse. She's a registered nurse at the University of Hartford Magnet School.

Tim McCarver, Bob, Ralph Kiner

Jane and I watched as many of the kids' games as we could, and Jane also shot video. We're both grateful to have shared such fun times together. And our grandkids are continuing the sports tradition. Sports has been an important part of our family life. Despite my broadcast schedule, we made attending their games a top priority.

. . .

Today's sports analysts keep getting better than ever. They're brainy guys, and they speak as natural athletes. New York City has an ample supply of top-notch commentators, but certainly no monopoly. Every major league city in all sports has its favorites.

In the earlier days, there were a precious few headline national sports analysts—Tony Kubek, Joe Garagiola, and Tim McCarver on baseball,

John Madden on football. Tony has retired, but Joe still does select games for Arizona, and Tim is still a World Series analyst with play-by-play caller Joe Buck. Old-time baseball announcers have long lives in sportscasting. Dick Enberg has returned to the baseball mike, now in San Diego as is another veteran, Jerry Coleman. Ralph Kiner still makes guest appearances with the Mets. Vin Scully, who prefers to work as a soloist, is going strong in Los Angeles. Many of the old-time play-by-play greats are no longer with us. But while they were broadcasting, and listened to game after game, they became more than voices. They were family friends, constant companions, always upbeat, always there.

Now New York baseball has a squad of analysts and play-by-play men: Michael Kay, John Sterling, Suzyn Waldman, Howie Rose, Gary Cohen, Wayne Hagin, Ken Singleton, Paul O'Neill, Al Leiter, Ed Coleman, Ron Darling, Keith Hernandez, John Flaherty, David Cone, Bob Ojeda, and Sweeney Murti. Field reporter Kevin Burkhardt exhibits excellent potential as a future star. Kimberly Jones is a well-prepared baseball interviewer. Missed is Bobby Murcer, whose charm and naturalness were wonderful additions to the Yankee broadcasts. And there are well-informed analysts on the pre- and post-game shows. It's a far cry from the early days when one sportscaster did it all on radio and later soloed on TV. The current number of announcers means that it's more difficult to become a household name, regardless of one's talent. Only the constant play-by-players get that chance through exposure. People used to tune in to hear their guy. In New York baseball, one can't be sure in advance who'll be in the booth except for Kay, Cohen, Sterling, Waldman, Rose, and Hagin. There are many other star personalities, but not daily companions.

Walt Frazier and John Andariese are mainstays of Knicks basketball analysis, Kelly Tripucka keeps developing as an analyst, Mike Crispino keeps adding to his schedule while Mike Breen delivers locally and nationally. Mike Tirico and Hubie Brown are an excellent pair on the national scene and Gus Johnson is a versatile performer. On the college side there's Bill Raftery, Kenny Albert, Ian Eagle, Jim Nantz, Clark Kellogg—all talented, skilled at their art. Content is vital, as is the ability to be concise with words. It's easier to sportscast basketball than some other sports. Players are easier to identify, weather is better inside, there's plenty of scoring and crowd roar. Little time for long stories and fast action takes away need for lengthy descriptions. An excited tone is important.

There's little room in sportscasting for being temperamental. That's different from the old days when a few stars were easily upset and found self-control difficult. Now just getting airtime is a major feat. Getting along with one's colleagues helps one's chances. Rising out of the pack for a starring role is a delicate art in a come-and-go business. In fact, getting the chance to play a starring or important role in a TV or radio line-up is usually a turning point in many prospective careers.

It bears repeating, "There's no test for the best." In sports or in business, one is constantly being tested to attain and then hold the top spot. There's no caste system. Treating all your co-workers as friends makes it an enjoyable experience for everyone.

It really doesn't matter how good any aspiring baseball broadcast team may have been. Jon Miller and Joe Morgan had a twenty-one year run on ESPN Baseball *Game of the Week* booth. Morgan is a Hall of Fame player, and Miller in 2010 became a Hall of Fame broadcaster. Their long run has ended. Individual styles and broadcast teams have to use new material, new stories and research to stay fresh over long periods, particularly to stay ahead of rising new favorites. Many teams break up for new opportunities. Some believe their partner is fading as a performer. Or they may be going great and the hirer wants a change. That's all it takes. Their replacements, Dan Shulman and Orel Hershiser have different styles. Jon Miller will continue to do San Francisco Giants games, and Joe Morgan will find other assignments as well. Both can be proud of their long record together.

In all major league cities, note how many broadcasters with play-by-play or analyst jobs continue for years and years. For many it's the equivalent of a lifetime job. Many top-flight aspiring baseball guys will never get this chance. Throughout the years, there's been little turnover.

Remember, though, that there are many other opportunities to win. Reputations can be built on other networks, other nights, and other sports. Many potential play-by-players become anchormen. One has to stay in the game to be recognized, and talent doesn't need a network to grow. There's always a spot for a new creative approach, but major league broadcasters do seem to live long lives. They don't have lifetime contracts, but many have lifetime jobs.

In the old days, when it came to the World Series I was thrilled to be Gillette's selection. Today with multiple sponsors, the network selects its own announcers and usually stays with the same people as long as they keep the rights.

Frankly, I don't know any other business where the performers can last longer than Major League Baseball broadcasters. There's no age limit on calling games and, year after year, the team broadcaster is a valued part of the franchise. There seems to be something about the daily excitement and camaraderie that is healthful. These broadcasters are treated in their cities like distinguished citizens. Idiosyncrasies are considered part of their charm.

Very few are worried about young competitors taking their place. Only a handful of minor league teams broadcast their games and those that do pay very little, so it's difficult to find a training ground for young hopefuls. They have to find other ways to supplement their income. Newcomers are mainly former pro players who are given a few innings to learn on the job, and this is mainly on the TV side.

Just note the longevity of all the baseball voices you remember. They may reduce their schedules at a late age, but retirement is rarely considered from a well-paid job they enjoy so much.

Pro basketball sportscasters and hockey and football broadcasters have fewer games each year to establish their roots; but, for the most part, they too can enjoy longevity and they, too, keep coming back for more.

. . .

Let's suppose you have shown outstanding talent as an on-air sports-caster or producer (or both) at a college or local station, and you feel you're ready for a larger role. You've sent out audition tapes, made phone calls, gone through in-person interviews—and have been offered a reporter-weekend anchor spot at a large city station. It looks like the big break you've been seeking, but there are two problems. First, there is no opportunity to do play-by-play. Second, the station's nightly sports anchor is entrenched with a big name and large following. There's more money to be made, though. You're single, so there's no family to uproot, and you feel that given a chance, you'll continue to progress. This is a difficult career decision. Many studio guys find it difficult to get back into play-by-play. This is when a sports agent may be helpful.

Sportscasting or sports producing is just like being a ballplayer. It's no fun sitting on the bench—at any level—unless there's a bright future in sight. Years go by, and now you're married with a family. Is this the end of the road for you professionally? The same thoughts go through the minds of the number two sportscaster or producer at small local, commercial or cable stations with less salary money and less exposure. More playing time is the goal of every bench-sitter, more airtime the goal of every TV or radio performer—and that sometimes means beating out the person in front of you.

Remaining a team player tests one's character. Moving to another station or network is a possible solution but is not guaranteed to help you reach the next level, and taking a completely new route may not be practical.

The frustration comes from believing you have the ability to do the job you desire, but not getting the chance to prove it. That's what show business is like—that's why there's so much movement in it—and that's why it's important to be different in one's approach and create one's personal image to avoid being part of the parade.

Always remember that winning is not based on being the best, but on getting the job. With that in mind, get to know others in the business—those involved in hiring. Any one of them could be your future boss. And the younger one gets started, the better one's chances.

If you don't get the job you want, consider another one in the business that will keep you in the picture. Hirers change, networks change, and sponsors change. Being at the right place at the right time can be a major factor in one's success.

15: Roar Of The Crowd

THERE'S MORE TO the sound of a game than the sportscaster's voice. Crowd roar is a vital part of the experience.

In the early days of radio, the lone sportscaster on the air controlled the entire tempo of the broadcast. When I entered the radio booth for the Rose Bowl or Sugar Bowl or Gator Bowl or any college game, or a World Series, the first thing I did was to speak to the audio engineer. "Do we have a mike to pick up the crowd roar?" I'd ask. "Does it pick up the whole sound of the stadium and not just a few fans in an isolated section?"

If I were pleased with the answer, I'd say, "Well, here's what I want you to do. Always keep the crowd level high—and let it get higher when my voice volume goes up. I want that crowd roar to confirm my excitement in calling the play. For listeners who keep moving from one spot on the dial to the next, I want them to stick with our broadcast because our game sounds the most exciting. Crowd roar should rise along with my voice."

This often gave my network a pretty clear edge. Many network audio engineers keep the crowd roar low figuring that the broadcaster wanted to make sure nothing would interfere with his sound. But I always felt that crowd roar was most vital at setting the mood.

On the national scene, one of the all-time most dramatic voices was Bill Stern. Bill used crowd roar as an extra gimmick. On a close football play in a hometown stadium—Michigan Stadium, for example—he'd say, "Now they're measuring. Listen to the crowd. They'll tell you whether the Wolverines made the first down or not. If they make it, you'll hear the fans in a roar of approval." When that sound erupted, Stern would then say, "First and ten for Michigan!"

Words and music go together on hit songs. Words and crowd noise go together on hit broadcasts.

Covering Madison Square Garden events, I made constant references to the sound.

"Listen to this crowd roar!" I'd say.

And in studio shows, with silence around me, if I were calling game highlights with just the video on the screen, in my mind I would imagine the crowd roar and automatically raise my voice with it. Crowd roar can make a game sound exciting. Lack of crowd roar makes a good game seem dull.

At the 2009 NBA All-Star game on TNT, the voices had plenty of excitement but when the players from each squad and then the starters were introduced, the crowd roar seemed muted, as if nobody was at the game. There should have been a reaction to each player. In the arena it may have sounded that way, but it was not heard by the TV audience. Crowd roar is vital to the game event—but only if it's heard. In 2010, the sound was excellent and so was the entire presentation.

I have watched a few boxing matches on TV where the crowd was sparse, the action was listless, and the roar of the crowd was deafening. They had a phony feeling and the suspicion arose that a tape was being used to juice up the excitement. Hopefully, that wasn't the case. Defenders might say that's how it's done in the movies. Movies are scripted with music and sound effects and TV sitcoms often employ canned laughter. But sports broadcasts should be genuine in every way—they should display a natural reaction. Volume can be controlled—high or low—but it should be the actual sound of the crowd—not a manufactured sound track.

One note of caution for sportscasters, though. Whether you're doing a network game or a local game, remember that an excellent play—an important hit or great catch—has to be recognized with the excitement in your voice, even if the home crowd isn't cheering because it's against their team. You have to recognize the artistry of the game on either side to be a fair and impartial observer.

On a network show this is mandatory. On a local broadcast, the sound may be a little more exultant when the locals come through, but the words should be the same. The praise for a great moment should be equal.

Players on both sides acknowledge great plays by their opponents. This is your obligation also.

16: The Importance Of Exposure

LET ME IMPART some vital information on how one advances in the sportscasting business. In one word—exposure. You have to make yourself known. When one is starting out, exposure is more important than money. Advancement is tied to exposure. Stations, networks, and sponsors all covet big names—names that folks at home recognize. They've had exposure. People with great exposure are usually referred to as "celebrities." Truth is, many are not celebrated, they're just well-known. Some "celebrities" with negative images are hired as sportscasters because they draw an audience.

Of course, exposure can be a detriment as well if one loses faith in the person or the product.

When Alaska Governor Sarah Palin emerged on the national scene as vice presidential candidate, her party believed that her charm, her down-to-earth quality, her attractiveness, and being a mother would be endearing traits and win public support. The risk was how much knowledge she had of world affairs. If anything were to happen to her running mate, John McCain, would Governor Palin be ready to be the nation's spokesperson and commander-in-chief?

Her national TV interview with CBS's Katie Couric provided a humorous but embarrassing answer to a direct question. Her view of Russia seemed to be provided by what she could see out of her back window. Had she appeared on that delightful TV show *Are You Smarter than a Fifth Grader?* and the topic was geography, Sarah Palin would have gone home empty-handed. Side-stepping answers is an art most politicians master early. Unfortunately for the governor, she didn't realize that sometimes silence is golden.

Tina Fey, a talented producer, writer, and performer on NBC's *Saturday Night Live* cashed in on this Palin appearance. Fey came up with an impression of the governor that was done so remarkably well—voice, looks, and lines—that Fey already famed as a multiple Emmy and Golden Globe winning writer and performer, was now the biggest television headliner of the year. NBC added extra shows to capitalize on this phenomenon, and put on an election eve special. Laughing at Tina Fey's impression may have had an influence on the election. She portrayed Palin as a photogenic but befuddled commentator on world affairs trying to cope with probing reporters. The political satirists jumped on this night after night as did the late-night talk shows—the result was a puncturing of faith in Palin's ability to lead the nation if anything were to happen to John McCain.

Palin's ability as a leader was not challenged, but her lack of knowledge for this job was a devastating blow. Better preparation for expected questions could have helped. Palin's perkiness, vitality, and strength should keep her in demand for future high-level jobs for which she's more qualified. For the veep job, she couldn't overcome the laughter.

Commercially, the economic fate of the book you're now reading is also dependent on the exposure it receives on TV shows, talk shows, guest appearances, print reviews, the Internet and radio, as well as word of mouth. Without exposure, sportscasters can remain dormant regardless of their ability.

So how does one attain exposure?

I've been helped tremendously by coming up with ideas that gave me recognition outside of my daily TV and radio work. Here are some that worked extremely well:

Publicizing my becoming Washington D.C.'s first television sports announcer.

Establishing a "Knothole Gang" for selected youngsters to get free tickets to the Washington baseball games. Giving the kids membership cards, and getting a sponsor to foot the cost.

Selling my scorebook at Griffith Stadium where the Senators played.

Putting together a singing group of baseball players—the "Singing Senators"—who put on a 45-minute concert on the NBC's *Today Show* from the Monument Grounds in Washington. I sang with them and played the ukulele.

Receiving national coverage when I did a radio interview between games with "a fan in the stands" in Washington who turned out to be the Vice President Richard Nixon. The veep played along with me and didn't reveal his name and occupation until I asked him in the final minute.

In 1952 I hit the jackpot by reading about a kids' football bowl game called the "Santa Claus Bowl" played in Lakeland, Florida.

I followed up on this with a phone call which informed me it was an invitation affair—four teams to be selected, one from each area of the country—for youngsters ages ten to twelve.

I contacted Coach Joe Branzell at the Washington Boys Club to see if he'd like to send a team there if I could raise the money for travel, rooms, and meals. After a resounding, "Yes!" I called Joe Tomlin, the founder of this game for the Pop Warner Foundation. Joe was looking for an Eastern representative; and after I told him about our club's activities, he told me that if we raised the money to transport our team and coaches, we would receive an invitation.

I was broadcasting a nightly radio sports show in Washington on WWDC and Ben Strouse, the GM, assured me I could solicit financial support on the airwaves. It didn't take long to bring in funds for a group of twenty-five.

Then I had a further inspiration. I called the Washington Redskins football team and asked them if they would support the

16: THE IMPORTANCE OF EXPOSURE

Boys Club team by assisting with coaches. They jumped aboard immediately.

My next call was to the *Washington Post*. What a great chance for photos, I said, the Redskins working with these young kids and giving them coaching tips. The *Post* agreed and we had pictures every day, including our group getting on the train on the way to Florida. My close friend Bill Gold, a most talented *Post* columnist and their radio station news director, had daily items about our team and pictures and stories began to appear across the country.

This became a national story when the National Education Association, in a statement, suggested that young kids weren't equipped for the pressure of a bowl game. I became the national spokesman on the network talk shows of the day, refuting the alarmists.

There was so much talk about the game that I received a call from Paul Jonas, the Mutual Broadcasting System's sports director, telling me that he was going to add the game to his bowl schedule. I was broadcasting Mutual's other bowl games at the time, and he was adding this Santa Claus Bowl game. And he wanted me to do the play-by-play.

Everything was falling into place. But there was more. Our D.C. kids won the semi-final; but the night before the final, some of my young kids were hit by a twenty-four hour virus. A large group was sent to the nearby Lakeland Hospital for a lonely overnight stay. The kids told me that they were comforted by an old man on the same ward who reassured them they'd be okay by morning and he would root them on to victory. And they were all ready on game day. I called the championship game for Mutual and Washington won. They were Santa Claus Bowl champions. But the kids never brought the winning game ball back to their victory case at home. The kids held a post-game meeting and decided to give the ball to that old man in the ward for keeping their spirits up when it counted.

At the victory banquet in Washington, I mentioned the story, saluting the kids for realizing that wins were great, but good deeds can be more important than winning or losing, and we all were so proud of their decision. There was no need of a further debate with the NEA.

. . .

When I became a regular commuter from Washington to New York to televise Madison Square Garden events—Knicks, Rangers, and the rest—the flight attendant on my ten o'clock flight kept noticing that I was always answering letters or working during the flights. One day she asked what I did with all the scribbling on yellow pads—did I need typing done?

"Yes," I answered, "I have to send it out to a typing service. Not too convenient, then I have to wait to get it back."

"Before I joined the airlines," said Jackie Dunn, "I worked as a secretary. I'm free with my flying schedule every afternoon. Just give me what you need typed when you leave the plane in New York, and I'll have it for you, all typed, when you board for the next flight."

Jackie was hired and became the cover story for a picture layout in the *Washington Post*. "The Flying Secretary," shown in her American

Jackie Dunn

Airlines uniform, started a second career. She later worked with me on preparation of my TV shows and other sports activities as well. Jackie eventually left for a new career—marrying Jim Dunn, an FBI agent, and starting a family. She remains a close family friend to this day.

An idea that received national attention had to do with another efficient, attractive secretary, Shirley Sager, who had left a law firm to work with me because she and her boyfriend were such avid sports fans.

In addition to televising and broadcasting the baseball games, I also owned, produced, and hosted all the Washington baseball pre- and post-game TV and radio shows. That meant I also selected those who would work with me.

When I was out-of-town with the team, for my pre- and post-game TV shows, I'd leave filmed interviews to use, but for the post-game TV shows I also wanted scores given. The most economical way was

Shirley Sager

to provide a filmed interview and let someone in the studio provide scores of all the games.

My idea gathered national headlines and a sponsor's checkbook as well.

I asked Shirley, my knowledgeable secretary, to become the nation's first "Scoregirl." Her job was to post all the nightly scores coming in and introduce my interviews.

But there's more. I had the scoreboard made up to look like the arrival and departure boards at airports. The teams were posted and the arrivals were the scores. Further, Shirley would dress in the uniform of a flight attendant and for fifteen full minutes, the name of that airline would be seen atop the big board.

United Airlines loved the idea and bought the sponsorship. We sent Shirley to spring training, where we took pictures of her chatting with players. The Scoregirl story and the pictures received nationwide publicity—"Scoregirl" was a feature of the *Bob Wolff Tenth Inning Program*—an idea that took off.

When I was broadcasting the Washington Senators, the team had put together a large network of other cities and stations to carry the games. The folks in those cities were listening to me every day or night. They knew me. I made use of this already attentive audience by sending a weekly column about baseball to the leading newspaper in each town. I then sold the column to a sponsor who put a small commercial ad in as presenter of each column.

On out-of-town trips, I'd do my nightly radio show on the phone to Washington, often using recorded material, and put TV shows on film with a studio announcer to introduce them.

. . .

Over the years my résumé has differed depending on which sport or activity I'm stressing. There's a different one for baseball, football, basketball, hockey, and academics. And throughout the years I've featured different aspects of my career.

I began as "the youngest telecaster." I'm now "the nation's longest-running sportscaster."

To show my versatility, I feature the fact that I am the only broadcaster to have done play-by-play of all four major pro championships—the World Series, the National Football League Championship, the Stanley Cup in hockey, and the National Basketball Association Championship.

Albums on Yankee Stadium include my two famous calls there—Don Larsen's perfect game and the 1958 Colts-Giants NFL championship, called the greatest game ever played. ESPN produced documentary shows about each event (available on DVD) featuring my comments along with my play-by-play.

Near the end of 2008, Major League Baseball Productions released *Yankee Stadium: Baseball's Cathedral*, where I appear throughout many times and which includes my Larsen play-by-play. Also included is my play-by-play of that classic football game when I'm on camera to discuss this Giants-Colts overtime championship thriller.

Wellington Mara

At Yankee Stadium with Rick Cerrone, former Yankees PR director

And if you happen to be in Japan, look for me on camera in a two-hour special which also includes the Larsen call. Producer Hideo Nakamura and his crew spent many hours with me. I guess they've started to promote it because on December 5, 2008, I received my first fan letter from Japan with a request for an autograph.

It's an individual judgment, but in my case, I would always take exposure over haggling for money. But I've always been a bit eccentric. For most of the big assignments I've had, I would have paid them for the privilege. Money paid our bills, but my pleasure came in doing the games. The more one is seen, the more new offers come in. When I began doing network shows with large budgets, I then hired an agent to handle all of the negotiating. Milt Fenster did that very well, ensuring that my talking was just about sports, not remuneration.

The greatest exposure, however, has come from the honors being bestowed on me in the sportscasting field. I spend time every day signing autographs on pictures or baseballs and answering letters from fans. It's a thrill to be asked and to read the comments. The Broadcast Wing of the Baseball Hall of Fame inducted me in 1995 with the Ford Frick Award, and my entire family was with me in Cooperstown for that memorable day.

The Basketball Hall of Fame honored me with their Curt Gowdy Award in 2008, in delightful ceremonies in Springfield, Massachusetts. Curt and I are the only two sportscasters in both halls. I also take great pride in being in the Madison Square Garden Walk of Fame, the National Sportscasters-Sportswriters Hall of Fame, the Sigma Nu fraternity Hall of Fame, the National High School Coaches' Association Hall of Fame, the New York City Basketball Hall of Fame, the Atlantic Collegiate Baseball League Hall of Fame, and the Halls of Fame in Westchester County, New York, where I used to live, and in Rockland County, New York, where I live now.

Sigma Nu Fraternity Commander Bob Anthoine, Bob, and bandleader Charlie Spivak

The Washington Nationals in 2009 provided a beautiful ceremony at the ballpark, along with a video tribute to honor me when naming the home TV booth the "Bob Wolff Suite." I'm pretty lucky, particularly when I realize that all I do for a living is talk—and that talk is about what someone else does in competition. That's the benefit of being a sportscaster.

There are many projects which are not designed as publicity ventures where the motivation is to bring pleasure to others.

When I was inducted into the broadcast wing of the Baseball Hall of Fame, Pat Waldron produced a half-hour special about my career for News 12 Long Island, a fine keepsake.

When I completed fifty years doing Madison Square garden events, Kevin Meininger and Roland Dratch produced "Bob Wolff's Garden Golden Anniversary," which I treasure.

Grandson John Wolff, Bob, and Stan Kasten, President Washington Nationals

Bob Wolff's Ninetieth Birthday

When I hit my ninetieth birthday and seventy-first year on the airwaves, Pat Dolan, my boss at News 12 Long Island, along with the News 12 family, put on a fantastic surprise celebration at the Carlyle on the Green at Bethpage State Park on Long Island. With a committee of Ann Bernzweig, Deborah Koller-Feeney, and Kevin Maher, this was a spectacular night. The birthday cake was in the shape of a football, basketball, baseball, and hockey stick and included a News 12 microphone. It was both authentic and delicious. The terrific video, produced by Dan Scotturo, was laugh-filled and sentimental, and the impromptu speakers related their favorite memories of our time together. The evening couldn't have been a finer one.

17: You Have To Know The Numbers

THE MOST IMPORTANT qualification to do play-by-play is to be a quick and accurate identifier of each person involved in the play. The ability to memorize names and numbers helps; having a strong work ethic is a necessity.

College football presents the biggest challenge, particularly doing the *Game of the Week* on radio. In pro football, the numbers on the players' uniforms are larger and some players stick around long enough to be identified without numbers, just by the way they move and look.

Hockey is difficult, especially if you're covering different teams each week. Most teams have no numbers on their uniform fronts, the lines change quickly, and a great identifying characteristic—the top of the head—is covered by a helmet.

Covering soccer from the football TV or radio booth is the worst. There are very few American soccer announcers who prepare enough to keep up with the play-by-play. Instead, they concentrate mainly on the few players they know and fill pauses with soccer talk and analysis. This slower pace is unlike hockey, where more identification adds to the excitement. The reason that soccer is so difficult is that team managements have never learned to put large numbers—or names—on their uniforms. The numbers on the players' are usually so small that when calling games from a high up in the stadium a sportscaster is forced to use binoculars. For many years, I broadcast the NASL's Tampa Bay Rowdies from the football press box in Tampa. The Rowdies, a team with creative management, drew big crowds. So did the New York Cosmos. Unfortunately, most of the other teams in the league didn't have enough box office stars. When the Cosmos' big names—Pele, Chinaglia, and Beckenbauer—left, so did the fans, and eventually so did the league. But when the Cosmos and the Rowdies were at their peak, their games drew huge crowds. Weaker teams couldn't draw. And there were more weak teams than strong ones. When the weak played the weak, sales and ratings went down. When leagues expand today, the same problem persists. The teams that can afford the big stars draw well

Soccer needs more scoring to conform to American tastes. Rule changes could make that possible. Numbers on uniforms have to be larger and better placed for school, college, and pro teams. Change is difficult to bring about in a worldwide sport. Soccer depends on nationalistic fervor to draw crowds. It's a sport with great artistry but little scoring, which makes it difficult to hold American TV audiences. A problem in selling TV commercials is that soccer is based on continual action without breaks. Sponsors now work in commercials with product placement, including superimposed images or by using a split-screen. In the NASL's early TV days, an embarrassment occurred when a player, on sideline cue, fell to the turf with a theatrical injury. Feeling his act was now over, he began to rise. The camera was still on him while he was waved back down again to continue his writhing. To my knowledge, that ended "injury timeouts."

Colleges in the United States will have to market their soccer teams and stars so there will be sufficient high-level, homegrown soccer players for a viable pro soccer league. Imported stars would then help teams win games instead of just appearing as special attractions. Teams need high emotional support—fandom just like the other sports. Today, more kids play soccer in the States, but don't attend pro games. If college teammates were playing, rooting interest would increase amongst fans of college sports. Unfortunately, most soccer games in the States are played in football stadiums with many barren seats. Smaller stadiums, crowded with fans, would help in marketing the sport. The MLS's Red Bulls moved from Giants Stadium to a much smaller stadium in Harrison, New Jersey. And if soccer announcers used hockey-type calls identifying the players, they would increase the excitement level.

Basketball is easier to call. The sportscaster is usually courtside, close to the action and the body shapes, faces, mannerisms, and running styles make a strong impression. Numbers just become a back-up when needed.

I remember when I took psychology courses at Duke, learning that the ability to memorize was a key ingredient in doing well on the verbal part of the SAT exams. I felt this was an acquired art and the key is intense preparation.

The New York Knicks had a terrific player, Jerry Lucas, who could top me easily in a memorization contest, though, and I was in awe of this mental marvel. For practice, Jerry would memorize pages of telephone numbers and record books. In fact, one time on a national TV show he stood in a theater lobby, asked the first two hundred arrivals to give him their name and home town. Then Jerry went on stage and as each person stood up in turn, he'd recite their name and home town. After identifying the first one hundred or so, the emcee congratulated Jerry, and he sat down to thunderous applause.

Jerry once told me to forget about bringing my record books to the arena. "Put a phone on the bench," he said. "Ask me any record and I'll have the answer for you." Nowadays, all needed information is available quickly, electronically, but knowing what's important, what to use, is up to the sportscaster's judgment.

Jerry and I often debated our memorizing methods. I didn't agree with his because it required an extra step. Jerry used an association method. Every name, face, or number would be associated with a picture in his mind. That worked for him, but I believed it involved more work. I preferred my repetition method.

Football, especially college, took the most memorization hours. After memorizing all the names and numbers, I then watched three selected game films supplied by the competing colleges. I'd play these at home, calling out the names and numbers remembering in my mind the extra dimensions of how each player looked. For the final session, I'd huddle with the coach on things to look for, offensive and defensive strategies, team specialists, the kicking game, injury problems, and anything else he could tell me to make this the best possible broadcast.

My next stop was the football field. Here in particular I wanted to check any pronunciation I wasn't sure of with the player himself, including any unusual hometown pronunciation. I knew the youngster's family and the folks from home would be up in arms if I didn't pronounce these correctly.

Then I went back to the hotel to read all the newspaper stories about the upcoming game, team brochures, and press notes. This process had begun earlier in the week; and I concluded by preparing a spotting board with a diagram for each team for offense and defense with all the numbers, heights, weights, home towns, player notes, and depth chart. For quickness, I'd list all the players numerically by number and name at the top of each board, so I wouldn't have to search. Quickness is imperative. There's no time to search for a number.

I'd pay attention to special teams, creating a list also of the kickoff specialists, punters, place-kickers, holders, captains, return men, officials, and prepare my own notes on the game's importance and what to look for. Having prepared so thoroughly, I'd be confident in calling the game.

On many college football games I'd use a spotter for each team—a fellow who usually had played on the team, perhaps now injured and sidelined—who knew the players just by their actions. They were cautioned not to be rooters, and asked to point on their boards at the number of each player who carried the ball, made the tackle, intercepted a pass or recovered a fumble. "Don't guess," I'd say. "I'd rather be late and correct than fast and wrong." When there was a pile-up on a tackle or a quick call on an intercepted pass or fumble—preparation paid off.

I looked at my spotting boards as little as possible, usually to confirm my observation with the numbers the spotter was pointing to. A second spent looking down or to the side would be a second I didn't want to miss on the field, so the fewer looks the better. And I'd be proud if I'd also pointed out the player opening up the hole or making a great block.

For the pros, I used only one spotter. I was familiar with at least one team, and the spotter could help with both. The numbers are larger, the players better known, and there are no graduations every year. Colleges are tougher. There are many more players, and in one-sided games, wholesale substitutions can occur. Parents are waiting by TV sets to hear their son's names.

The spotters were my insurance, never a crutch. I wanted to never take my eyes away from the game. In most games, I rarely used the spotter's services, but they provided security if needed. The viewer expects perfection, and so do I. I'd do a final review on game day.

For a significant game, like the Rose Bowl or Sugar Bowl or Gator Bowl, I'd invest about forty hours of work mixed in with my other broadcasts. With all of this preparation, I went into each assignment confident I could get an "A." No one ever called or wrote to say I didn't make a mistake. My gratification was that no one ever called or wrote to say I made an error, either. It takes a lot of preparation to be at peace with oneself after a broadcast. Fortunately, I was able to experience that feeling. The toughest call to make is on a touchdown plunge a few yards from the goal line. The press box is at midfield and if there's a pile-up at the goal line one has to be correct on the carrier. On TV, I confirmed my look at the field with confirmation from the TV screen where a close-up camera was on the play. If on radio, I always requested a TV monitor in the booth in front of me.

My inner drive was not to draw applause, but to avoid messing up a big chance. I didn't want to even contemplate that possibility. My safeguard was my preparation and I was never concerned about the hours that took.

In many TV booths or table locations, the TV monitor that the announcer watches is off to one side, which demands he look away from the play, or the monitor sits in front of him blocking his view of the game. In Washington, I devised and had installed a monitor at my TV baseball table which was inserted and sunk down into the table itself so that its viewing screen was directly in front of me, level with my notes and papers on either side. I watched the game and just had to glance down to confirm what the viewer was watching. That's the only way to watch game action and use the monitor simultaneously. It still remains a rarity in too many places covering baseball, football, basketball, ice hockey, and other sports.

On my pre-game checklist was listening to the volume of the public address announcer. Particularly on nationally-televised games, I had the feeling that some PA men sometimes turned the volume up as if they were auditioning coast-to-coast.

I asked the TV director to take over the chore of controlling that output so it wouldn't sound like a competition going on. I also made sure that all the pronunciations which I had checked personally with the players were being announced correctly on the P.A. It would sound bad if I gave one pronunciation and the P.A. announcer blurted out a different one. I never relied on what the coach or the trainer or even the college publicity guy called a player. I checked with the player personally to be one hundred percent sure.

One of the all-time great public address announcers was John Condon at Madison Square Garden. Before every game I did at the Garden, I made sure to read John what my pronunciations would be. John and I never had a conflict.

At game's end in basketball, college or pro at the Garden, I'd give the leading scorer. By this time the arena was clearing out, and on the P.A. they'd announce the leading scorers to the press loud and clear. On rare occasions, the P.A. would give a different point total for the leading scorer than I had. My stat man, Harry Robinson, a newspaperman I had hired to work all home games with me, would just shake his head and point to his chest, signifying he was right. Harry double-checked everything, always, I stuck with what he gave me, and after the game we made sure the press guys were not misled by the P.A. announcement. They went back to recheck and Harry was always correct.

And speaking of public address announcers, no one is more revered than Bob Sheppard, who was still the voice of Yankee Stadium into his nineties. Some gave him the ultimate celestial title of "The Voice of God" as well. An amazing gentleman. Yankee Stadium was sometimes called "Baseball's Cathedral." Bob's eloquent speaking style and dignified manner provided the tone that made every visit there something special. Bob left us as the most famous public address announcer in history. A good friend, his voice will continue to remain in one's memory as a vital part of the Yankee tradition and the New York Giants as well.

On the subject of boards, I always used a smaller board for basketball, and for hockey as well. There's no time in these two sports to use a spotter. I would use a statistician for both sports and also in baseball. In baseball, I'd keep my scorecard, which is essential to keep up with the flow of the game. On my scorecard I also show the defensive alignment of each team, just for security if I have to look down quickly.

I also like to hear (at a low level) any announcements made in the press box that have a bearing on the game—injuries, records, next day's pitchers and scoring comments. In most places that sound is heard in the announcer's location. If it wasn't, I'd make sure to tell the team's PR guy it's essential that a note be handed to me containing any important information announced, so that TV and radio has it as well.

The point is—it is important to ensure that the viewer or listener does not miss any vital information. If that were to happen, it would override anything the broadcaster said in the game. Suppose, for example, in a baseball game, the manager came out during play to speak to the plate umpire, then the other manager joined the discussion and play was held up. I'd be ad-libbing in the booth, musing on possible reasons for their discussion—perhaps the bat being used— but the audience was waiting for something more concrete. I'd send my stat man down to the field, hopefully to get word from the plate umpire at inning's end, or have him go to the PR man in the press box to call the dugout. I always felt an obligation to somehow let my audience know what was happening. In recent years, a sideline reporter became a valuable asset in these situations.

All of this preparation and pressure to cover all the bases before the telecast, including production meetings, is not glamorous stuff but it makes or breaks the show. The public is not interested in what effort goes into it—they expect the performer to be at his peak at all times. After all, he or she is being paid just to watch games and speak about them. Right?

The most tiring part is what happens before the games. The games are exciting—the crowd roar is a great stimulant. That's the fun. The homework is the key, though. I would never go to sleep until I felt prepared. And the sportscaster must get to each game early. Injuries, last-minute line-up changes, and breaking stories can all change one's plan for a broadcast.

What I found the most discomforting was not the preparation. It was the monastic life away from home—the air travel, the delays in airports, going to bed after late plane arrivals, changing time zones, strange eating habits, and the loneliness of hotel rooms, particularly when big family events were being missed. There's a sameness of going to an airport, a stadium or an arena, a hotel, an airplane. Trying to remain fresh, upbeat for every show, every day, and every night can be difficult. The glamour of being on the road wears off. If the team one is covering is in contention, this is a powerful stimulant. Regardless, one has to be "up" for every broadcast, win or lose. Every game, every show is a performance. That's a sportscaster's obligation—to keep performing at the highest level—all the time. A lot of tired people, working tough jobs, or seeking any job, depend on sportscasters to bring a little excitement into their lives. That's what sportscasters do.

Rick Wolff, Jerry Lewis

There was never any boredom in calling games, though. It didn't matter what was at stake. The setting, the competition, the crowd roar, the excitement—each game was a new test and I tried for high marks.

Particular fun came doing the National Invitational Basketball Tournament. Now, many preliminary games are played at competing college sites. For many years all the tourney teams would play at Madison Square Garden. As the Garden's TV announcer, I'd telecast play-by-play of two college games in the afternoon and two more at night. I loved this challenge—a constant parade of new faces, new numbers, new notes. It was stimulating, not tiring. There was plenty to shout about, and I did.

MSG photographer George Kalinsky

18: Ways To Stand Out In The Field

⎯⎯⎯⎯

I **LIKE SPORTSCASTERS.** They enjoy what they do—and so do I. Talking sports is the next best thing to playing them. There are some very bright sportscasters, but being brilliant intellectually is not a requirement.

It's like playing, managing, being a comedian, an artist, a designer, an actor or an actress, or a musician. Those who succeed have an aptitude for what they do. Many are truly gifted in their specialty, but their talent—if that's the word one uses—is not reflected in graduation rates, SATs, ACTs, or diplomas. Since 1939 I've worked with so many skilled people in the communications field, many of the top news and sports performers in the country, hired many of them just starting out and never knew their grades or test scores, never asked and never cared.

The people I write about in this book all have the knack of being sufficiently appealing in what they do to be hired. Some are good journalists, while some stress personality. Many write well or speak well, while some are average in those regards. Ethical codes of conduct differ considerably. Basically, the ethical standards of sportscasters are far higher than those of movie stars who lust to make the gossip columns, regardless of how negative the story may be. But remember, movie or TV actors don't portray themselves. They speak someone else's lines.

To many, getting a job means success. But define success. Is it in being recognized or making money or doing well in an art form? How about being admired as a person? How does success affect families? Is success defined by how well a person is known—or by one's reputation or one's talent or appeal? To even be considered a success, one has to be seen and heard. Being a successful athlete may not ensure being successful in other ways. Some are, some are not.

The statistics tell the story in no uncertain terms. The hours devoted to sports, particularly with all the night games and travel can put a great burden on a sportscaster's family life, especially if the sportscaster's wife has her own career ambitions. I've been very fortunate. My wife has always been a vital part of the team, and somehow I've used my odd working hours to spend increased time with our children.

Remember though, sportscasters report what others do. They depend on stations or networks to get game rights and put on sports shows. Viewers and advertisers or subscribers are needed. Sportscasters depend on others. It's amazing how many last in what can be a precarious business.

My wife and I believe that family success is more emotionally rewarding than individual attainment, and we try to share the good fortunes that have come our way with our family members.

Watch any nightly TV newscast and count the negative stories that are reported—stockpiled one after the other. The lone bright or humorous story is saved for the end of the show so the half hour is not one of complete gloom.

This means that sportscasters trying to look and sound upbeat have to search for ways to bring a pleasant distinctive touch to their telecasts or broadcasts. Sports are considered the fun and games department and its benefits should not be overlooked.

Playing sports, whether competing individually or as a part of a team, teaches human relations and physical development in an exciting way—character development in wins and losses that are not part of the classroom curriculum. Leadership, courage, strength, sportsmanship, and fair play are all being taught daily through sports. They are all vital values to our society, to our way of life. That's why negative sports headlines, when they occur, are given such attention. How did people with so much opportunity to develop go so far astray? Their number is small; but when those cheered in competition don't measure up away from the sports spotlight, the public reaction is disappointment.

TV and radio goes in for trends. If something happens that works, others jump on the bandwagon. But maybe it was the personality that attracted the audience, not the format or the method.

Nightly sportscasts and pre- and post-game shows overload with people all vying for a line or two where they may stand out from the crowd. Quickness is vital. Keep the shows moving. No long stories regardless of appeal. One liners, please. Get emotional. Look like you're having fun. Keep smiling. What is said seems to be merely incidental.

With this rapid high-voltage banter, how does anyone plan to stand out in the studio bedlam? The networks keep looking for that one sure-fire personality—negative or positive—who will immediately make each show the biggest audience-grabber of them all.

Like Howard Cosell or John Madden, Don Meredith's ability to puncture pomposity played well against Cosell's pronouncements.

How about Dennis Miller, whose scripted one-liners sounded out-of-place when inserted during the natural flow of *Monday Night Football* play-by-play? Was this going to entertain the masses? Or was the fan asking, "Who's this guy and what's he talking about?"

What role could Tony Kornheiser, a talented sports columnist, play with two partners talking about the game?

Sports teams are cast to form a desired picture. The image one creates is part of the selling process.

. . .

The New York Knicks' first championship team (1969–70) featured players who stressed teamwork on the court and individual attainment off of it. Going on a road trip with them was like sitting in a study hall. They used their time wisely.

Guard Dick Barnett, whose number is retired at Madison Square Garden, used travel time to read books on public administration. They didn't feature exciting plots, but they contained valuable information for his future. Dick was working towards his master's degree while still playing; and once he received that, he moved on to his next goal—a doctorate. Dr. Barnett continues to work assisting youngsters who need a guiding hand.

Hall of Fame guard Walt "Clyde" Frazier made headlines as a man-about-town, a flashy dresser, and a multi-talented player. That was what the public saw. I always observed a quiet man who never revealed excessive emotion in winning or offered excuses in losing—a consistent, thoughtful performer. On road trips, he brought with him books on increasing and improving one's vocabulary. *New Ways to Word Power* and the like. Not the standard reading material. Walt used all this as a broadcaster, first in a humorous way with his emphasis on alliteration, rhyming basketball words such as "running and gunning" while fans were "rooting and hooting." Walt made vocabulary a strength. How many other sportscasters can you say that about?

Sweet-shooting forward Bill Bradley—Hall of Famer, Rhodes scholar, senator—brought his political books with him and did some writing during journeys. Hall of Fame power forward Dave DeBusschere always had three new novels on the trips. His later career included being coach, general manager, and league commissioner. Phil Jackson, a reserve forward, went on to fame coaching the Chicago Bulls and the Los Angeles Lakers. Phil gloried in discussing philosophical concepts of a loftier nature than pick-and-roll-strategy.

Hall of Fame center and captain Willis Reed, a coach and general manager has continued to serve in top executive capacities.

As a unit, this group personified the type of teamwork that all coaches seek but few attain. Each player had all-around skills, looked for the open man, played excellent defense as well as offense, and

Walt Frazier, Bob Wolff, Mike Breen

gloried in assists and unselfish play. No Knick was in the top ten in league scoring, but more important, no Knick cared.

They had the right coach in low-key Red Holzman, a modest but authoritative man whose temperament was just right for this group and whose mind was constantly thinking of new strategies to win. Red used trainer Danny Whelan as his goodwill ambassador to do some humorous needling if the team's energy ever lagged. Danny did this with a laugh and it was well-received.

Red also made good use of a brainy bench and convinced each player of the importance of his role.

All-Stars all, but the product of this team was even greater than its parts. It was the smartest team I'd ever covered, perhaps tied by the '72-'73 Champions which included two more bright fan favorites—Earl Monroe and Jerry Lucas. In fact, Lucas became nationally recognized as a memorization expert.

. . .

A great way for a nightly sports show to gain extra recognition is to develop a weekly feature which stands out from the crowd and eventually may spin off to a show of its own.

Marv Albert began a compilation of wild, funny, wacky moments of video clips in sports for his weekly feature, and eventually used it for countless appearances on David Letterman's show. Marv's put-down commentary drew big laughs. A local extra became a network feature.

Len Berman had a similar venture which was used locally, and occasionally on network shows. Len had a knack for punch lines and this was a great way to utilize this. At year's end, he had a ready-made hour-long show. Len used to tell me the first lines he wrote for his nightly sports show were his punch-line endings.

Scott Clark, also with a nightly TV sports show in New York, featured his "Out of this World" sports clips of an unusual nature with similar success. Scott is one of those happy sportscasters who always seem to have a ready smile and this was an added asset with his presentation.

A relative newcomer to the New York City TV studio scene on NBC-TV is Scott Sanford, who utilizes a wry sense of humor for two or three humorous observations on his nightly segment. It adds a different approach.

In airing my call of the Don Larsen perfect game in the 1956 World Series as part of the documentary *Yankee Stadium: Baseball's Cathedral,* ESPN producer Meredith Eckert asked me if I remembered the words I'd used. When I said yes, she replied, "well, let's hear them." I shouted my call from memory, and on the show she played my exact words—those on air in 1956 and those I recited to her in 2008—alternating back and forth—presented in an unusual sequence with the effect of a strong echo. It was a novel stunt that received a great audience reaction.

Humor is the key to noteworthy extra features. Most of my colleagues in sportscasting are quick-witted fellows, but few have the

Don Larsen

chance to prove it due to the fast pacing of studio shows. A good opportunity to use one's wit is during the ample time of baseball games, but only a few take advantage of this. Most with wit and humor try for sports panel shows preceding or following games or for roles on sports talk shows with longer airtime.

For a few seasons in Washington, I was joined in the broadcasting booth by Chuck Thompson. Our back and forth banter just seemed to click and for our next few years together, we had a natural flow going. For this reason, I loved rain delays. Trying to top each other was a treat. I wish we had kept recordings. In Minnesota, I also worked one season with Ray Scott and we had a similar rapport.

One can't do that with all partners, though. Some combinations just click.

In November 2008, it was a treat to work with producers Marc Kinderman and Mark Durand on a two-hour ESPN documentary—*The Greatest Game Ever Played.* The game was the 1958 National Football League Championship between the Baltimore Colts and the New York Giants—the first overtime game ever played in the NFL. The Colts won 23 to 17, and the game had such impact across the country it put pro football at a brand-new high level of recognition which has carried forward to this day. My broadcast of the game is utilized in the film as are my comments. A decision was made to put cameras on ESPN sportscaster Mike Tirico and myself bridging segments in the show with our observations as the action unfolded.

I had never met Mike before, but did know that he was an ESPN star, well liked for his natural, amiable style. We came to New York to tape these segments.

When we met, I wanted to make sure that we'd look like a team—not two strangers meeting for the first-time—so I asked Mike what he wanted to say so I wouldn't intrude on his thoughts. "Bob," he said, "you called the game, you were there, I'll just ask you the questions and that should do it."

We did all the bridges in one take with no repeats, nothing written, nothing on teleprompters, no rehearsal—just two guys talking and enjoying each other's company. It was pure television, and I was thrilled to be a part of it. When I watched the completed show at the December 3 press preview, I was elated to find no cuts had been made in our comments; and an ESPN producer commented to me on what a fine team we were.

I treasure that experience. When one has the right partner, there's something special about the result.

I had received one tip about Mike about a month earlier. When I was inducted into the National Basketball Hall of Fame, Hubie Brown, a Hall of Fame coach who partnered with me on NBA telecasts on the USA network, told me how much he enjoyed working with Mike. Having worked with Hubie, I valued his judgment. He was correct again in his evaluation.

. . .

For thirty years or more, under different titles, I've prized the opportunity to do features—both humorous and serious—expressing my personal views. This adds a distinctive touch to the usual scores and highlights. But my viewpoints are my own, and this has added a personal angle for Madison Square Garden Network, News 12 Long Island, and myself.

There's money involved, of course, and exposure, and fortunately Emmy awards; but I've always considered the greatest value the privilege of stating on the airwaves how I feel about any issue or person in the sports world, and I prize this aspect of the work above all others. I've done thousands of these segments, and no boss has ever interfered with my freedom of expression. I'm truly grateful for that.

A note of caution. When giving on-air critiques, particularly if charged with strong emotion, make sure that truth and research are on your side. They are your allies. Be wary; remember, just one phone call from the higher levels can send you packing. There's a bit of courage involved in standing up for one's beliefs, and a tremendous amount of inner satisfaction. Tip: use humor to make your strongest points. One can be factual without being vindictive. The truth is a sufficient weapon.

There's a big difference between those who battle for higher standards—whether it's in journalism or in life—and those whose aim is for notoriety through words or thoughts which are distasteful, offensive, demeaning, or dangerous. Some seek glory in wallowing in dirt, selling degenerate shock as entertainment.

Some hirers sign these performers for the sleaze market. They perform at the lowest level in a sordid part of the entertainment industry. The problem is the obscene and immoral performers are also in the entertainment business and are judged financially by the size of their audiences and the money they generate. Negative sells as well as positive, if not better, and as the years go by, the dividing line between clean and dirty becomes more blurred. Fortunately, the four-letter word comedians are getting fewer shock laughs, as garbage becomes boring.

Let me tell you what's given me great personal satisfaction during the years: Having the chance to tell my colleagues how much I've enjoyed their specific stories or lines or play-by-play calls. I've always taken pride in being part of this talented group. There's no envy—we all use the same source material—but in different forms, different ways. I've always been excited about this association.

The organizers of most big sports-related dinners love to load up with "celebrities." It's a public relations trade-off. Tickets are sold because a celebrity sits at each table or on the dais. He or she is introduced with a mention of station or network or team. It's a trade-off considered good business. If one isn't seen or heard frequently enough, "celebrity" status can quickly disappear. In the media, celebrity means being recognized—for whatever reason.

And for years celebrities have been used as spokesmen or women for charities and other causes. Many are honored for their work and their name attracts dining patrons at the dinners. This is a positive contribution, but be wary. Sometimes appearances are for good money instead of good will.

The shelf life for most celebrities is a short one, though. Celebrity has to be enjoyed while it lasts. Most audiences are more impressed by the present than the past.

19: The Delicate Role Of Sportscasters In The Marketing of the Team

THE SPORTS MARKETERS work at making fans so passionate about their sport and their favorite teams and players that they'll buy uniform shirts, caps, autographed balls, pictures, videos and accessories demonstrating their allegiance, along with tickets, the sponsors' products, luxury suites, and memorabilia. If one wants a seat from the old Yankee Stadium or a patch of grass presented artfully, Brandon Steiner, in association with the Yankees, has it framed, ready for purchase at Steiners Sports Gifts and Collectibles.

The more intense the rivalry between the teams, the better this is commercially—the greater the demand for tickets and products. The bigger the audience, the bigger the potential buying audience. The ball clubs, stadiums, and networks count on the sportscasters to build the audience with their broadcasts, win or lose.

Fortunately, no employer or sponsor has ever spoken to me about slanting my calls to favor the home product. They knew what my reaction would be. I pride myself on objective, honest broadcasting. I enjoy bestowing praise, but errors, fumbles, and interceptions are part of the game and can be reported without being vindictive or accusatory. Some aspiring neophytes believe they're solidifying their bond with management by prejudiced verbal outcries such as, "our team is being robbed" by the officials and "we won't stand for this!" Doing this destroys the public faith in the broadcasts and the broadcaster. Honesty, not homerism, is still the best policy.

One-sided "homers" may be known as characters in local markets, but networks prefer calls fair to both sides. Marketers don't lack for supporters, though, who become part of the selling team. The new role of the public address announcer is to whip up enthusiasm for the home team with vocal excitement.

The early public address announcers in the country played it straight. No frills, no enhancement, no bias. Today, however, many P.A. guys raise their voices in wild exultation giving their home-team line-ups and then almost whisper the names of the hated opposition. They serve as the crowd's cheerleaders—they get the audience steamed up, just like the warm-up comedians before some TV comedy shows begin.

These fellows pull out all their vocal tricks. Their counterparts are TV game show hosts—who are near hysteria when they give away the giant jackpots. And the announcers who introduce the stars on TV make this the most important announcements of their lives—every night—"Heeeeere's Johnny!" or "David" or "Jay"—as loud as any winning touchdown in the Super Bowl.

Before the announcers and the P.A. guys joined forces in this act, there were the scoreboards which urged the fans to yell—or shout—or clap—or just make noise. For years, I was able to figure out myself when to cheer—but now guidance is given in how to raise the decibels. The fans are made to feel part of the show while retaining their amateur standing.

And to keep the fans revved up for the entire ball park experience, blaring music makes it difficult to continue one of the joys of watching baseball—conversing with friends between pitches, discussing game strategies.

Yet, it's tough to argue that this is bad business when attendance at the major sports is greater than it's ever been. Minor league players refer to Major League Baseball as "The Show." This is the show—lights, camera, action—the juiced-up version of the old national pastime.

A great example of how marketing can profit from emotional sports involvement is the Olympics. The early Olympics were good-will affairs where the world's top athletes could come together and compete to set new records. Just as important was the opportunity for nations to bond as friendly competitors as mutual respect grew into an admiration of others who shared a love for sports. This was sportsmanship at its peak—but it didn't sell. Friendship is great—but where was the emotion?

The Olympics were then for amateurs, but some sport stars were being paid by their governments, competing to bring glory to their countries. The United States had their own leagues of professional athletes but kept them away from amateur competition. In 1980, a United States Olympic hockey team composed of amateurs—mostly college kids—defeated a team of Russian "pros" in an emotional, classic game charged with nationalistic fervor, viewed by a large TV audience. Emotion brings ratings which, in turn, bring sponsors.

Individual competitions were the focus of the early Olympics, which were fun sporting events—but then became more of a business.

How to sell them? The answer was evident. Emphasize nationalism. Country against country. The sporting equivalent of war. Play up nationalistic pride—jump on any unfriendly incidents to get the fans stirred up. Bring in flags, chants, noise, excitement—and make medal counts a vital part of the coverage, country against country. Let the pros come in to make the playing field fair for all. Get the spectacle on worldwide television. Attract major sponsors, advertisers. Supremacy is at stake.

The money poured in. TV rights hit new heights, TV ratings escalated—the marketers had won. They had harnessed emotion to dollars. Advertisers gloried in supporting the emotion, a plus not delivered by the average TV program or newspaper ad. The Olympics became a profitable venture.

Selling sports is based on emotion. And marketers help to make it pay. Sportscasters are expected to be reporters of the Olympics, not cheerleaders. With the emphasis on national pride, this can be a difficult assignment. It's always refreshing, therefore, to note the respect that many athletes, win or lose, exhibit for their competitors after their event is concluded. Handshakes and embraces are emotional in a positive sense.

There's been an increase in use of positive human interest stories about the athletes' lives, regardless of which nation they represent. Bud Greenspan, an excellent TV producer who died in 2010, produced memorable Olympic documentaries portraying all the Olympic personalities he covered in a most positive light, emphasizing their courage, determination and will to succeed, regardless of obstacles in their path. To him, an Olympian was a winner, and a gold medal wasn't required.

20: The Agony Of Choice

WHAT'S MY LINE? used to be a popular television show. On it, a guest would come on stage, sit down at a table, and be quizzed by a panel of experts trying to determine what his or her occupation might be. If the guest was a well-known public figure who could easily be recognized, the panel members would first put masks over their eyes before the questioning began.

An early television humorist made use of this guessing game. Steve Allen put the camera on people walking down a busy street and got laughs by coming up with bizarre occupations they seemed to be suited for.

Sportscasters are easy to recognize—by look, sound, and demeanor. They come in all sizes and shapes, but they share recognizable traits. Good humor, natural or contrived. High energy, hearty personalities. Enthusiasm. Excitement. Sportscasters enjoy being the middlemen—or women—between the action and the audience and appreciate their public. They speak louder, smile more, laugh easily, they're gregarious people—in essence they are the extroverts. Day after day, night after night, their voices are upbeat, speaking in excited tones about the sports they cover—whether their teams are winning or losing.

On screen, they never tire and are always friendly, courteous, electronic companions one can count on, season after season, year after year.

In actuality, sportscasters lead normal lives. They do go to doctors and dentists, pay bills, have diverse interests. They try to make time to devote to their families while preparing for each assignment, whether it's a game or a studio show. They have to keep a careful eye on their popularity, their ratings, and their relationships with their colleagues, those who hired them, and those hoping to succeed them. The longer they stay on the scene, the more secure they feel. Sportscasters seem to live long lives with long employment with teams, sometimes extending from one generation to the next.

Game after game, they're exulting, "What a game!" "Home run!" "Look at that catch!" "Great play!" "He scores!" "Touchdown!" and the rest. They become part of the scene, yearly increasing their value to club owners and sponsors.

You'll never hear a sportscaster say during a four hour or longer stint at the mike, "Pardon me, friends, I have to go to the men's room, but I'll be right back." That would break the mood of the show.

My record without leaving the mike is over seven hours. I did this while broadcasting every inning of a baseball doubleheader plus the pre- and post-game shows and then following that with another late sports show that night. In those early days I worked solo, but in nine decades of broadcasting games, I believe I've maintained my natural emotion, my excitement, and my desire to be at my best regardless of audience size or game importance. That's my job and my obligation to my employer and to the audience. Sportscasters don't complain about being too hot or too cold or too tired. They're performers who know that such admissions would spoil the show. The audience would laugh at guys complaining while being paid to sit in choice press box seats and talk about their discomfort. The only exceptions could be a few baseball characters who might do it to get a few laughs.

With the constant air travel to get to games, the change in time zones, strange eating schedules, the countless hours spent in preparation, the many production meetings and obligatory public appearances, there are worries or concerns of personal disappointment at not attending important family events. Home games are much easier.

When the mike is on or the camera is focused on every expression, one needs total concentration—the vocal tone comes alive—and the sportscaster knows he's being judged solely on this performance. How he did in the past doesn't count. It's acting in a way, but it's staying positive, acting natural—saying what one feels should be said, what one thinks, and above all, appearing in a good mood.

There's a certain subtlety in standing out from the crowd, making those in hiring positions aware of one's capabilities without appearing too pushy. In production meetings with producers and network executives in attendance, I've seen an aspiring candidate use his most theatrical tones in the conference room—monopolizing the occasion by giving a lengthy lecture on an unimportant opinion or asking needless questions mainly to make his presence known—and in doing so, lose the battle.

An obtrusive method would be immediately recognized by the show's producer and the sportscasters' colleagues. A producer who turned down a strong candidate for a job remarked to me some time later, "I've worked with that guy before. Has talent, but insists on telling everybody how to do the job. I can live without that." It's not the loudest who wins.

Sportswriters, as a group, are brainy fellows who, by nature, are more reserved. In a quiet way, most have a great feel for the big story and disdain for small talk. They go in for substance, not bombastic look-at-me fervor. They're perceptive, without the overwhelming need to win applause.

Producers have a great intuition for what will and won't work with sportscasters to enhance the product. In temperament, they're more like the writers.

In TV's early days, a sports programming firm in New York run by an enterprising young executive, Ed Scherick, put together sports programs and sold them to ABC-TV. In essence, they were the sports programming agent for the network. As Washington's first television sportscaster, I was seen and heard on early pro and college games on the DuMont TV network, which mainly broadcast in Washington and New York, and NBC Radio used me to broadcast the post-game show following Bill Stern's game.

Scherick's firm and ABC-TV selected me to host their pre- and post-game scoreboard shows. I would give the football highlights verbally—there were no video highlights available then—and I'd have a partner to read other scores between my longer highlight descriptions. I had different partners during those years: Jim Simpson, Pat Herndon, and Jim McKay. During my final year on this program, ABC decided to add a new programming venture, the *Wide World of Sports*.

ABC *Wide World of Sports*

My major source of income during the summer was as a telecaster and broadcaster of the Washington Senators and all their pre- and post-game TV and radio shows, plus nightly TV and radio shows in the nation's capital. In the fall, I added commuting to New York to telecast all Madison Square Garden events on WPIX. When I began doing network shows in New York, Milt Fenster approached me about becoming my business representative. Milt impressed me with his personal interest in my career and family. We joined forces and it proved to be a wise decision. Milt represented me in signing with NBC-TV as their *Game of the Week* telecaster, and in bowl games and other national ABC-TV assignments.

One of our first major discussions involved what I wanted to attain in my career. "Milt," I said, "I'm off to a great start in baseball and the

NBC TV Game-of-the-Week

other major sports, and my ambition is to be a World Series broad-caster and to do championship events in the other sports as well."

Milt said, "You now have the baseball. You're doing Madison Square Garden events, football bowl games and your network foot-ball scoreboard show. ABC-TV mentioned to me an upcoming *Wide World* series. I believe Jim McKay will get it. Frankly though, I didn't pursue it. It would mean giving up all you already have and I didn't express any interest."

"Milt," I said, "You played that just right. Traveling around the world for smaller events is not something I want to do. Jim McKay is an excellent choice for them. He's a top-notch reporter. I might consider doing a few *Wide World* shows for the network, but not on a steady diet. I want to keep doing what I have now."

The outcome was that Jim McKay proved to be outstanding on the *Wide World of Sports*, which became a TV hit. I became a World Series announcer, left ABC-TV to become the play-by-play broad-caster on the NBC-TV baseball *Game of the Week*, did NBC's Rose Bowl and Sugar Bowl broadcasts as well as their college and pro-basketball, and in 1995 was inducted into the National Baseball Hall of Fame. I did add a few *Wide World* shows to my schedule, covering events including the Surfing Carnival in Australia. McKay grew in stature with his *Wide World* program and became a sports-casting great.

Staying in the States, I had the chance to watch my children par-ticipate in their various sporting events. No part of the sports scene has provided more personal pleasure than that.

A career in sportscasting is full of choices. Some decisions prove correct, while others prove otherwise. Many decisions are not made by the sportscaster. They're made by the network, the station, the spon-sor, the economic times, the ratings, and ever-changing personnel at the top. A network or station may lose its rights to cover a particular sport or team, which can end the sportscaster's precarious climb up the ladder. I marvel that my steps were continually guided in the right direction, and I have always been grateful for the guiding.

Of all the qualities that one needs to survive in a local market, wearing well with the public, the sponsors, and the ball club that okays your presence on their games may be the most important key to longevity.

Particularly in baseball, but also now in basketball, hockey, and football, the local team broadcaster becomes an old friend to the listener. His style might not be suitable for national coverage, but his manner, sayings, and delivery become so accepted by his daily listeners that his value to sponsors is increased. These local personalities become more entrenched with each passing year, and there's a long list of those who are still active at a late age. Maybe their health is helped by getting steamed up every day. The fact that so many continue generation after generation increases the difficulty for younger announcers to find opportunities. In addition, more and more openings are being filled by former ballplayers who start as analysts and gradually move into the role of color commentator or the play-by-play field.

There aren't that many play-by-play opportunities with minor league teams or independent clubs and those who go this route to gain experience usually have to supplement their income from the games by also handling PR work or other business activities for the club. The upside is the chance to develop one's style and make an audition disc to use for larger opportunities. An easier route is broadcasting college sports, bypassing the minor league route. Doing high school play-by-play is a good place to start as well, but there are not many radio or TV stations covering these games. Those few that do may favor a more seasoned sportscaster. If there are games to do, however, and you can convince the hirer you're the right person for the job, it's a great way to learn.

Unlike college or the pros, where the public relations departments provide team handbooks with player information, game notes, and game spotters if you don't have your own, information for high school games has to be pursued without assistance. You have to check on injuries, line-ups, pronunciation of players' names and hometowns, and records made during the game which would be announced in the college and pro press boxes. And then there are last minute number changes. It's imperative that one gets informed, and not be embarrassed by reporting the wrong person do the scoring.

On the high school football scene, the reporter gathers all this himself. Further, college numbers are usually easier to read, and in the pros, they're not only large, front and back, but sometimes the player's name is also on his uniform top. If one can do high school games well, the transition to college and pro games is an easy one. The college and pros have far better press facilities, even including men's rooms not available in most high school press boxes.

School games are a great way to learn the business and make tapes of your work to study. There's not much money involved, but they're a valuable learning base. And on local cable stations, covering local teams has a greater importance with video replays and highlights, which are important parts of sportscasts.

Be aware, though, that no matter how good you may sound, colleges and pros are not scouting your work on high school games. Local cable is primarily a learning position and a confidence builder. One needs tapes in applying for a job. A big part of the sportscaster's job is selling himself or herself to a station or sponsor. The audition tape has more impact if it's a higher-level game.

Suggestion: Find the nearest college team, make friends with their PR guy, prepare to do a broadcast with your tape recorder, sit in a vacant spot in the press box, and make sure you are also hearing the roar of the crowd with the call of the ball game. Then pick out four or five minutes of your work and use that as your audition piece. That should be the easiest way to give the audition tape some impact. If the cable station does both college and high school games, choose the college. Or go to a top college or pro game, bring a tape recorder with you and make your own broadcast.

Half the battle is getting the job. This is one way to do that.

And one important note on building one's image: You know how on drug commercials these days how the advertiser is forced by law to state all the possible dangers in taking the pill being advertised—well, in trying to impress on one's audition tape, remember that the emotion in one's call has to be natural—not fake. Screaming, shouting, and getting hysterical at a routine call will demonstrate that you have no idea what's important and have lost touch with reality. It's show-off emotion, and shrill, hoarse voices are unpleasant sounds. A few seconds of that will turn off any would-be sponsor. Today's most in-demand sportscasters like Jim Nantz, Bob Costas, and Joe Buck show emotion with clear, excited tones, but don't go berserk.

Your good judgment should rule. Natural emotion is what one wants to achieve. The top stars in the pros have learned that lesson.

In college philosophy classes, they'll debate "is a sound a sound if one can't hear it?" Well, in TV and radio, the sound of your voice—no matter how pleasant—will not aid in advancement unless a hirer is watching or listening. And not just the sound, it's what you say and how you say it. Those who get the big assignments sell themselves or work closely with someone who helps the selling process. Sportscasting is an art, but it's also a business.

PART THREE
Getting
The Extra Edge

21: Tricks Of The Trade

HOPEFULLY, YOU'RE NO longer thinking in terms of being "the best sportscaster."

There's no such thing.

First of all, you haven't heard them all. Does your favorite do all the sports? On both radio and TV? Perform play-by-play, provide analysis, or anchor? Local, regional, or network? On what criteria are you judging?

Getting hired doesn't mean one is the best. It means he or she was hired. All of which means you, a novice, have a chance—all you have to do is be hired and then prove it was a wise choice. I've had the good fortune to be seen and heard on all the national networks and the top cable networks, as well as a slew of regional ones and local stations. Regardless of the outlet I'm the same person, with the same effort, same ability. Ability is in the eye of the beholder—the hirer—and hirers' opinions vary. Many make excellent choices, but many deserving candidates don't get a chance.

Let's concentrate on the first step—getting the opportunity. Be aware that some great sportscasters have never had the thrill of calling a championship game or one outside their local area. Since broadcasting ability can't be evaluated numerically, it's tough to prove how well you perform. It's not like having a high batting average in the minors or setting a home run record. If you want to contend for a higher-level position, you have to maneuver to sell yourself. So the initial search is for an opening. Next one has to find the hirers and sell yourself to them.

I remember well when I was a teenage professional sportscaster at WDNC, the CBS station in Durham, North Carolina, while attending Duke University. My older colleagues would sit around some days listening to the voices of announcers on the national shows. In frustration, one would say, "I can't believe this. I know I sound better than that guy. Tell me honestly, don't you think so, Bob?"

"Absolutely," I'd agree. "But remember, the guy in New York who does the hiring doesn't know you. That announcer you heard undoubtedly is a good salesman and the hirer liked him." I didn't add that this whole business of sound was overrated. Some voices do sound more pleasant than others on the airwaves, but most people just assume that if you're on the air, the sound is better.

Just being hired is not enough, though. Then you have to hold the job.

Wearing well is an art. All one needs to enhance broadcasts is curiosity. I chatted every day with the players on both teams. I made notes on what they told me. This was made easier as I worked out with the Senators, pitched batting practice to them, and was treated as one of the guys. I could talk inside baseball—techniques, how pitchers set up batters, bunting skills, base stealing, fielding tips— the stuff talked about in the dugouts and the locker rooms. I needed fresh material for every game. This is vital to keep people listening to a losing team.

I welcomed the advent of television. It provided the chance to supplement the visible action and point out the thought processes going into each pitch, each at bat, each managerial decision. When exciting moments incurred, that would occupy the complete focus.

As an objective sportscaster I don't wear a team's cap or jersey or championship ring. My role is to report impartially. This has nothing to do with personal feelings. A great play is a great play, regardless of which side makes it.

Bob pitches batting practice to the Washington Senators

Knowing what's important is the key to being a topflight reporter. Ever had a classmate who was despondent? The one who memorized all the notes, wrote down everything expressed by the professor, knew all the dates, but never received the grades he or she hoped for? The student knew all the details except the most vital—the meaning of all those facts and figures, their importance, the trend or pattern they revealed. In essence, they couldn't identify what was newsworthy. A journalist has to have that knack or should be in another field.

Here's a great test for you.

You've just been assigned to cover a baseball game in person. The anchor will throw it to you for an on-camera thirty-second report of what happened. You'll ad-lib this, of course.

That's nine innings to recap in a thirty-second time. What should you mention?

The same things you would shout to your family, your friends—now to an audience—if they were waiting patiently to find out. This tests your editing skills. Just the facts, please.

"What a win for the Monarchs. Six to five over the Tigers. Tom Jones's home run in the bottom of the ninth won this thriller. That's the third time this season Jones has had a game-winning homer. Sid Alexander gets the win in relief, Joe Clarey is the loser. The Monarchs now lead the Tigers by one game in the Eastern Division standings. Ted Leonard from the ball park, returning to Steve Smith in the studio."

The audience wants the main facts quickly—and you must be animated in telling them. That's it.

As for rising in the business, the first step is a true evaluation of what talents you may have. Are you a natural storyteller? Do people gather around you to hear your views, your adventures, and your opinions? Do you have a strong personality? How's your voice, your appearance? How well do you know sports? Which ones have you played or coached? Where did you attain your sports knowledge? Do you know the rules, the players? After this self-examination, where do you think you qualify? What should you emphasize as your selling point or points?

The next step is to prove yourself. To get your foot in the door, you have to establish your credibility; an ex-athlete or a coach or sports writer or sports executive has a built-in advantage. If you don't qualify on those counts, you're an announcer, and have to emphasize your strong points—voice, wit, judgment, content, education, looks, charm, opinions, style, or success in a related field like acting, performing, or work you've done in the sports field. The next step is to make an audio (or preferably, a video) tape—include a few opinions, an editorial, a short commercial reading, and a touch of humor.

Baseball provides the best medium because there are so many ways to score runs or make defensive plays. Colorful baseball language abounds—a sportscaster's delight. Baseball is the top storytelling sport, with plenty of room to demonstrate one's ability.

Football is next, particularly with its time between plays. Football, with its physical side, adds a whole group of contact words. On a short plunge for a touchdown, the fullback can "ram over" for the score, "rumble in," "blast through," "crash through," or "squeak through"— the list goes on.

Calling basketball doesn't allow such leeway. "He makes it," "It's good," "Lays it in," "Banks it in," "Yes!" "He scores," and "He does it" pretty much represent the entire gamut. And let's not overlook the "she's," although lady basketballers are still said to play "man-to-man defense." Radio usually involves a guess at the distance of the shot. On radio I told fans all distances were "estimated." On TV the viewer sees

Rogers Hornsby

Vince Lombardi

the distance. I never gave it on TV except for a record shot by Jerry West that I called in a championship series which I knew would be in every newspaper story. The three-point shot when it came into being gave telecasters a vocabulary boost.

On radio calls, many sportscasters give the numbers—"an eighteen-footer" or whatever. There's no use of the word "estimated," but that's what it is.

Let's look at two different calls of the same basketball action for radio and TV.

On radio: "Inbounds to Wright, he dribbles down the right side, crosses the center line, is tied up and passes to Clyde Cook in the right corner. He's closely guarded and sends it back out to . . . " Radio describes, TV supplements the picture.

On TV: "You might note how often Wright moves down the right side when he crosses the line. The defense has scouted him well. Defensively, the team shifts quickly into almost a zone defense with an excellent chance to intercept a pass or stop penetration on that side. They have the outside guarded as well . . ."

Bob Lanier

Anybody can say, "These teams are working hard—they're both up for the game, it should be a real battle, there are great stars on each side, and there should be plenty of excitement." If delivered in an exciting manner, you've filled some airtime, but you won't win points as an analyst. Good content means meaningful comments.

Speak in short sentences, particularly if you're using statistics. Newspaper readers can go back and read them again; listeners can't ask you to repeat them. Go easy on the numbers, dole them out sparingly. During a televised game, they'll be flashed on the screen to supplement your play-by-play.

This is just the beginning, though. The first job is to get a professional springboard to put you in the competition. Can you afford to take a low-paying job to gain experience and exposure? Can you afford to travel away from home to do so? How does your girlfriend or wife feel about the matter? How about family obligations? Would you be content just to work in your small local market if there's little chance to continue upward? Do you need additional income to support your family?

There's the possibility of a great adventure ahead, but no guarantee. It's hard to feel secure when changing markets, when one is not assured of steady employment and opportunities to grow economically in that market.

Learning how to sportscast well is just plain basic preparation, but fun to do. If one is doing play-by-play, it's learning the names and numbers of the players, the rules, and compiling notes about the players and their techniques. Adding these to the broadcast will enhance the action.

Preparation demands a concentrated effort to know each upcoming event so thoroughly—its strategies, stories, offense, defense, records, rules, names, and numbers—that you feel you could coach either team. Knowledgeable viewers or listeners need to believe that they're listening to an expert. In bantering with a color partner, an analyst, one should ask questions that demonstrate knowledge, not ignorance.

I always felt confident that my calls would be accurate. Mistakes can end careers. Make an error, and the volume of calls and letters can be extraordinary. Being correct takes more perspiration than inspiration.

There's no relaxing once you get the job. Now you have to hold it against all the others waiting to take your place if you falter. The hazards include ratings and management changes. TV and radio critics—sharp people—are quick to note mistakes; just one can override hours of preparation.

22: Vocal Suggestions To Hold Any Audience

MOST YOUNG SPORTSCASTERS believe the faster the action is, the faster they have to speak—to keep up with every detail of the excitement. The result is a jumble of words, few of which stand out with meaning.

The trick is to stay in control—it's not how many words you use, it's how you emphasize them. That higher the tone one reaches with distinct pronunciation and full vocal force, the greater the attention-getter.

Keith Jackson used to do this on football games.

The average sportscaster might say, "It's a great day for a football game." Keith wouldn't waste that line. He'd say, "It's a GREAT day for a football game," and that extra emphasis made you believe it.

Bob Costas has this knack on studio shows. He makes each word sound important.

Marv Albert's concise, staccato burst of words with the emphasis on each is an integral part of his exciting style.

Doc Emrick on hockey has his own method of capturing attention. Too many announcers going along at an even pace suddenly burst out full force to describe a goal or a penalty or a beautiful pass. That's exciting, but jarring. Doc does the whole game with a pleasant level of excitement but as the pace intensifies, he glides up with his voice to the next level and then glides down after the excitement of the moment passes. He captures the ups and downs of the sport in an easy manner, just as a great singer goes from low to high notes on a song in a controlled, comfortable style.

In horse racing, Dave Johnson sets the stage for excitement by proclaiming full voice, "Down the stretch they come." That puts the call into high gear.

Mets' broadcasters, Gary Cohen, Ron Darling, and Keith Hernandez on TV and Howie Rose and Wayne Hagin on radio, make for good listening. They're always up for the game and do lively shows. They reserve their full vocal outbursts for the most dramatic occasions to give them the most meaning. If one yells at everything, what's left to shout about?

Working with Hubie Brown televising network basketball, I was impressed with the thought he put into becoming an outstanding analyst while I handled play-by-play. Hubie watched the play like the ultimate scout. Players' movement and techniques were instantly noted. Hubie added a dimension that statistics rarely showed. What an enjoyable experience it was to work with him.

Few sportscasters ever reveal their off-the-air likes or dislikes— books, movies, music, or other diversions. They stick to the game. But I have always enjoyed those who, when appropriate, add some light humor with comments of a personal nature. It's always a plus, I believe, to hear of their interests and opinions outside the sports realm.

Tim McCarver, in his early network days, was adept at this. Tim was one of the first to make "inside baseball" observations vital to his commentary. Joe Garagiola pioneered that type of technical information with both insight and humor. It was a treat to be Joe's NBC-TV network partner. Jon Heyman is another outstanding TV and radio analyst.

On sports talk radio, family men Chris Russo and Mike Francesa used to share bringing-up-kids observations with their listeners. Dave

Letterman on his nightly show has expanded his viewership with family observations and a genuine curiosity in everyday problems which have nothing to do with show business.

Jon Miller, the talented broadcaster for the San Francisco Giants, is a great impressionist. He does superb imitations of Vin Scully, Harry Caray, and Bob Sheppard, the legendary former public address voice of the Yankees. Jon even includes the stadium echo that accompanied Sheppard's distinctive voice.

It's not mandatory to have a distinctive style. I try to be different, but I pay more attention to my content than my voice. I have no unique style—or unusual sound—or mannerism. I don't expect to be imitated. I do show my natural emotion. When the action heats up, so do I. I don't work at this—it just comes from within me.

Mike Breen, the Knicks' TV announcer and network basketball play-by-player, paid me a nice compliment on a TV show. "Bob," he says, "gets a kick out of asking perceptive questions. He has a natural curiosity that he shares with his viewers." Having an interest in others has been an asset. Coming up with interesting stories is a fun part of my business.

I haven't heard any Breen imitations. It's difficult to imitate a person who is prepared, intelligent, and straightforward in his remarks, without any apparent quirks. He's a good guy who gets the job done right.

There are no imitators of Jim Nantz, CBS-TV's top sports guy on major events. Jim's so smooth, so polished, and so sensitive in his comments that he commands complete respect. He makes the show happen right and never hogs the spotlight. He brings graciousness to the booth. Jim has called the Masters golf tournament for years and his tone fits that sport just right. He also has been CBS's lead announcer on the NCAA post-season basketball tournament. He covers the event in his authoritative style, but is not a basketball screamer. His partner, Clark Kellogg, provides the high-pitched proclamations as the analyst.

This is a reversal of the usual play-by-play and analyst style. For years, the play-by-play has worked as the primary enhancer with a more excited game call while the analyst speaks in a calmer manner. Pat Summerall and John Madden reversed those roles on football with Madden becoming the shouter; Nantz and Kellogg do the same on basketball, with Kellogg handling the exclamations. The reversal fits the personalities of the performers, and both partnerships have been highly successful.

Dick Vitale, who vibrates with energy, is a high-voltage speaker on and off the microphone. One rarely notices his play-by-play partner.

Dave Sims is a major league baseball broadcaster who has learned the trade well. He is quick-thinking. Dave has branched out to football and basketball for ESPN and does exciting radio calls for the Westwood One Network. Dave began as a sportswriter, learning to look for the big story. That's evident in his broadcasting techniques. A good baseball player, too, Dave's a power hitter who was my catcher when I pitched in TV-radio games at Yankee Stadium.

Charlie Steiner, the LA Dodgers play-by-play radio broadcaster is another who made the move from the east to the west coast to continue his career.

Gus Johnson is another versatile sportscaster with an animated style who continues to rise, particularly in basketball.

Michael Kay, the Yankee TV announcer, also began as a sportswriter. His interviews on the YES *CenterStage* celebrity series are outstanding. Mike listens, makes the guest comfortable, is quick to smile or laugh, keeps the pace going, and makes each program an event worth repeating, which the network does. Each program is well researched, bringing out unusual events in each guest's life. A skilled play-by-play man, he demonstrates also the art of listening with his responses and reactions. Phil Rizzuto also was outstanding in this overlooked art, which he did with the ease of eating a cannoli.

Another surprisingly good interviewer is Boomer Esiason, the former pro quarterback. Boomer quickly moved from the gridiron to the microphone. He asks good questions, is well-researched, and exudes confidence in his style. He's a quarterback in the studio too, calling the plays. He also teams well on a talk show with the outspoken Craig Carton, who employs an irreverent approach. Craig was more reserved when he took my sportscasting class in college, but his present outspoken approach has brought him faithful followers. It's a good combination.

John Dockery is another former footballer—with the Jets—who gets right to the point with newsworthy interview questions. John has a masterful manner despite an overflow of publicized present athletes who are brought in to be the pedestrian questioners of the newer crop of stars. John asks frank, right-to-the-point questions. Chris Myers is also a network practitioner of that art, as are Jim Gray, Craig Sager, Chris Fowler, Tracy Wolfson, Erin Andrews and many others. Many women excel in basketball like Madison Square Garden's Tina Cervasio.

Kimberly Jones on the YES Network has made her name in baseball as has Suzyn Waldman. Kimberly is a well-prepared sideline reporter with probing questions.

Former *SportsCenter* anchor Keith Olbermann loves the give-and-take of questioning and is a witty, well-researched observer of sports and politics. He gets right to the heart of a story in a forceful manner. Keith lands strong blows with comments on the political scene, but is always in a serene mood covering baseball.

When the 2008 presidential debates were going on (and the vice-presidential ones, too), Keith would immediately tell his MSNBC viewers of every factual error that was made, which bolstered his opinions of their content.

But sports are also part of his life. A baseball historian, Keith's calling card shows Keith in a baseball uniform. He's worked by my side for many years at Yankee Stadium as I do the play-by-play and Keith the color for the Yankees' yearly Old Timers' Game. It's a fun assignment for both of us and 2010 was our tenth year together. I look forward to this annual reunion with a long-time friend.

Too many former sports stars take jobs as TV interviewers, then ask the same silly questions they spent their playing lives answering. The result is too many queries like, "Did you enjoy winning?" or "Were you upset when you lost?"

Keith Olbermann

It's unfair to put athletes in this position without proper training—the ability to hit a curve ball does not confer the ability to ask a meaningful question. Many hirers don't seem aware of this. Athletes can learn on the job, but a preparation course would make their paths easier.

Speaking well can help land a significant sports related job, even if it's not directly on the airwaves. Cal Ramsey, my former broadcast partner with the Knicks, is a community relations leader for the New York Knicks, representing the team at a large schedule of community events, including meetings with youth groups. Cal speaks at most of them, a voice for the team off the court, and as a New York City Basketball Hall of Famer and a former Knicks player, his comments have meaning.

Cal Ramsey

Hockey Hall of Famer Rod Gilbert does the same type of service for the New York Rangers. Rod adds his French charm and accent to his well-chosen words.

Both men are also constantly seen and heard on TV and radio interviews. They're respected and talented spokesmen for their teams and the Garden organization.

Analysts are becoming the bigger booth personalities in many sports, particularly because they express strong opinions or add humor and insight to the entertainment.

Sports talk radio usually features two-person partnerships, and if the day's sports news is dull, they can always take opposing sides on a larger issue. This can be a dangerous practice unless both do well in these debates while showing great respect for their partner. If they don't appear to like each other and the public gets involved, their fraternal act can come to an end.

Harry Howell Night

Vin Scully, an all-time great, honed his speaking style and pacing to exactly the rhythm he wanted and prefers to work alone. Because of his ability and clout, for many assignments he's allowed to do so.

Radio, with its lengthy sports talk programs, has more time for lively and heated debates on sports issues than TV provides at present, and dotes on outspoken guests. Both media have given the fans more involvement than ever before.

Unemployed coaches or managers keep their exposure at a high level by taking TV jobs which keep them in the public eye and help ease a possible return to field positions.

Newspaper columnists and book authors who can express opinions well have found openings on their airwaves also. Columnist Maury Allen, for many years was an in-demand guest. He died in October 2010 and will be missed. John Feinstein, known for his sports books, now has a radio basketball show; and boxing historian and writer Bert Sugar, known for his ever-present hat and cigar, livens up many a sports show with his sharp comments and devilish wit.

Entertaining personalities—storytellers—are always in demand.

Bert Sugar

23: The Art Of Ad-Libbing

I **LEARNED A LOT** from my playing experience at Duke. I learned that to evaluate oneself, high school stardom is not a true test. A college with top-level athletes gives one a far better appreciation of how one rates on a national level. And hard work is a factor only to a certain point. Some people have a natural gift for what they do—and don't appear to be even working at it.

Ad-libbing to me has always been the easiest act. It's like having a conversation with a friend. There's no worry about the words—they'll just come to you. Just know how to start the story, hold the attention of the listener, and have a good close.

More difficult is compressing a story into a short time sequence. Each word counts.

In the 2009 baseball playoffs and the World Series, I did a minute and a half TV analysis on camera before or after each game. I used the same routine I've used for years and I recommend it.

I take a theme, write down on a small card the points I want to make, and rehearse those points in my mind. It's like telling a story to friends—the words may change slightly, but the story remains the same. I do this aloud once or twice. This gets me ready. I know the story and memorize a few names.

I don't need a stopwatch—I know in my mind how long I'm taking. I used the same technique for years on ABC-TV and at Madison Square Garden. Occasionally we did those pre-games on tape. It may have been luck, but they always came out without a problem. When I taped them, occasionally I'd ask for a second try to put more energy into it. I think the pressure of hitting it live on the first try helped me to concentrate. And frankly, I wanted my first try to be perfect so, if my analyst was standing beside me, he wouldn't have to repeat as well.

Prior to Game 6 (which the Yankees would win, earning them a 27th championship), I made these pre-game story points:

"Here at Yankee Stadium, this is a game for the ages.

"Alex Rodriguez, now at the mature age of 34, has been at his peak in this post-season, swatting home runs and doing his job in the field.

"But it's pitching where age is making the headlines. Andy Pettitte, now 37, was asked by the Yankees to come back this year and help them win this championship. Andy has already won the clinching game in the Division Series and did the same in the American League Championship Series. Now he has a chance in the World Series to make it a clean sweep of big-game playoff victories. Andy is already the number one pitching winner in post-season play.

"His opponent is a year older—Pedro Martinez, the crafty old-timer pitching for the Phillies. He's 38. Pedro has to win to keep the Phillies alive for a seventh game.

"If the Yankees take the lead and hold it, in the bullpen they have baseball's greatest closer—Mariano Rivera. Mariano is 39 and still going strong. As I said, it's a game for the ages.

"Incidentally, I always celebrate Mariano's birthday. I was born on the same day and month. The years are different, though."

"From Yankee Stadium, I'm Bob Wolff for News 12."

When teaching at Pace University and St. John's in the mornings while broadcasting in afternoons or at night, one of the unpleasant chores I faced—along with other professors—was giving out grades. Some kids deserved As for effort, but not for the ability they displayed in classroom

Bob Wolff, News 12 at Yankee Stadium

discussions. Others had the knack of answering test questions right on target, even if they rarely showed that energy in the classroom. In grading, I wanted to recognize effort, but couldn't overlook ability.

Aware of this, in the course I taught on public speaking, the students really graded themselves. I explained to the youngsters that the content they used in answering questions verbally had to demonstrate excellent preparation, research, and ability to communicate a story or an idea. It also had to hold the audience in an appealing manner that would induce a strong positive reaction from the audience—applause, laughter, tears. The worst outcome was a negative one or no reaction at all—indifference.

Success was measured by the positive reaction it provoked, and that's how students were being graded.

I warned them that this would be different from other courses where one memorized answers and just spouted them back, so if they

BOB WOLFF'S COMPLETE GUIDE TO SPORTSCASTING

were worried about grades, it might be wise to consider classes where effort would correlate with grades.

I explained that in speaking, the best stories come from the speaker's own lives. They're unique to each person. Further, they're easy to remember and more emotional because they're part of you, not somebody else.

And then I let each student speak, without preparation. Tips on how to improve would come later. First, I wanted to see how much each brought to the assignment.

How does this fit in with sportscasting? Say the start of the game is being delayed—maybe the lights in the arena are not working—your order is just keep talking. Or on TV, the picture conks out. Keep talking. You need confidence to do this. When broadcasting I enjoyed this type of challenge; I knew I had material to use.

I used a variety of tough test topics in the classroom to prepare them for this possibility.

My most popular: "Speak for two minutes about the importance of paper clips. Starting . . . now."

Some would get up, take their turn by mumbling, "Paper clips are used to hold paper together—and, er, er—for other things, too," and then sit down. Others might last a minute or so. One or two would actually give a full two-minute dissertation, but without an appealing presentation.

Most were laughing at each other for their ineptness. They were sharing a similar experience. There was nervousness and a fear of being embarrassed.

I explained to them after this exercise that being nervous was a natural feeling, not one to be alarmed about. Every top performer suddenly put on stage like this should be nervous—if not, they're abnormal, and it's difficult to perform if one is abnormal.

Then I explained a surefire way to perform on the fly without preparation: by calling on what they know, what they've observed, read, or experienced. This draws upon a lifetime of preparation. Preparation they weren't even aware of.

If you're called to walk up to the stage and perform, I said, think quickly of how you'll delve into the subject of paper clips in a way to capture attention—and then how you'll hold the audience. And end with a good closing line.

Imagine a book about paper clips—with each chapter as a separate topic. If you think of these topics, each one is good for several minutes, particularly if embellished with personal stories.

"All right, class," I'd say. "Let's list some chapter topics on paper clips."

Hands were raised with topics: "Different sizes of paper clips," "color of paper clips," "cost of paper clips," "inventor of paper clips," "other uses of paper clips—instead of buttons, for example," "shape of paper clips," "making little figurines with paper clips," "personal paper clip stories," "danger of paper clips," "design of paper clips," "selling paper clips," and more.

And as a possible close, "So, friends, in this great world of ours, let's always remember that a little paper clip, such as this one I'm holding in my hand, is the greatest unifying force of all."

Exit to applause. All this preparation is already within you. Just call on it when needed. At year's end, we had some great ad-libbers.

In the early days of television, comedian Milton Berle was its most famous performer. One day, I was waiting to do an interview with him in Washington where he was appearing in a stage show. Berle was late arriving at the studio, and there was barely time for me to ask what direction he'd like to take on the interview.

"Milton," I said, "what topic do you want me to discuss before we talk about your show?"

"Bob, just ask me about any sport. I've got two or three gags about them all." The show began, I went from sport to sport, and it went great. Milton had arrived prepared. He knew he could lead any conversation into his sports bits.

Milton Berle

In choosing topics for class discussion, there are a few surefire ones I'd use to help students work on ad-libbing, their confidence in delivery, and their audience appeal.

"Tell the class something about your life that you find both unusual and emotional." I've heard answers that left our group in tears and some that left us laughing. Content and execution rated top grades.

One girl, who seemed rather shy, had the class spellbound as she told of her constant search to find and meet her true parents. She loved the couple that adopted her, but yearned to know where she came from and what circumstances had forced her parents to give her up.

That was a silent room when she ended. There was no applause—just sympathy—a most difficult way to fulfill a school assignment.

There was also a youngster from a foreign country who told us of the ritual that was an old tribal custom in the initiation of going from youth to being declared a man. Armed with only a knife, a boy had to spend time in the jungle, protecting himself, feeding himself, finding a spot to sleep, and finally emerging, now admitted to manhood. I don't remember all the details of this ordeal, there was no script, but it certainly held everyone's attention.

The assignment focused on how vital a story is in journalism, but it also showed the students they had that power within to make people listen. Further, as a group, each moved from being just a student to becoming a full personality in the classroom, an event that doesn't happen too often in class routines.

Another good exercise is taking the other side of a current hot topic— the unpopular side. I borrowed this idea from my philosophy course. I was fascinated by the dialogue between the greatest minds of their time, who would argue topics such as "what is beautiful" or "what is honest" or "is sound actually produced if one isn't around to hear it." There was never an absolute truth in these answers, never a winner. (No one, no matter how clever one is, can prove most of these declarations.) These mental duels between philosophers were fascinating. Tolerance was being preached, for while one may not agree with an opposing viewpoint, it's worth listening to and considering. In other words, the debates provided a valuable lesson in seeing how words, right or wrong, can influence opinions and judgments. Being true to one's convictions is vital, but truth, philosophers concede, is difficult to define.

There are a number of challenging topics. Speak on the benefits of tobacco, of jail, athletic scholarships, aluminum bats used in Little League, an unpopular political candidate, or about a losing team. Speaking about winners is easy. Remember that except for a lucky few, the majority of sportscasters who do play-by-play or analytical work for the pros or colleges, have called or have played for contending teams. On audition tapes, a truer test is not how the sportscaster sounds on a winning touchdown or home run or basket, but how he holds an audience when one's team keeps losing. That's the real test.

Always remember, in the NCAA basketball tournament at the conclusion of the hoop season, sixty-eight teams are invited to participate. sixty-seven teams leave as losers.

I always believed that ad-libbing helped me as a sportscaster. The ability to tell impromptu stories to hold one's audience is a valuable asset when a game is delayed by weather or some other problem. And it doesn't always have to be a sports story. It might be related to sports, but it's good to have other knowledge as well.

Nowadays, most delayed games return to the station for filler pro-gramming—and the audience plummets. This does not sit well with advertisers who have paid for large numbers to view or hear their commercials.

When one is doing a ballgame—whatever the sport—there is no time for long stories.

The worst mishap is starting a story that relies on a strong punch line, finding that the first two batters have quickly gone out on fly balls or pop-ups—and you're only halfway through your engrossing story.

If the next batter flies out on the first pitch, it's commercial time—and your story has not reached its conclusion. Keep long stories for the right time—when the punch line is not rushed. During action, make story points quickly, don't intrude on the action.

Analysts have to be quick, darting in and out with pithy observa-tions. Joe Garagiola, my partner, had terrific timing, creativity, and humor.

During rain delays on those games, NBC would stay at the field. The reason was financial. Each contracted team would play the game even if they had to wait hours for the rain to stop—they got paid only if the game was televised. So Joe and I stayed on camera, tell-ing stories, swapping opinions. In my pocket, I always carried a list headed "Rain Stories." Just the titles; I knew the stories. These were the long tales, pre-tested in conversations or at banquet appearances, that I knew would hold an audience but were too long to tell during the game itself.

Joe could go on stage for an hour or more also spinning his yarns. We were well-matched for this possibility and could trigger each oth-er's thoughts.

I remember, before I left ABC-TV to join NBC-TV that Mets General Manager George Weiss had spoken to me about how I would compete with the Yankees' Mel Allen.

"Mr. Weiss," I answered him, "Mel Allen is an all-time great. His voice is his weapon. He also has had the benefit of being with winning teams. He provides good news. Mel is big on the old-time greats, so my content is different. Mel loves to reminisce. I deal more with stories about our current players.

"With the Washington Senators, my battle was to generate excitement for a losing team, to keep people listening and the sponsors happy. I relied on stories to fill in the silence of a losing series or a team out of contention. I always thought better days were coming. My content and my excitement were vital to the Senators' broadcasts and, if I took your job, I believe I'd provide what's needed for a developing team."

While I was doing national telecasts on NBC-TV without an analyst, on one National Invitation Tournament basketball game in the early 1960s, I had a good chance to illustrate ad-libbing to Tom Gallery, the network's sports director.

Mel Allen

It was St. Patrick's Day, March 17, and I was at the mike for the Navy-Duquesne game. I had just started to welcome viewers across the country from courtside at Madison Square Garden when the game director's voice in my earpiece told me there would be a delay in the start of the game. It seems that the St. Patrick's Day Parade had stalled traffic in New York City and some workers who were expected to be at courtside were late in arriving. He told me to keep ad-libbing.

I was prepared for such a possibility. I explained what to look for in the game. I told the viewers that Navy coach Ben Carnevale always prepared scientifically for a game and noted which opposing player would take the most shots and which one the fewest. Ben planned his defense accordingly.

The go-to-guy for Duquesne was Willie Somerset—a small guard with a great shot who had led his club in game after game.

His main feeder for shots was a wily passer named Bill Stromple, who averaged around six points per game. In some games, I said, Bill would attempt as few as six shots. Chances are Stromple's defender will help with Somerset, I declared. Assists and defense were Stromple's specialties. I had taken time that week to watch both teams work out and gave a half-hour rundown of what to expect from players on both sides.

My finals words before tip-off, "So watch for Stromple's defensive man to fall off him to help with guarding Somerset. That's been the defensive-type plan that Coach Carnevale has used so successfully against top scorers during the season."

The game began. Stromple's man gave him freedom to shoot while moving closer to Somerset. Stromple hit three shots in a row for Duquesne—and Navy never recovered. Duquesne won the game. I was proud of my preparation and NBC and the NIT Committee were especially pleased.

Some years later, I needed a statistician assistant for a TV game I was televising in Pittsburgh, home of Duqesene. I thought of Bill Stromple and gave him a call; he was surprised to hear from me, but joined me to work in the booth. We had a great time reminiscing after the game. Bill was surprised but delighted that I had remembered his role.

24: Your Mind Can Be Your Secret Weapon

I BELIEVE MANY PEOPLE don't know how great their minds can be because they don't take time to test them.

A large part of sportscasting is memorizing names for quick identification during games—and by quick, I mean instantaneously. It's a conditioned response. See the number and give the name of the player automatically without pondering. If a spotter points to a number or if it's flashed on the TV monitor, then in the second or so while you're looking for it, the runner may have picked up five or more yards. Memorization wins.

At my peak, I was broadcasting an average 250 games including double-headers and day and night events each year. With seasons overlapping, on weekends I'd broadcast a college football *Game of the Week* in the afternoon, fly to another city (sometimes with a rented plane and pilot), telecast a hockey or basketball game that night, fly to another city after the game to do a pro football game on Sunday, then fly home and continue with more games and daily shows all week.

That meant memorizing hundreds of numbers every week—and that, in itself took time. College Games of the Week were the toughest. Different teams each week, different players each season. With the pros, many players were the same from year to year—they didn't graduate.

I found it amazing how a mind works. By game time on any Saturday afternoon, I knew the numbers—had them down cold—no hesitancy calling every player on both teams. And there were large football squads—most schools dressed everybody. Twenty-four hours later, I could store all those numbers in another part of my brain, and knew both pro squads without confusing them with the previous college game.

For NIT basketball at Madison Square Garden, I'd telecast two games in the afternoon, another two games at night, and repeat this schedule the next day. Numbers, day and night.

Here's what I learned about memorization. It can't be done well at one sitting. Spread it out over days. Plant the seeds and overnight they'll grow. On a Monday, I'd take my first look at the roster, run my eyes down one team's list and see how many numbers I'd remember. I'd keep repeating that. Then I'd take four numbers at a time, going down the list, then up to eight, increasing as I went along. Oddly, there was always one or two that I kept forgetting. I'd go back and work on them. After about one half hour or possibly an hour of this on a Monday afternoon, I'd write each number on a separate small card, and after dinner or maybe when taking a plane or being driven to an airport, I'd turn up cards to see how many numbers I now could name. The next day, I'd remember many of them, including ones I'd missed the previous day, though there were some I'd still forget.

I'd separate the ones I'd miss and go through them three or four more times. Then I'd put the numbers away and let them sink in by themselves. The next day, I'd repeat the process and see how many of the numbers would give me instant name identification.

By Thursday, I was ready for Jane or our three kids to start asking me numbers—sometimes we had contests as to who could memorize the most names. It was a fun game to play, and it was nice to discover how well the young kids could do. Not only would I know the numbers, but also I'd respond automatically without having to think first.

What astounded me is how quickly one can shuffle yesterday's numbers away and learn the necessary new ones. What also amazes

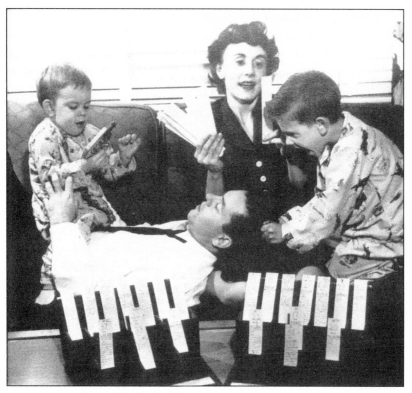

Learning numbers with the family

me is that, years later, I'd meet a college player for a team I called just once, and I could flatter him by calling out his number.

I learned early on that for television coverage, it was vital to have the TV monitor (the set I was watching during the game) right in front of me, sitting low into the table desk, so it didn't bother my view of the field. It took years before I could get this set-up on road trips. If I'm speaking about the quarterback and the picture shows the coach shouting something from the sidelines, the viewer wants me to shift my words to acknowledge the coach, too. The picture rules. That's a primary lesson for all TV sportscasters.

When I did bowl games on the radio networks, I always asked for a TV monitor in the booth as well. Camera close-ups of short plunges for touchdowns magnify my view from fifty yards away. On hockey I wanted a monitor so I could identify deflections.

On baseball, I wanted to see replays. Basketball is the easiest. One is sitting closer, there are fewer bodies in play, and player heights assist with identification.

The ultimate in quickness occurs when one follows the same team for a season. Numbers are no longer necessary to identify a player, and are replaced by body movements, mannerisms, size, and physical characteristics such as red hair or no hair.

Doing basketball with numbers memorized and sitting close to the action, I would follow the ball naming the passer and receiver, and who was guarding the hot shooter. Paramount was always giving the score. Viewers want the essentials. Scoring totals, fouls, time left and all the rest are important, but giving the score takes precedence.

In studio work, I tested my brain in another way—and found my brain responded. When I started doing college and pro scores shows on TV for the ABC Network, I was selected to do the highlights of games while my partners would give scores. I worked with three top-flighters, one of whom, Jim Simpson, I had hired in Washington as a young fellow with potential just starting out. Jim kept moving upward. Many years later, I got a big kick out of watching Jim on ESPN College World Series games with my son Rick as the analyst.

Jim was succeeded on the scoreboard shows by Pat Hernon, another talented fellow, and then versatile Jim McKay, who continued with ABC to win renown on the *Wide World of Sports.*

On the scoreboard shows, game highlights came in from news wire services, from all around the country. Some games had ended, and I rewrote those stories to make them about thirty seconds apiece and to have them sound more conversational. For late scores coming in, I hired a terrific young writer, Phil Pepe, to do the same using the same approach. We usually did two shows—one for the East, one for the West, so some made the second show. This was on camera, but there were no video highlights—scores were put up manually on a standing

Bob Wolff, *Wide World of Sports*

scoreboard by a young fellow, Jim Spence, who went on to become a top ESPN executive.

I found out that instead of having to look down during the show to read the highlights, I could glance down for just a second before I went on camera and memorize the entire paragraph with a visual picture. People used to marvel at my performance. How did I have all the important game details on the air so quickly without reading them? A little training is all it takes. It's only fear that keeps others from trying this. Just take one quick glance down at the story before going on camera. The picture stays in your mind. It takes practice, but it can be done. One just has to feel confident to try it. One glance can give the brain a picture of a paragraph full of words.

In later years, when giving highlights on camera at ballparks or giving longer pre-game notes on camera, I'd take a small white card, put down a few key words, hold this out of sight, it was only for security, rehearse in my mind what I wanted to say, and begin. No reading required. In later years, when teleprompters arrived and adhering to exact running times became important. I'd use prompters in the studio but not at ballparks or arenas. And gradually I'd forget about the security cards. I put in my mind the points I wanted to make and didn't worry about the words.

I didn't need exact words. A salesman who knows what he needs to say doesn't read a sales pitch. Same goes for on-camera work. Know what you want to say, add enthusiasm, and that's it. Being natural is the best way.

And except for a few formal occasions where each word has a special meaning, like an induction speech at Cooperstown, or the Basketball Hall of Fame, or the Madison Square Garden Walk of Fame, I just ad-lib, whenever possible—on radio and on TV.

Television producers prefer everything to be written for many shows as the timing is vital. Producers know what's coming next. If video is needed along with one's comments, the script shows when it should be added to the spoken words. Your words are listed as "voice over." There's also a record kept of all shows. Studio news-sports shows are scripted, except for an occasional wisecrack or banter among the anchors and the reporters.

I always prized the banter as the personality part of the show. Great chance to inject some ad-libbed humor and informality.

It's odd, but true—it's more difficult to compose words to fit a short time slot than to speak extemporaneously at greater length. Pruning one's copy to have the same impact with fewer words is an overlooked but important art. I value the editors who eliminate some of my verbosity—as long as they leave my laugh lines untouched. Those are the ones that really count.

When I taught classes at Pace and St. John's, I knew what I wanted to say and so spoke without notes. It certainly establishes a closer bond with students than reading from a book. For many years, I've given talks at Fordham University's Sports Workshop, run by Bob

Ahrens. I use the same method. If nothing else, it shows students how it can be done.

Two important notes with credit to one's brain. For years I broadcast a fifteen minute radio sports show. This is not like writing a book or letter, where one may, on second thought, decide to make a couple of changes. One has to be aware that a late story may change what you planned to say.

I'd sit down, dash off a script for the show in one take (in those days on a typewriter), and read it on the air. There was no time for anything else, I did this between a bunch of other programs I was doing.

One day I thought, *Why am I typing these words and reading them? If I can write without changing the words, why can't I speak like that? Why not let the words go right from my head to the microphone? Why am I writing them down first?*

I decided to bring in any notes I might need—the story order and any necessary numbers—and just ad-lib the entire show. It worked then and it still works today. Most sportscasters who read off telepromters try to sound as if they're ad-libbing, with natural pauses and throw-away lines. Top actors who memorize lines try for the same effect.

An important note for play-by-players, particularly those on the radio: Your broadcasts can't have a stop and go flavor. When calling a play, if for any reason you don't see the number or can't remember the name, don't stop to look for it, don't guess for it, don't call out the wrong person. Call the play, keep your rhythm going, and then give the name.

Unsure of the carrier? Here's how to handle it: "Quick plunge off right tackle—good for four yards. That moves the ball to the 34 yard line. And once again the Lions called on that hard-hitting halfback, Tim Green, to keep his team advancing. Second and six coming up." Delaying the carrier's name—while still providing useful information—gave you time to watch him get up and spot his number. Chances are the listeners won't notice, as the rhythm stayed the same.

An amateur would hold up the rest of his call until he determined who carried the ball.

Here's a finesse call of an unidentified interception: "It's intercepted at the forty, a quick cut to the right sideline, across midfield before Tom Drake brings down Jimmy Papillon, who's been outstanding all afternoon. That's his third interception."

It's far better to identify the defender as he intercepts the ball if you can, but the example above provides a viable back-up plan if needed.

I would be remiss if I didn't explain another way the mind can give a sportscaster a decided edge.

Sideline reporters are hired to get a quick comment from a coach or manager, report on an injury, or to add a new look, or a big name, or a smile to the broadcast, but they're rarely more than a payroll luxury. It's tough to do anything meaningful in sixty seconds or so. For the performer, it's a payday with good exposure.

Most interview questions are innocuous, designed for what they receive, short stock answers. Of course the interviewer has to appear energetic, excited, and delighted with this opportunity. Remember though, the audience watching the game is curious about plays, calls, decisions, and anything relating to the game. They're looking for answers. Ask questions to satisfy their curiosity. It makes this short interview more than a social visit.

I do my interviews without notes or cue cards, but I know in my mind what I want to find out. The tone of the program—a friendly conversation—is designed for natural appeal. The players were all relaxed, they weren't on guard or wary—they trusted me. Unscripted, I could move in any direction.

My questions were designed to elicit answers which were informative and entertaining, the same goal sought by Johnny Carson, David Letterman, and Jay Leno. Every good interviewer wants lively conversations which hold attention.

It helps to come prepared with research on each guest. The more you know about the guest's work, his strengths, his background, his interests as a person, his family background, his talents, the more at ease the guest will feel.

I didn't need notes. Notes would detract from a natural conversation. If I had to look down for my next question, it would prevent a natural follow-up to an answer the guest had given me. That's where the gold lies—in the follow-up.

So what did I rely on to keep the flow going? In one word, curiosity. That's the key. I came ready to ask questions I was curious about. I didn't work at being curious. I'm intrigued by people, I'm curious to find out more about them. There's no shortage of questions and I was bound only by the time of each show.

Here is a sample of a few of the questions I asked Ted Willams when he was my guest. I asked them, without notes, because I was curious.

"Ted, why do you take so many strikes?"

"Ted, why do you keep flexing your fingers on the bat?"

"Ted, why don't you try to hit to the opposite field when they shift defenses on you?"

"Ted, have you changed your batting style during the years?"

"Ted, who's the fastest pitcher you've faced?"

"Ted, does what you do in batting practice reflect how you'll do in the game?"

All good reporters have to be curious and eager to find answers. If they ask the questions they and the public what to know, they're on the road to become winners.

Curiosity also supplies content for the play-by-play man to weave into the game or surrounding shows, observations worth listening to. The most curious sportscasters become the best-informed.

Being curious is the best weapon a sports reporter can have. This field is wide open because not all hirers realize that their interviewers need an inquiring mind.

25: Being Different Is An Asset

BEING A WELL-PREPARED, conscientious journalist does not mean that one can't be entertaining on TV as well. College professors are learned intellectuals yet are rarely hired as news anchors; people you see on the screen must also have personal appeal as performers.

Walter Cronkite, the "most trusted man in America," never finished college, but no journalist was more respected. Walter was an authoritative person. Personal appeal is the extra that all good performers have. Appeal is what convinces stations, networks, and sponsors to hire you.

I've always enjoyed the lighter side of TV communication. It adds a little entertainment to the serious tone of the daily newscast, where negative problems receive the greatest coverage.

For years I've done weekly light humor essays as a supplement to my basic sportscasting work. Serious points can be made through humor. On play-by-play and studio shows, I tried to inject observations which will bring a smile. In banter with colleagues, nothing is better than ending one's segment with a hearty laugh shared by all.

A good, unexpected line can be remembered more than any other part of a show. America's late-night hosts, with assistance from their writers, are experts at making conversations with guests amusing. Not just idle talk, but fun. That's why they last so long.

For years, I did all the interviews with the winners at Madison Square Garden events on the MSG Network: the Westminster Kennel Club Dog shows, the Millrose Games track meets, and Virginia Slims tennis tournaments—one interview after the other, live. I wanted to capture the euphoria of winning, but also the informality of a personal conversation, not an inquisition. My baseball interviews were first used in Washington, New York, Boston, and other major league cities and then nationally.

In my mind, I divided each interview into three parts, each designed to get a different reaction.

Suppose I was talking to a victorious runner. My first question would be a conversation opener. "I understand your favorite snack before a race is a tuna sandwich. Was that your diet tonight?" That should bring a smile. My second question was for newsworthiness. "When did you decide to put on that finishing kick that won the race for you?" The last question sought to send us off with a happy response, "Right after you won, I saw you wave to someone in the stands. Was that somebody special to you?"

My technique was like a quick three-act play. A relaxing question, a newsworthy point, and end with a smile—that was always the goal.

For thirty-three years, I televised a change-of-pace event at Madison Square Garden, the Westminster Kennel Club Dog Show. The show had a large TV audience as it appealed to all ages and most viewers rooted for the breed they loved. The climax was the selection of the "Best in Show" from all the group winners, a stern test for the well-qualified and impartial judge.

To make it as fair as possible, audience applause at the Garden was not to be considered, nor was the competition dog against dog, or handler against handler. The winner was the dog that came closest to perfection in the standards of its particular breed.

I also enjoyed coming up with taped light humor stories for these two-day events. There was time to run these features as the ring at the Garden was cleared between each group of dogs.

In one, I appeared on camera and told the TV audience that I was about to reveal, for the first time ever, what was really meant by those

Bob interviews canine friend

words always heard on broadcast sports events, "We pause for station identification." Then I pulled a miniature Chihuahua from under my tuxedo coat and held the little dog right in front of the camera. "Here they are, friends, exhibited for the first time, 'wee paws'—for station identification." I know the guys in the control room were laughing, and hoped the audience would be, too.

One night I started the show with an excellent impersonator, Dan Myerson, interrupting my early on-camera remarks. Dan was adorned with a Groucho Marx mustache, glasses, a cigar in one hand, wearing a long frock coat. I had just opened the show talking about the dogs at Madison Square Garden. I asked the Groucho look-alike why he had come to the show. Dan held up a hot dog, took a big bite, and proclaimed, "I heard they have the greatest dogs in the world here." He then took another bite, swallowed, winked at the camera, and when I said, "I agree," he said, "You said a mouthful" and sauntered away Groucho style as I resumed my opening comments.

These little pieces were taped. My main conversations didn't make light of a serious event. The people who show dogs work very hard at their craft and have earned respect. Ozzie, our family beagle, was a wonderful friend for seventeen years—loved and treated as a family member. I didn't want to displease any fellow dog fanciers—but dogs are fun, and I didn't want to turn my back on that—so always discussed possible reaction to a skit with the producers before including it. There were no complaints.

One year I dressed in a uniform top that had coach written across it. Their handlers brought about twenty dogs into a locker room and I gave them a fiery "pup talk" getting them ready to show.

Another night I consoled a dog who had lost. Lying on a table in front of me, the sad-eyed dog seemed to appreciate my trying to be a dog's best friend, a reversal of the usual relationship between canines and mankind.

Another time, I staged a parody of the Miss America Pageant. I put on a Miss Personality competition, composed and sang a song for the occasion, and used some little kids as judges (though I dismissed one from the panel when he told me on camera, "I have to go potty").

The shows aired not only on the Madison Square Garden Network but the USA Network. When the judges got down to choosing the final winner, there was the same terrific tension of any human sporting event. Every championship I've done—in every sport—has that elation of winning—or disappointment at a loss. It's live—the audience shares the emotion.

The TV audience for the dog shows was a large one. Most people have a favorite dog breed to root for. The show appeals to all ages with excellent demographics. Adding little unexpected hijinks provided an extra special touch.

The two producers on those early shows, the talented duo of Mike McCarthy and Howie Singer—added to the spirit of the occasion. They produced "Westminster Wiggle" to appropriate rock music, and a dog soap opera. It was great fun to work on this show for thirty-three years.

I also sang songs with humorous lyrics that I wrote about the dogs, "And now we're at the end, just let the credits roll, this Westminster prize, is like the Super Bowl." I'm no Frank Sinatra, but I can stay on key and my lyrics fit the occasion, so I got by. I put my ukulele down eventually and asked Eddie Layton, the legendary organist for Madison Square Garden, Yankee Stadium, the Nassau Coliseum, and countless network shows to accompany me.

I loved our recording sessions together. When we did one that clicked, Eddie would say, "That's it!" That was praise from the master. One day, Eddie, aware as I was of how big a business dog life had become, suggested we put out a dog show album together. People bought dog food, dog vitamins, dog paintings, dog grooming, dog houses, dog clothing, dog books—why not dog records? I was flattered by Eddie's suggestion, but told him, "I'm not sure how many dogs would buy the album."

I've always thought, however, that if I compiled the dog show skits and added some bark-by-bark competition highlights, it might make an amusing package for a dog show sponsor to use as a show or a giveaway. That project would take time I couldn't spare. It's still in the file cabinet.

While dogs are frisky, the most amazing thing to me about the dog shows is that those champion dogs didn't bark at each other. When I did the National Horse Show for many years, those animals were regal and didn't lend themselves to horse tricks. Yet I wouldn't refrain from contemplating an attempt at debunking a commonly held belief about them.

I had heard for years that "You can lead a horse to water, but can't make him drink." I exploded that myth on camera. I personally led a horse to a bucket of water—and the horse drank. Buoyed by that success, I was eager to disprove the myth that, "You can't change horses in mid-stream." There were no streams in Madison Square Garden to prove it could be done, but if I do an outdoor horse show in the future, I plan to give it a try.

One stunt that worked I have never tried again. Milk-Bone dog biscuits was the sponsor, and I offered the sponsor's biscuit to a winning dog. Immediately, my heart was in my throat. Suppose the dog wouldn't eat it? Everybody would think that was funny—except the sponsor, the Garden, the network—and me. My job could be at stake.

The dog devoured the biscuit, and I was a hero. But never again would I gamble on a dog's appetite. Frankly, if the dog had sniffed the treat and turned away, I might have tried to eat it myself, to prove its quality. Dog biscuits, though, are too hard for human teeth. I do know that sponsors don't want to get laughs at their product.

I also learned that I can no longer pull off stunts which fit my early days. One year at Westminster, on camera I asked John Ashby, a famed dog photographer, to take my picture. "John," I said in a little sketch I had outlined for him, "I find it hard to get a good picture of myself, understandably, but you're an artist, can you help out?" John said "Yes" and I said "That's great, John, should I stand over here?" John shook his head, "Bob, I'm a dog show photographer, that's what I do. Just hop up on my table, get down on all fours and look happy. I'll get the picture." So I hopped up on the table and looked at the camera. "Bob," John said, "I don't like the expression." He held out some vile-smelling stuff, which proved to be liver. "Sorry, John, I don't like liver." John pulled out weapon number two—a small rubber mouse he called Squeaky. He squeezed Squeaky, but the sound had no effect on me.

At this point, a good-looking girl walked by, pre-arranged, spotted me on all fours and laughed at the sight. I grinned at her as John snapped the picture and shouted, "Great, that's it."

I thanked the attractive dog show patron for helping out and the feature drew praise.

But times change and so do bodies. I couldn't use that feature today for two reasons. Number one, I wouldn't risk jumping up on the table. Number two, I'm not sure what the reaction would be of an older man using that big smile for a young beauty. The smile would be genuine, but what would be the perception?

So one keeps changing the nuttiness throughout the years. There's always another way to perform the unexpected. Just make sure that the joke doesn't backfire.

One day at a Virginia Slims tennis match at Madison Square Garden, I was interviewing a woman on TV who was the handler for tennis star Martina Navratilova's dog, nicknamed Killer Dog. Killer was the size of

Chris Evert

a puffed-up marshmallow, small enough to lie at the top of Martina's gym bag and gallantly guard over whatever valuable possessions Martina stored there. Obviously a position of trust.

During the interview about the handler's unusual occupation, I mentioned my friendship with dogs and reached over to pet my anticipated new one. The result sent our studio crew into hysterics and became a fixture on the Garden's highlight reel. Killer Dog jumped out of her resting place as my arm came toward her; and before I could draw back, Killer Dog nipped my shoulder, sending me sprawling off my interview stool and onto the floor, where I signed off this segment. A great moment in Garden history.

During another Garden interview, I was demonstrating the technique to get the proper head on a beer, which I had mastered when I was doing commercials live. This time the beer didn't cooperate. It came out of the bottle like a volcano. I was covered with suds, a pool in my lap, with beer running down my face as well. I had a gusher. That was my last on-camera beer pour. Fortunately, the audience loved it.

And changing an expected line always helps. I was covering a tennis match at Madison Square Garden for WPIX Channel 11 in New York, and the indefatigable Tracy Austin was keeping the ball in play from the baseline. She'd wear out all her opponents. Every half hour I'd say, "Stay tuned for 'the Prisoner of Cell Block H'" at the end of the match.

We were now in early morning hours when the director said, "Say it again." I began the same way, but then couldn't resist. "We'll have 'the Prisoner of Cell Block H' on at the conclusion of the match—if he's not already out on parole."

26: Agents And Public Relations People

ON A LOCAL level, agents really aren't a necessity because all the doors should be open to you. Local broadcasters become part of the town. However, in New York with its multiple TV, radio, and cable stations, if one is seeking contract renewal, a larger contract, or greater network exposure, an established agent is a valuable asset.

They are particularly helpful in negotiating contracts. Let the agent do all the talking about your worth and the money that you should be paid for your services. It's not appropriate for you to discuss this. It's immodest to be boosting yourself or bickering over contract stipulations—that's the agent's job.

The more established agents have the best connections with the hirers—usually on a personal level—and they're skilled at follow-ups.

Be aware, though, that the top agents represent in-demand performers, most of whom already have big exposure programs. Agents are always seeking even more lucrative contracts and further opportunities for their clients. The more established their stars are, the better the agents can do for themselves as well. They'll occasionally add a few young talented sportscasters who have made local reputations in major cities and appear to have network potential.

Younger agents without established stars may take on promising newcomers, but rarely do so unless they feel they have excellent potential for advancement. The plus side is that they have more time to devote to the selling process, but don't have the strong contacts as yet at high levels.

Despite years of doing network play-by-play along with my local shows in Washington, I didn't sign with an agent until I moved to New York. Milt Fenster had an excellent reputation and was a skilled negotiator. Milt impressed me as a person, and hiring him proved to be a wise move. He's been both a great friend and guide in many business decisions.

Steve Porricelli, a former student of mine, handled all my later negotiations with News 12 Long Island. It's been a wonderful relationship and I'm indebted to Al Primo for getting it started.

Bob Costas, an excellent play-by-play man on NBC-TV, saw his network lose the World Series game rights. FOX, using Joe Buck, Tim McCarver, and reporter Ken Rosenthal took over these coveted games. Bob joined the new MLB Network in order to stay closer to diamond activity, leaving his HBO studio show to do so. Pursuing what one wants to do is a difficult path. Being with the right station or network can be a major part in fulfilling one's sportscasting ambitions.

The most unusual publicity representation I've had was the late Mike Cohen who was so well-liked and admired in media circles that a recommendation from Mike would always be listened to and acted upon.

Mike made his mark in a most unusual way. First of all, he was a brilliant newsman—he recognized the type of story that would always make it into print or on-air reporting, and he knew instinctively which columnist or reporter or newspaper or magazine would go for it. Whether one-liners, features, or human-interest stories, Mike's material kept appearing in local and national columns. Mike was a fighter—for causes and for those he represented. He was also a friend and an advisor.

Mike never bothered with press releases. He made contact personally—either over the phone or through private notes to the top columnists. When Mike called, people listened. Mike's creativity was a great source for column material—and usually was ladled out on an exclusive basis. Many writers were indebted to him for the behind-the-scenes revelations he provided.

Mike developed a whole squad of young PR people and then helped them get jobs at colleges and stations in the New York area. They were all his people. Mike's influence was widespread.

The remarkable part of Mike's approach was his bluntness, his honesty, and his refusal to be a "yes man" to any network superior if he disagreed with how a PR problem was being resolved.

Mike's personal critiques were a constant source of assistance to national broadcasters who would seek his counsel at half-times of games with quick phone calls to make sure they were living up to his expectations. Marv Albert and Charlie Jones were just two of the network stars who made sure to check with Mike.

Mike knew every sport, but had a particular passion for boxing and track and field. When I worked those Madison Square Garden events, I always prepared with Mike.

Mike worked up the ladder handling boxing and harness racing on the way to the top sports PR spot at NBC-TV. He later opened his own agency.

But it was his outspokenness that meant such a difference in his career and his closeness with the media. The top media moguls whom Mike worked for were afraid to cross Mike by making decisions in public relations that Mike didn't approve of. The fear was that if Mike left them in protest, people would assume there must be flaws in the executive's thinking, not Mike's. By saying no to the powerful, Mike held power. Mike Weissman, the talented NBC-TV sports chief for many years, was one of Mike's strongest boosters.

Mike could increase his client's contracts. He'd arrange lunches with competing network bosses, mention his client, and somehow the word would appear in gossip columns that his client might be considering a better contract with a new boss. This bit of make-believe usually resulted in a long-term boost in pay.

Quite aside from the PR business, when I was the commissioner of the Atlantic Collegiate Baseball League, a proving ground for prospective draftees, Mike was the president. I took bows, but Mike made the tough decisions.

I always got a chuckle out of his power. If I ever phoned a major network person to set up an appointment for an idea I wanted to propose, my call would always be accepted immediately. The first question I'd be asked was, "How's your friend Mike doing?" Columnists feasted on the notes he fed them. He was a remarkable person, a great personal friend, who took an unusual path to the top of his craft. Mike passed away at an early age, but his impact on the media is still felt with his many disciples. When I televised a major event, I'd call Mike to check on my grade. I miss Mike.

At the higher sportscasting levels, creating publicity and keeping one's name in the papers are great assets in getting jobs. And I mean exposure in a positive way.

Exposure doesn't mean the performer has more talent. It means that the person is better known, which increases the chances of attracting a bigger audience and higher ratings. That's how stations make money, by selling ratings. Newspapers do stories about bigger names, that's an important part of being recognized. The better known are labeled celebrities. They qualify through exposure.

Most top performers are well aware of the benefits of publicity. And the more publicity a sportscaster receives, the more valuable he or she becomes to an agent.

At the networks, PR people are assigned to help with interviews, promotions, and guest appearances. This is all part of the creation of stars, and stars sell.

Not all publicity is good, though in Hollywood, it doesn't seem to matter, good or bad, except to one's personal life. In sports, however, poor publicity can not only cause personal problems, it can also scare off advertisers who pay the bills. It can cost jobs. In movies, it may actually help the box office receipts.

For some years now, I've worked with Scott Cooper as my PR representative. Scott fits in with the way I'd like to be represented. He's low-key, has sound judgment, is trusted, and accepted as a good person by those he speaks to at media outlets—a personal contact who is never afraid to give me a "no" answer as well as a "yes" on a suggestion. Marty Appel, a former Yankee public relations director and bestselling author, handles my PR on this book. Marty has a great news sense. For special placement contacts, I've added Skyhorse Publishing, whose experienced staff also spreads the word.

All the PR people I've worked with through the years have continued as my close friends to this day. Chuck Stogel assisted me for many years while writing for various publications. He's an excellent craftsman and a prized friend. With PR outlets shrinking along print lines, those who succeed need even greater creativity finding outlets. Their job is made easier if the public likes the book. Same with movies or Broadway shows.

Publicity has helped to shape careers. With newspapers folding, a valuable source of promotion is no longer as accessible. Yes, there's the Internet and sports-talk shows, but the well-read printed newspapers of yesterday are dwindling down to a precious few.

27: Different Ways To Win

INJURIES ARE A part of sports. Sometimes, however, they shape new careers. In 1964, I was hosting the World Series pre-game TV shows on NBC-TV. I talked about the previous day's game, showed film highlights, then spoke about the game coming up, discussed the pitching selections, and interviewed a different manager on each show.

On one show, I had not been able to find an available manager, but there was an injured player with the Yankees who would not be playing—Tony Kubek—and, at the ballpark, I arranged a meeting with him.

"Tony," I said, "your teammates tell me you're great at discussing 'inside baseball,' and I'd like to use you on my show which we'll tape in the morning. As you watch the game today, I'd like you to look for strategies, or techniques, or important plays that most others won't notice so we can avoid traditional questions. I know you can do this. Would you like to go on with me and do it?"

Tony said he'd give it a try. We met after the game and he told me the points he'd like to make, the show was aired, and Tony received an excellent response.

"Tony," I said, "everybody loved your comments. I've been doing this show for some years now and have never had a repeat guest. If the

Series goes seven games, the seventh game is still open for a guest, and I'd like you to be my first to repeat." He agreed.

Tony was on again and was superb.

A couple of years went by and one day, I received a phone call. The caller identified himself as a vice president from NBC-TV and said the network was looking for a baseball analyst for their games.

"Do you remember the guest you had on who was so outspo-ken—in fact, he was on twice with you. We made a note at that time to consider him if an opportunity ever arose."

"Of course—that was Tony Kubek."

"Do you know where he lives?"

"I believe it's in Wisconsin. I'll find the address for you."

Tony got the job, and worked with many greats including Jim Simpson, Curt Gowdy, Joe Garagiola, and Bob Costas. All Tony needed was a chance to be heard. His talent took care of all the rest. His final seasons were on the Madison Square Garden Network.

I was so pleased that Tony's outspokenness and his participation on my pre-game shows caught the network's attention. That's really all it takes. And there was more excitement to come. In 2009 Tony Kubek was inducted into the broadcast wing of the Baseball Hall of Fame with the Ford Frick Award. In 2010 it was the enjoyable Jon Miller, who made the Hall. Jon was a great mimic of many of baseball's great-est voices before his own voice earned national recognition.

It took a long time before sportscasters could be called "outspo-ken." That's understandable. Pro sports are businesses. Ball clubs are in the business of selling tickets. They don't want announcers depre-cating their product. Sponsors sell merchandise. They don't want to lose listeners or viewers who oppose the announcer's opinion. Upset fans may take revenge by not buying whatever the sponsor is selling.

Yet sportscasters have to be objective to have credibility. The bet-ter ones describe the games as art forms, enthusing over great plays on either side or describing events or mistakes in judicial not scornful tones. They present both sides of a question. The way to survive is to be honest and forthright—with civility. Be critical, but not disparaging. Don't let scorn affect your tone of voice—be a judge without rancor.

National broadcasters cannot, and should not, take sides. Local broadcasters can root internally, but on the air should root for a good, exciting game, just as reporters root only for a good story to write. "There's no cheering in the press box" is an axiom all journalists should abide by. Local broadcasters who openly root on the air may court local favor and management support but are not considered objective reporters. For many years this enabled the networks to keep their own announcers on big games, claiming they were more impartial for national play calling. Among others who had to prove impartiality and did so was Tim McCarver. Mel Allen proved he could root for either side but Phil Rizzuto's open rooting for the Yankees took him out of national contention along with others. I personally stressed the artistry of the game with equal volume.

The roar of the crowd or the desire to cozy up to home management should not cloud one's calls or one's choice of words. One can be completely honest and emotional just stating the facts without getting too wrapped up in winning or losing. The announcer doesn't control the game's outcome. An opinion—based on what the announcer sees and what the replay confirms—must be given in a factual manner even if it clashes with the home team's version. Gaining respect is a vital asset to the play-caller. Respect comes from favoring the truth, not the home team. The crowd is important. On home games, if the team is winning, one's voice rises over the crowd roar. If they're losing, the tone has to stay up and not sound mournful or disinterested.

Tony Kubek was frank, outspoken, honest, and unconcerned with consequences. When he worked Yankee games on the MSG Network, the Garden's executive producer at that time, Mike McCarthy, had to make sure that Kubek's frank comments were not endangering his relationship with management. The front office is always looking for positives. If the analyst doesn't sound vindictive and makes his points diplomatically, friction can be averted. Tony survived on his own terms on the way to the broadcast hall at Cooperstown.

Today many sports-talk shows are far rougher—but those announcers are not paid or approved by ball clubs they talk about. Their salaries come from the station. Network announcers and those paid by stations are not as beholden to the ball clubs.

I viewed players as if they were my family. I never swear or curse in my personal life, so I had no fear of doing so on the air. I worked hard to use the right shadings in my comments to be correct in my interpretations. The facts usually speak for themselves; scolding can cause resentment.

At no time in my career did any club owner ever talk to me about my content. I figured they hired me for how I think which results in what I say. The chances are they knew that if they had a gripe and tried to influence how I expressed myself, it would take away my freedom of expression which I prize. I would never yield that. Fortunately, my resolve was never tested by management although, on a few occasions, I expressed my concern to advertising agencies regarding unseemly commercials, particularly those that intruded on the drama of the game itself with ad-libs to be inserted at key action points to extol their products. These can only irritate audiences, not increase sales.

Win Elliot was an outstanding early TV announcer and broadcast partner with the New York Rangers, a talented man and a fine personality. But I had heard management grumbling that Win seemed to always favor the Rangers' opponents. The management never heard Win do home games because they were at the Garden, but they were glued to the telecasts when the Rangers were on the road.

I listened to Win's road work and quickly discovered the problem. On the road, the crowd roar, the shouting, the clapping is all for the home team. If the Rangers scored, there was silence. Win went up with his voice level to rise above the home crowd—and so always sounded more excited when the opposition scored. By contrast, he seemed less emotional when the Rangers got a goal.

I took Win aside and told him he'd better watch his voice meter—go up more for the Rangers, cut down on the decibels for the opposition. That solved the problem.

The level of emotion can be more important than the words.

I have always told my audio men to keep the noise level high—but balanced for both sides. If people are changing stations, I want them to tune in where there seems to be the most excitement.

I know that the sportscaster's voice is important, but frankly nothing beats crowd roar. Tim McCarver never holds back on giving strong opinions on World Series telecasts. He's at his best on inside baseball, sharing the knowledge he acquired as a big league catcher before moving to the broadcast booth. Keith Hernandez in New York adds spice to TV with his comments.

Speaking of vocal theatrics, there are two important factors that make a sportscaster's job easier than a sports writer's.

The first is inflection. The inflection of one's voice changes the meaning of words.

Here's the text of a call: "Cabrera the batter—grounder to deep short—Ramirez moves to his right—tries to backhand the ball—it's off his glove and into left field." Start raising your voice at "tries to backhand the ball," and raise it some more when you say "off his glove"—it sounds as if Ramirez gave it a great try.

Now use the same exact words, but lower your voice and emphasize "off his glove"—it sounds like Ramirez has let the team down again. It becomes a disparaging description.

Inflection is a vital factor in broadcast communication. Print journalists are limited without it.

The second factor is pauses. Nothing holds attention more than a pause. Too many sportscasters are afraid to use them. They work, though—and add to the drama. Example: "Friends, there is one important aspect of this basketball game that is often overlooked. (PAUSE.) It's this. (LONGER PAUSE.)" The audience is now quiet, leaning forward to hear your next words—and will wait patiently for them. "Free throw shooting. That can make a winner or a loser." Try this. It works.

The wise broadcaster should avoid demeaning inflection or rancor in his words—many analysts use their tone of voice more to condemn than report. It's a delicate job, but criticism can be aired without being vindictive. Use the tone that a father uses in speaking to his children—parental, not demeaning.

Dick Vitale used a unique positive approach to become a national star, combining tremendous energy along with an enormous appreciation of basketball artistry. His gushing over great plays was fueled by his knowledge of the game. The former coach erupted with shouts of "Awesome, bay-bee!" and other verbal accolades that players sought and audiences appreciated.

Fran Healy was a major league catcher who received an opportunity to do some color on Yankee games after his playing days were over. Fran provided quick-witted give-and-take in the bantering art particularly when working with Phil Rizzuto. An amiable fellow, Fran made friends at the top level when the telecasts were put on cable, and developed a larger role including play-by-play on the cable games.

Fran realized, however, that he needed something more than his voice could deliver to ensure future mike duty and his found the solution in his outgoing personality. He became an asset to his Cablevision bosses with his readiness to represent them at community and personal events and above all, to develop one's own shows and bring in sponsors. Some of his programs received national distribution. Fran found that being a quick-witted businessman was a great asset. In television, bringing in money is an important asset for survival.

Being a journalist begins with having a mind curious to learn and an ability to express one's thoughts well, either verbally or in writing (or both). A natural curiosity should be the number one asset for all interviewers. The interviewer has to be the link between the interviewee and what the viewer or listener is anxious to know.

Unfortunately, many hirers relegate this job to former star athletes with little journalistic experience. Most have spent careers answering questions, not asking them.

The great pitcher, Bob Gibson, after his glory days on the mound, was placed in the awkward position of network post-game interviewer, and one of his first guests was pitcher John Candeleria, who had just pitched a no-hitter. It was an exhilarating moment and the audience waited to hear Candelaria's elation. Gibson's first question took all the smiles away. "Will you ask for a better contract now?" In an exciting moment, the interviewer has to share the joy.

Another Hall of Fame pitcher—Sandy Koufax—also was given a similar assignment interviewing a young pitcher after a victorious outing. "Will you explain to our viewers how a curve ball is thrown?" asked the master of the art. A golden opportunity for an all-time great to expound on his specialty had been transferred to a newcomer.

Both pitchers happen to be brilliant men and all-time greats on the mound—but were rookie questioners who were not afforded any preparation in the art. Both were in the spotlight as all-time great pitchers, but neither craved the spotlight as TV performers.

Most sportscasters are self-taught, but it does help if someone in the business gives them a helping hand. Experience is a great teacher, but that doesn't mean that all those with experience are good teachers. Being great in one art form doesn't automatically mean one can do the same in another. Michael Jordan is considered basketball's finest by many people, but discovered that baseball was another matter.

28: Words Influence Images

I'VE ALWAYS MEASURED success by my latest performance and whether I lived up to my expectations. It's always been the most recent program that counts. I taped most of them and graded myself. I'm a tough grader, but seemed to earn my best marks on national events.

I viewed sports I had not played or broadcast like new subjects in school. I could learn them and make good grades through determined effort—just plain hard work.

"Can you broadcast this sport?" I'd be asked by a station, network, or sponsor. "Absolutely," was always my reply. And then I worked to prove it, putting in hours and hours of preparation. Whether it was the Australian Surfing Carnival, the National Gymnastics Championships, the National Horse Show, the Westminster Kennel Club Dog Show, bowling, tennis, track and field, or boxing—I always said, "Yes, I'm ready." The proof came in being rehired for the same assignment year after year, eventually becoming accepted as an expert in each field. This took perspiration, not inspiration. Study is not glamorous—but it's vital.

The biggest risk involved fitting all these events into my schedule, particularly in the 1950s and most of the '60s while I was still doing a full slate of major league baseball, pro and college football, pro and

Carl Lewis

college basketball, and hockey. On most of these events, I was the solo play-by-play caller, with no substitute. Most assignments provided no color men to set the scene—I was the sole voice. One can imagine the dire consequences if I didn't get to the microphone for an event, be it local, regional or national. Not only would I be fired—but the disgrace would last a lifetime as well.

Rocky Marciano

I never thought of these consequences, believing somehow I'd make it from city to city just in time. It was the confidence of youth, not the wariness of age that sustained me—and somehow, I averaged around 250 play-by-plays a year traveling all over the country. But in retrospect, I shudder at the close calls. To say I was lucky is a complete understatement.

I missed only one when snow grounded all planes, but had time to get a replacement. I had many scary moments, though. If I hadn't survived them all, I wouldn't be writing this book. Sometimes I arrived just seconds before I was due on the air. I realize how lucky I was, but have never hesitated at taking chances with transportation and weather. My closest call resulted in doing television play-by-play of a Knicks game from a TV set in the Empire State Building instead of the arena in Cincinnati. The Knicks had arrived in Ohio for their tilt against the old Cincinnati Royals, but my plane was grounded in New York when a snowstorm closed the airport. We piped in the picture and the crowd sound and on the air I said—"Our picture comes from Cincinnati and audio from New York." Nobody questioned the arrangement.

An odd thing about sportscasters, they work together for hours, but very few pal around together. When the game's over, they're off to separate lives.

There are a few whose air work I don't admire, even though others do. Still, I do admire that somehow they got the job. That's the material side of winning. Maybe that's their art— getting on the air. Their on air style may make me cringe—just like the power hitters who've become millionaires through steroid use. Some may defy the standards of journalism I believe in, but appeal to the public regardless.

One can't define what's right in this business. Usually the test is— will it sell? That includes the performer and the product.

And who's in the audience? The demographic experts now jump into the picture.

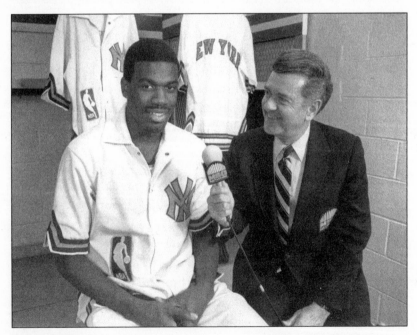

Bernard King

The public tastes keep changing—in humor, in music, in the presentation of sex, in language use, in standards. It's always been mandatory for me to keep aware of my content and stay fresh in my approach—while remaining true to my conscience.

So, I just keep changing my act to what works at the present time.

I do believe that some sportscasters have more class and good taste than others. Some get laughs with crass humor and play to a lower level. Some thrive on put-down humor, getting cheap laughs by embarrassing or belittling others. Freedom of speech is a necessity, but how about taste? Demeaning others is cruel treatment and no laugh is worth it. Yet, somehow my friend Don Rickles has thrived as a comedian needling celebrities and audience members who wait in line for the honor of being ridiculed by him. Maybe Don's knack is knowing that his targets are celebrities of such stature they don't experience much sting in Rickles's exaggerated comments. Incidentally, most comedians are terrific baseball fans. Like sportscasters, they work mainly at night. During the day, many would go to the ball games

Bill Veeck, Jerry Lewis

261

Derek Jeter

with me, sit in the broadcast booth, and listen to my broadcasts. At night, they would ask me to watch their shows if I were available. Some made their TV debut as a guest on my baseball shows—Jerry Lewis, Jonathan Winters, Danny Kaye, and Shelley Berman, to mention a few.

During a recent baseball season, for a week or so sports sections and sports shows teemed with stories relating the "fact" that Yankee stars Alex Rodriguez and Derek Jeter were not bosom buddies.

For one thing, Jeter was single at the time, and Rodriguez was married. Did someone expect they'd be hanging around together at night?

I've been with ballplayers for over half a century—and they're just like sportscasters. They play together, work together, respect each others' talents—but when the game's over, they too go their separate ways.

Their bonding is done as a team—they share memories but rarely extra time together.

So this book includes many names, but this is not a tell-all confessional. Frankly, I'm not privy to anything more than the average fan in the stands sees—I just have a better seat.

But I've been close enough to understand that athletes, sportscasters, and entertainers should be judged as skill models, not role models. I've broadcast the sporting heroics of thousands of outstanding men—but I'm also aware that a few skilled athletes, despite their talent, unfortunately have made headlines as racists, or egomaniacs, or liars, or drunks, or druggies, or cheaters, or assaulters. Being a fine athlete doesn't ensure being a fine person. The same is true in all society. The current economic problems have shown that there are some businessmen, politicians, entertainment stars, and other citizens we trust who have taken the wrong path.

An on-the-road lifestyle doesn't facilitate a normal life, particularly for a sports family. Underneath all the friendly spirit of playing or performing together, there's the constant competition to get maximum playing time. It's rarely discussed, but it's always there. It's a continual battle for sports survival. Some handle this better than others. Life on the road is difficult—and, for the most part, boring. The games are fun, but otherwise it's a one-dimensional existence, devoid of normal social activity. In baseball particularly, one copes with more failure than success. Sportscasters with a losing team have to keep up their enthusiasm on the air while knowing their club just isn't good enough. Some sportscasters rarely, if ever, get a chance to broadcast championship or national events, and spend their careers with non-contenders.

Remember, amateur players in high school, colleges, and recreational leagues play for fun, for the love of the game. Their biggest fight is to make the team—and then win the title. For most, money has not entered the picture. Winning for money or sports survival is not always character building.

Some players make strong, positive impressions on me by their specific actions quite aside from their playing abilities.

Though some players are sociable only after a game they've won, there are stars who stood out as always being accessible regardless of how they played.

Gary Carter was always available to be interviewed and always upbeat—whether the questioner was a big-name sportscaster or writer or some kid just hoping to get a few minutes on tape. Gary, now in the Hall of Fame, didn't need any more publicity. Still, he was delighted to help anyone. Many kids breaking into the business got their first interview with him.

After his playing days, Gary's desire to let others know of his availability to assist at high-level jobs did bring a few detractors. That job availability is better served by agents. I always found Gary's efforts to be genuine.

David Cone

However, his discretion was challenged when Jerry Manuel's managerial job with the Mets was threatened and Gary expressed his interest.

Win or lose, pitchers David Cone and Al Leiter never left their lockers till all questions were answered, while Ron Darling took everything in stride. They never let their emotions interfere with their straightforward answers.

Don Mattingly also played that role, always taking time to give his autograph to the clamoring group of youngsters waiting near the dug-out. It was an obligation he felt sincerely about, win or lose. Hockey great Pat LaFontaine was always accessible, as were fellow icers Rod Gilbert and Andy Bathgate and basketball legend Julius Erving. Joe Torre and old-time managers like Chuck Dressen and Al Lopez never offered up excuses after a loss. Optimistic Chuck would say, "I've got a great plan for tomorrow."

Some players are gracious enough when they lose to acknowledge the skill of their opponent. The most vivid example of that came when I broadcast the Baltimore Colts defeating the New York Giants in the NFL's first overtime championship game. Players from both teams described it

Chuck Dressen

as "the greatest game ever played." When the losers say this as well as the winners, it means something. In addition to the excitement of being the first NFL championship overtime game, it turned out to be a spring-board for the league's tremendous growth which continues today.

And for even disposition with thoughtful answers, manager Joe Torre, whom I covered with the Yankees, was exceptional with his calm demeanor, first class in every way. Joe was outstanding in his sensitive appraisal of his players' performances.

How would you describe Billy Martin? Feisty, combative, street-smart, strategist, maneuverer, fighter, dirt-kicker, legendary?

I covered Billy Martin from a reporter's perspective for his entire career—eleven years as a player, sixteen years as a manager. Brash, lively, opinionated, at times charming, sometimes irascible, some-

Rod Gilbert, Bob Wolff, Willie Mays

times crude—he always seemed to be in a constant battle for respect, for understanding.

Billy was more than talk, though. He gave his all to the game and proved dependable in the clutch. In 1953, for example, he personally carried the Yankees to a four games to two World Series victory over the Brooklyn Dodgers. Martin batted .500 in the six-game series, going 12 for 24, tripled with the bases loaded in the first game and drove in the winning run in the final game to give the Yankees their fifth consecutive World Series crown.

As a manager, he demanded complete control and became embroiled in battles with Yankees owner George Steinbrenner (known by many as "the Boss)."

That was Billy's image: excitable—often out of control—a battler— a wild horse that needed taming, yet the type of brawler who commands respect. That was the image I saw and read about.

Billy's playing career as a second baseman was winding down in 1961. I was broadcasting the Minnesota Twins in their inaugural season, and Martin arrived that June in a trade with the Milwaukee Braves. Martin

THE NATIONAL BREWING COMPANY

BALTIMORE, MARYLAND

H. E. HUDGINS
DIRECTOR OF ADVERTISING

January 2, 1959

Dear Bob,

I've just heard the tape of your broadcast on the Championship game.

Throw out the fact you had a lulu going, but Robert, it's the most spine tingling job I've ever heard, anywhere.

This one will go down in radio memory. (God, that doesn't sound like me, but that's the way it is!)

Dempsey-Firpo is nothing. Likewise the crash of the Hindenberg!

Great job, Bob.

Sincerely,

Bill

H. E. Hudgins

HEH:kd

Mr. Bob Wolff
3063 Harrison Street, N.W.
Washington, D.C.

P.S. Yes, you'll get a record of it!

Colts-Giants game sponsor letter after championship game

Jackie Robinson, Joe E Brown

added some spark to the team but not much offense. There were rumors that he might be considered for a future managerial berth because of his fiery disposition, win-at-all-cost play and knowledge of the game.

On a rather uneventful afternoon game in Minnesota, Twins Manager Sam Mele removed Martin at the midway point for a pinch-hitter. Martin, who had been in the on-deck circle, slowly walked back to the dugout.

My eyes followed him, but the TV cameras did not—they focused on the pinch-hitter. I watched as Martin stood in front of Mele, flung his bat and helmet at the manager's feet, and then stormed off to the locker room.

I had to make a quick decision—should I mention this on the air? If I did, the story would embarrass Mele and certainly put a blot on Martin's future managerial aspirations in Minnesota or elsewhere. I determined that it was not mandatory to use it in the context of the game itself and I passed on it.

But that evening, in the airport before boarding the plane for our next road trip, I told Billy I wanted to speak to him in private. "Billy," I said, "I didn't report on the air your actions with Mele in the dugout because I'm a believer that you'll be an excellent manager some day. Suppose you were the manager and one of your players had put on that act with you in the dugout. I can imagine your reaction. I hope you're a manager some day, and I'll still be in your corner if you agree it won't happen again." We shook hands and that was the end of it.

The years went by and I covered Billy managing the World Champion Yankees. Twenty years after that Minnesota episode I was at a Yankees'

Son Rick Wolff playing for Detroit Tigers

Old Timers' Day luncheon in New York. There was laughter and old baseball stories being retold at an adjoining table where Billy and many of his teammates and former players were enjoying lunch together.

Billy spotted me, got up from his table, walked over to where I was sitting, found a vacant chair, and in a low voice said, "Bob, I want you to know I've always remembered your words to me and how much I appreciated them."

We shook hands. As Billy stood to return to his group, I added, "And, Billy, I'm certainly proud of my decision."

His comments showed me a different side of Martin, his sensitivity, and I was impressed.

I found it interesting that Martin's first major league managerial job was with Minnesota, in 1969.

I also found it a wonderful coincidence that, a few years later when Martin was managing Detroit, our paths crossed in an unusual fashion. My son Rick had just been drafted by the Tigers and was on his way to their spring training camp in Lakeland, Florida.

I was telecasting the Knicks games for the Madison Square Garden Network and found it difficult to get away to get to Florida for a quick look at how Rick was doing.

Then one day, I found a solution. National Airlines was offering a special—a day in Florida as a short stopover before continuing on to the West Coast, for an extra charge of only five dollars. I was scheduled for a Knicks-Lakers game in Los Angeles with a day off for traveling.

The exhibition schedule showed the Philadelphia Phillies at the Tigers. I could fly to Tampa in the morning, travel by car rental to Lakeland, watch half the game, drive back to Tampa, and continue my plane trip to LA.

I got to the ballpark during pre-game batting practice, waved to Rick, and went into the Detroit dugout where I spotted Martin. After greeting him warmly, I explained I had flown down there to visit with Rick, a draftee, but after half a game, I had to return to the airport to continue my trip. Before I left, I told Billy I just wanted to say hello to him.

Both teams had their regulars in the starting line-up as they were approaching the end of spring training.

What a thrill when over the public address system came the announcement, "Rick Wolff now batting." Rick reached base on a fielder's choice, the next batter walked, then suddenly the pitcher whirled and threw to second—the throw was wild and into center-field, Rick moved to third and the runner on first went to second. Next up was home run slugger Frank Howard who was walked intentionally. However, the Phillies survived that inning.

I had to leave the park, but before I did, I leaned into the dug-out and said, "Thanks, Billy." He answered, "Have a good trip, Bob. Don't worry—I'll take care of your kid."

It was difficult for me to remain objective talking about Billy Martin. To me, he had a genuine regard for family values. Watching out for my son provided further proof. This was rarely observed and a great contrast to his combative nature and problem with alcohol. I remember the cover of a Yankee Yearbook that showed him kicking dirt on an umpire and thought of the saying "You can't tell a book by its cover."

29: How To Find The Right Route If You're On The Wrong Path

I'M A LUCKY guy. I get excited easily. Just comes with the body, I guess. When something happens—in sports, on the stage, in daily life, I'm up applauding, congratulating someone. It could be a competitor, an opponent, makes no difference—if someone moves me, I'm grateful for the chance to enjoy artistry.

That certainly helps in sportscasting. There's no script for most of what I do. When I get excited, I share my glee with the audience. And I believe one of the reasons I've survived in this business is my natural emotion, which emulates the reaction of the listener or viewer. As electronic friends, we're watching together and our feelings are the same. I let my feelings be known. I extol the positive, but realize that adversity is always a possibility.

In retrospect, there really aren't that many superb games or plays that stand out forever. I remember the impact at the time they occurred and have been fortunate to broadcast some of those headline events for teams and individuals.

I've used the word "great" thousands of times in broadcasting sports—too often, I guess—but at that moment when I shout, "What a great game!" I mean it. Like a satisfying meal, the game was completely fulfilling. And I try to explain succinctly why the game was so significant.

I keep seeing new pulsating games, more comebacks, more game-winning plays, more spectacular saves, more tremendous performances, so the list keeps increasing. Many moments are remembered, though, only because of their significance or in replays.

Of course, certain ones still remain personal favorites. I couldn't have been more excited than I was in the 1969–70 season when the New York Knicks—after twenty-four lean seasons—were on the path to their first World Championship.

I was at the TV mike when, after trailing Cincinnati by five points with less than a half minute to play, the Knicks came back to win their eighteenth straight game. That win set an NBA record at the time for consecutive victories and helped make pro basketball a major sports attraction. The Knicks continued to sellout the Garden and won a second championship in 1973. Neither of those great teams had one player in the top ten in league scoring, but their teamwork and defense thrilled every sports purist. My call of the games reflected my excitement.

During the '72–'73, season the Knicks scored 19 points in a row to defeat Kareem Abdul-Jabbar and the Milwaukee Bucks on their way to another NBA championship. To accomplish this they held Jabbar and his teammates scoreless for the final five minutes and fifty seconds, an unbelievable feat. I shouted, "This is one of the greatest comebacks of all time" and no one ever refuted that statement. What a wonderful experience.

From an individual standpoint, calling Don Larsen's perfect game in the 1956 World Series was a once-in-a-lifetime thrill. Broadcasting the Baltimore Colts' victory over the New York Giants in 1958 in the first National Football League overtime championship game, "the greatest football game ever played," was a great privilege. That game is considered the turning point in making pro football the success it's become.

While I was screaming my accolades on the airwaves, I was the voice of the listeners. On the air, I was their representative. That's always been my belief.

Dave Sims, Jane Wolff, Fuzzy Levane, Allie Sherman, Bob, and Dave's wife

I don't want to downplay the need for accurate, informative, well-researched, and analytical opinions, but the broadcaster also has the privilege of adding vocal excitement and emotion to his words—that's the music added to the lyrics—that's the impact that makes for a great broadcast. This is natural reaction, not scripted. It has to be genuine and one has to be qualified to render an accurate evaluation and judgment—and of course, one needs the urge to do so. But the vocal tone, the urgency, the volume, should have a musically pleasant sound, under control excitement, a natural outburst—not a shrill, barbaric scream as if the announcer is being strangled.

There's a current pattern on network and local game telecasts, TV and radio, to begin with a succession of taped highlight calls to set the emotional scene for the game to follow. Most of the calls of game-winning plays are radio ones where announcers go berserk with strained shouting designed to hit the jackpot with sheer hysteria. They're not only too loud, but they're laughable in their excessiveness as well.

Voices have to remain musical, clear with a strong tone, and the sportscaster has to keep from excessive embellishment. Listen to today's top play-callers—they impart excitement but don't overact. Bob Costas, Jim Nantz, Mike Breen, Greg Gumbel, Al Michaels, Dick Enberg, Mike Tirico, Joe Buck, Verne Lundquist, Kenny Albert, Dave Sims, Ian Eagle, Vin Scully, Marv Albert, Doc Emrick, Tom Hammond— the list is a long one, but all of those broadcasters remain in control of their voice levels. A voice should sound strong, not frantic. Many top personality sportscasters have distinctive voices.

On Tuesday night, October 6, 2009, I sat in front of my TV set at home to watch the Minnesota Twins play the Detroit Tigers in a one-game playoff for the chance to play the Yankees in the Division Series beginning the next night at Yankee Stadium. The Twins had finished the season, winning 17 of their final 21 games to tie Detroit.

Watching would be fun, but also business. The next day, I'd be doing a pre-game TV feature from the Stadium, and this game would be part of my preparation. From a personal standpoint, I had an interest in both teams. When the Senators moved from Washington to Minnesota in 1961, I went with them to be a TV-radio voice of the rechristened franchise. I was joined by sportscaster Ray Scott. As the Twins' announcers, we meshed well and it was an enjoyable experience. My son Rick later was drafted by Detroit, so I had a connection to both teams.

I never display a rooting interest as a broadcaster. My job is to be fair and impartial. I do root for my broadcast to be my very best. When my emotion erupts during the game—it's because of the artistry of the play, the execution, the unexpected, the comeback, the courage, whatever grips me for either side.

As a one-game playoff to play the Yankees in the Division Series, the Twins-Tigers' thriller started with built-in tension. There was no tomorrow for the losers. and euphoria was in store for one team, despondency for the other. I hoped that whoever won would do so on merit, not on some error or misplay that would haunt the loser forever.

Ray Scott, Halsey Hall

I don't know TBS sportscaster Chip Caray personally. I do know that he comes from a sportscasting family. His grandfather Harry, a Broadcast Hall of Famer whom I knew, was an emotional personality, relating everything at full volume, personally involved in every game, with a strong following. Chip's dad, Skip, also an announcer, was more laid back with a droll sense of humor. Skip, who is deceased, also had a large fan base.

When Chip appeared on camera for the one-game playoff, he seemed relaxed and ready, a good-looking guy with a pleasant voice and an easy style. In 2009, I was listening and watching Chip's color man on the games, Ron Darling. I already had my evaluation of Ron's ability from his excellent work on the Mets games in New York. Working with a top-notch play-by-play caller in Gary Cohen on TV, and at times with showman Keith Hernandez, an outspoken analyst, Ron's perspective remarks and insight of the game proved to me he was on the way to future stardom. The 2009 Mets didn't provide much to shout about, but if a raised voice was needed, Gary's play-by-play supplied it.

Casey Stengel

The Twins-Tigers game was the type of playoff that could become the highlight of a sportscaster's life. But Chip's words and tone of voice didn't equate with the fantastic dramatic value of this game— the same game I was applauding as a viewer. This was one of those rare games that every sportscaster yearns to call, but Chip didn't share this exultation with his audience.

The game had roller-coaster ups and downs, pitchers getting out of impossible situations, great fielding plays to stave off defeat, timely hits to keep hopes alive—all this and extra innings, too, with the constant suspense that one team would proceed to the Division Series, the other would end its season. You couldn't write a better script.

The game evoked a wide range of emotions, feelings that the announcer should share with the audience. If I'm moved like this, I know the other viewers are too. But Chip did not bring out this enhancement—didn't mention the uniqueness of this game.

Chip did say, "This is a great game," but it was more an acknowledgment than a standing ovation. Unfortunately, his verbal mistakes began to pile up as the broadcast progressed as well. Correcting his new partner would have been a delicate role for Ron Darling to play, not a gracious one, and Chip left little room for banter. Later, in the Championship Series, Buck Martinez joined the booth as the third member of the crew and made his presence known, but Caray kept making miscues. He made a call too quickly and tried to turn back awkwardly in mid-sentence. Chip said, "It's a line drive, base hit, for an out." A tricky situation, but a rookie mistake. "Hit" can be a noun, as in "He has two hits," but "hit" can also be a verb, as in "He hits a line drive." The sportscaster should say, "There's a line drive, falling in for a base hit" or "There's a line drive to the center fielder for an out." The name of the fielder should be mentioned as well.

Chip also said, "There's the winning run on second" in the top of an inning. The home team had not batted. It could be described as "the possible winning run" but calling it "the winning run" displays little baseball knowledge. Chip's baseball terminology didn't seem to be right for the occasion, his statistics were from a previous year, he was weak on baseball rules, his tone was more declarative then conversational, and he had a problem with depth, seeming fooled on the difference between routine flies and possible tape-measure homers. His main problem, though, was not understanding the uniqueness of this game.

Here's what others had to say about the game, just a small sampling of the praise that was majestic and voluminous:

- "This is one of the all-time best," Frank Viola, a former Cy Young winner with the Twins, told the *New York Times.*
- "This is absolutely the most unbelievable game I've ever played in and seen," said Minnesota shortstop Orlando Cabrera on-camera with Craig Sager on the post-game show,
- "This is the best game by far I ever played in, no matter the outcome," said third basemen Brandon Inge of the Tigers, despite being on the losing side.
- "A game so exciting and stressful on both sides that only superlatives could describe it," Pat Borzi reported in the *New York Times.*

But there were no superlatives on TV.

That's just a small sampling of quotes. How was this impact not understood and emphasized by the play-by-player calling the game?

Al Lopez

It's the first lesson in sports journalism: knowing what the story is—and how to present it, in print or on the air. What a missed enhancement opportunity.

Knowing how to avoid errors is part of the learning process. Chip has come a long way without learning lessons at a lower level. That's the remarkable part. He might have been helped by any number of producers, directors, colleagues, critics, fans, and baseball people before he reached the high exposure test. It's learning by experience. Chip has learned the hard way, but that's the past. His ability should make for a bright future and I believe he has that potential. It was good to see that just weeks after being let go by Turner Sports, Fox Sports South hired him to do play-by-play of the Atlanta Braves.

In Washington, my friend Bill Gold, news director of the *Washington Post* radio station and columnist for the paper, would give me seven or eight typewritten pages each month critiquing my work—no holds barred. When I got the chance to broadcast my first World Series, I was ready for the challenge. The more one learns early, the better prepared one is.

Thom Brennaman, like Chip Caray, comes from a broadcasting family—his dad Marty is in the broadcast wing of Baseball's Hall of Fame. Thom would also use powerful TV tones when he began. Now with a more conversational style, his football and baseball calls have both drawn national praise. TV voices are more conversational than radio tones, particularly in baseball and Thom now excels at both. Thom also brings a warm personality and a pleasant manner to his work.

Mel Allen, one of the all-time greats, didn't do many interview shows. His style was to tell a story on TV to his guest and then ask the guest if that were a big moment in the guest's life. The guest would answer yes and Mel would then tell another story, eliciting another "I agree" answer. Nobody would dare say to Mel, "Just ask the guest about the play he made last night and let him talk." Mel didn't get many interview assignments, and no one wanted to explain to an all-time great why this was happening. Suggestions are rarely made in sportscasting.

When I was telecasting the NBC-TV *Baseball Game of the Week*, I always went to the ballparks for batting practice to get used to the flight of the ball from the booth. If one wants to be fast on calls, this is an excellent aid. It takes a while to get acclimated.

I once asked a terrific manager, Al Lopez, how he could see the field so well, including the strike zone, sitting in a dugout, "Bob," he said, "after years of sitting in a dugout, my eyes were trained to do just that. What I can't understand is how you TV guys call games from those high press boxes." The answer is much the same—it takes practice, it's not a given talent.

Oddly, sportscasters rarely help each other with tips on improvement. Maybe they feel advice would be resented. After all, sportscasters progressed without tips from a competitor. Whatever the cause, it rarely happens.

A tough agent may offer some suggestions, but playing back one's calls with a knowledgeable friend at your side is a method that works. In the long run, your eyes and ears should be trained to evaluate yourself, if, of course, you have the ability to do so. Regardless, this is part of the job. As in the games, it's a question of getting runs and hits—but avoiding errors. Long runs are short on errors. The more you prepare, the fewer errors you'll make.

PART FOUR
Survival Techniques

30: Different Sports Demand Different Techniques

THE GREATEST CHANGE in sportscasting since its early years was moving from providing descriptive radio calls to commenting on the TV picture with insights about players' techniques, strategies, observations, player notes—in essence the mental side of the game.

This opened the door for a whole new group of sportscasters and former players who could bring inside information of their sport and, hopefully, sufficient voices for audience appeal. Distinctive voices, a strong vocabulary, and knowledge of grammar are still prized, but the new wave of headliners had enthusiasm, personality, insights, and a wear-well style that appealed to listeners and viewers.

Mel Allen and Red Barber were the first two baseball sportscasters to enter the Baseball Hall of Fame's broadcast wing. They were describers with memorable voices and, in their time, that was what the public wanted. They rarely strayed into "inside baseball." There was no demand for it then. Barber would occasionally explain the difference between hit and run and run and hit; Allen would recite the infield fly rule—and that was about it.

Regardless of the sport, however, it's a positive boost if one is a storyteller. I'm not speaking about fictionalized yarns. I mean continual new game-related material which the sportscaster comes up with—content that holds the audience. Stories which have an intriguing beginning, a newsworthy middle, and an excellent climax—surefire stuff to hold any generation. This material is gathered by getting to games early, asking questions, and doing a lot of reading. Those who have played sports should have ready-made stories about techniques, personal experiences, players they know well, and strategies of the game.

Stories are better suited for baseball, though, than fast-action sports like basketball, hockey, football, track and field, boxing, gymnastics and the like where the action has to be one's main focus. On fast sports, content can be used on interviews or features. I had a stat man with me for football and used spotters, too, but on baseball and other slower action sports, just a stat man, no spotters.

Baseball is tricky. Disaster comes when one starts a long story but there are three quick outs before the punch line. Timing has to be just right. On average, baseball games last for more than three hours, only seven or eight minutes of which contain frenzied action, so it's necessary to fill the remaining time with entertaining human-interest material, strategy discussion, analysis, and newsworthy information. Humor is a great plus for a storyteller. Too many use this golden baseball airtime opportunity for meaningless statistics. Numbers are important only if they tell a story.

Statistics can relate mathematical results, but they require further explanation—which demands knowledge of the game being played and insight as to how circumstances contribute to the numbers. For example, there are two major reasons baseball games are longer than they used to be. One is that the commercial time after each inning was increased from one minute to two minutes and twenty seconds, and as much as three minutes for network games. The second reason is that complete games are becoming rarer, as the current reliance on pitch counts making 100 pitches the norm for most starters. The parade of relievers adds to the running time. But like a good book, it's the content that counts—not the length. Extra innings add to the excitement. Baseball has no time limit, which is a plus. (It would be nice if night games started earlier, particularly for youngsters and those who have a long drive home.) Despite the longer games, baseball is drawing more than ever before. And those extra commercials help pay today's larger salaries. It's not just that games last longer—it's that the game has changed, with more pitchers involved. There's a greater fear that multi-millionaire starters may come up with sore arms. Regardless, there are more fans today.

When I was broadcasting the Senators, Washington had a versatile infielder, Pete Runnels. A left-handed line-drive hitter, who rarely pulled the ball, but instead stroked drive after drive to deep left for outs. He was traded to Boston where he topped all the Red Sox in hitting, including Ted Williams, and twice led the American League in batting. The statistics showed that his average improved—but they didn't say why. Pete's new ballpark was a major part of the story.

All those long outs in Washington with its cavernous left field became extra base hits at Fenway Park against the friendly Green Monster, a short inviting target.

Hall of Famers Nellie Fox and Luis Aparicio at second and shortstop were all-around players who got on base and scored runs. Each managed just a homer or two per season. In today's power game, they might have been bypassed, but in those earlier days, they were the ideal table-setters for the long-ball sluggers. Fox went a record 98 games one season without striking out! Today, the homer guys may strike out a lot, but when they connect, can win the game— and also draw people to the ballpark. Thus they're always in the line-up. The old-fashioned game was one run at a time, Fox and Aparicio were ideal for that style. Players strike out a lot today, but a homer with men on can win ball games and long-ball hitters are in demand. Club owners who invest millions in top pitchers might fire managers if they believe they're jeopardizing their hurlers' future with overuse. But why is it that old-time pitchers pitched so many complete games and stayed healthier than today's well-conditioned crew?

Stories hold audiences. Too many stats are irrelevant and just clutter up the TV screen or the airwaves.

Pete Runnels

Ad-libbers in the early days were in demand, as they could fill the airwaves with words to minimize dead air or to hype an event.

Times keep changing. Today, simply generating a slew of words is not enough to hold an audience— content is what's important. This takes preparation and a knowledge of what's newsworthy. The latter quality was not demanded from too many early sportscasters.

TV was a great factor in changing techniques. As Washington's pioneer TV sportscaster in 1946, with a professional radio career that began in 1939, I quickly learned that the pictures on the tube were the new stars. My job was to enhance that picture for the viewer by adding information or insight or emotion to make the viewer's enjoyment even more complete.

In my early days doing major league baseball, I had to forage for statistics about the players. I could get the home team's batting averages,

Bob and Willie Mays

but rarely the visitors'. I remember one day when Marsh Samuels, then a Cleveland executive, handed me the Indians' averages before a game. "Thanks, Marsh, this is great." Back then, such information was rare. Today, it's all on the Internet.

Now, every club hands out a book of notes—usually in small print—before each game. It requires extra effort to go through them and determine what information is pertinent. There's not much time to skim through all the pages, underlining the most newsworthy points to use on the air.

There have been changes in the techniques for calling TV or radio, as well as changes in the techniques for the individual sports. Each sportscaster has to choose which style is best suited for his or her presentation.

For years at Madison Square Garden, I worked with Jimmy Powers, a sports columnist for the *Daily News*. I did the play-by-play, Jimmy did the color. Jimmy was a pleasant man with a ready smile. We worked well together, but I never once shared a conversation with him off the air. Jimmy would show up just before airtime and leave the moment the game was over.

Jimmy landed a big contract when the Gillette Safety Razor Company hired him as their TV commentator—a solo job—on their boxing events. Jimmy's technique was simple. He identified the fighters by the color of their trunks, mentioned the round coming up, the seconds to go when the round was ending, and then the number of the next round when it began. He then let viewers hear the judges' decision—and that was it. Certainly Jimmy was never accused of over-talking.

Some years later when Howard Cosell was doing boxing, he never stopped talking or showing emotion.

Other boxing announcers have used their own techniques. Now it's usually a pair of announcers—play-by-play and analyst. On the radio side, Don Dunphy was a long-time favorite with his crisp, quick blow-by-blow.

Joe Louis

30: DIFFERENT SPORTS DEMAND DIFFERENT TECHNIQUES

When I did boxing on the Madison Square Garden Network, my analyst was the popular public address voice of the Knicks, John Condon, later the Garden's head of boxing.

I remember one day as some grease was being applied to a boxer's battered eye, I said to John, "Have you ever wondered what that stuff is?"

"What's that, Bob?"

"The guck."

"The guck?" repeated John, looking surprised.

"Yes, John, it's really called that. I looked it up one day, it's called guck in the dictionary, defined as 'oozy, sloppy dirt or debris,' just like it sounds. I wonder where they find that stuff?" It must have been one of the strangest boxing conversations John ever had.

One reason Gillette loved boxing is that the round ended every three minutes, giving them another chance for a commercial. Knowing this, when boxing went out of fashion for a while ratings-wise, I went to Gillette with a series of individual sports events shows for out-of-season athletes. The format would include frequent breaks in which to sell their blades. Who's the faster runner, the most accurate thrower, big names competing in many categories for monetary awards. I didn't sell this show to Gillette, but came close. A few years later a production company used a similar idea for a network replacement show, but Gillette wasn't on it.

Some sportscasters do TV well but are not suited for radio. Some radio men aren't as enjoyable on TV. It's much easier to switch from radio to TV than the other way around. Radio demands quicker identification, precise word use, and a higher voice level. TV emphasizes fewer words and comments with impact and emotion to enhance the picture.

One test I gave when I was teaching sportscasting at Pace and St. John's was designed to find out one's capabilities.

Here it is: With men on first and third, the batter hits a long drive to left-center field. It falls between the left fielder and the center fielder. Give the name of the pitcher, the catcher, the the outs, batter, the base runners, the relay man, the umpire—and all those who are involved in the play.

First describe the ball being lined as it falls in for a hit and rolls out toward the fence. Next name the runner scoring from third. The left fielder picks up the ball—name him. He makes a relay throw to the shortstop, the cut-off man—name him. The man on first is rounding second and is close to third—name him As he is being waved home. The shortstop fires to the catcher—name him. It will be a close play at the plate. Give the runner's name and voice rising, relate the action as he makes his slide—he's safe. The umpire—name him—gives the sign. Two runs are in—give the score. The batter—name him again— is on second. Give the number of outs, then repeat the score and the inning.

A quick, prepared radio sportscaster can make that call—and be right on the play—with all the names in the proper sequence. He should be considered for the job.

A TV broadcaster, brought up on this medium alone, with proper excitement in his voice, can simply say, "Fastball from Jones." What a shot to left-center, appears good for extra bases." Then name of the runner scoring from third, give the name of the second runner now rounding third, also attempting to score. "Here's the relay from short-stop (name him), it will be close, (runner's name) is safe." Give the ump's name that made the call, then name the batter on second. End with the score, number of outs, and the inning, and the audience will accept this abbreviated version. They get the key points in TV form.

Take a recording device out to a ball game and see if you can make the TV call, then try that radio call as well. Good radio broadcasters can do both. Those who are strictly TV callers have not been brought up on full descriptive plays and usually concentrate on adding to the picture, with details later.

I benefited in my career because I was mainly a TV sportscaster, although I did many radio games as well on the national networks. I personally prefer TV because I find it more challenging to add comments to the picture than just describe the action, but most of the top early sportscasters seemed to prefer radio where they were in charge of the entire word output and not bound to switch topics when a celebrity's picture came up on the tube and needed to be identified and woven into the conversation. I enjoyed this and found it a fun challenge to include new picture notes along with my play-by-play call.

Many players remain with a team for a number of years—the sportscaster knows them well, but new faces are always coming up, and visiting teams have to be learned. If one is a team's regular broadcaster, identification becomes easier as the season progresses.

Goals in hockey aren't frequent events (and they're even rarer in soccer), so it's vital that one gets them right. There's always the problem—was the shot deflected on the way to the net?

I called TV soccer as I did hockey, naming each player who received a pass or kicked the ball, or each stick-handler passing or receiving or shooting the puck. It increased the excitement level. The announcers who cover soccer's World Cup are more commentators than play-by-play men, which is also an acceptable style.

Radio callers need to have a TV monitor in the booth, as close-up shots provide closer player identification. I always pre-arranged this but sometimes the monitors were off to the side, which made viewing difficult.

For wordsmiths, baseball has the best chance to show off one's verbal abilities. Home runs or great plays provide ample opportunities for description—and plenty of time to make an exciting call. There are many ways to describe the action: a rising voice is a great enhancer, colorful phrases, a liberal use of synonyms, shared exultation. Some broadcasters take a safer ground—signature calls—and make them part of their act. They have to make sure this repetition continues to appeal to their audience. They do know their signature call will be recognized as part of their personal style.

Basketball is difficult for wordsmiths. A shot goes in—it happens in seconds. How poetic can one be in that time? How many variations are there on "it's good" or "Smith makes it?" Here the announcer's voice—the tone—is definitely the enhancer, not the words. On TV I never used "it's no good" or "it misses." That makes the game sound too negative. Instead, I'd give the name of the rebounder and if the shot was good, give the updated score. In double figures, I'd mention the total points by the scorer, the number of points the team has scored in a row and other newsworthy notes if time allowed.

Some broadcasters are good at all sports—fast or slow. Others are better suited to fast action calls, others to baseball's slower rhythms. Track is a challenge, particularly on sprints with a large field. Getting the winner's name out quickly in a short sprint is a real test.

In football, the announcer gives the ball carrier or receiver, the gain or loss on the play, sometimes who threw a key block, the tackler, the yard line where the ball is spotted, the down coming up, and the yards to go for a first down—with frequent references to the score, the quarter, the time left to play and what other player or game notes the sportscaster can weave in.

Then comes the analyst with the replay, the opinion, maybe banter, and the same formalized system continues. Little time remains for storytelling.

Basketball has many other fill items, compiled by the stat man, including the largest margin a team has led, the biggest deficit, number of lead changes, number of ties, second chance points, individual scoring, individual rebounding, assists, steals, blocked shots, player notes, shooting percentages and quick banter with the analyst. It's not a storytelling sport. Those who do so usually sacrifice the reporting of the game, which should come first. That's what the viewer cares about, the score and who made the basket. I rely on a top-notch statistician by my side, someone who is quick and accurate is posting numbers on his score sheet which I can read or feeds me slips of paper with numbers he believes are newsworthy which I might want to use.

Some basketball sportscasters do tell stories, but don't keep giving the score and which team is leading. That jeopardizes audience appeal. My preference is to give the score after each basket. That's the continuing drama of the game.

Hockey action is so fast, there's little time for storytelling. The toughest part of broadcasting this sport is identifying the players. This is made more difficult since there are no numbers on the front of the jerseys and every player wears a helmet. One has to spend sufficient time to know the players by body movements.

Soccer, for some reason, uses uniform numbers so small they're difficult to read.

There's so little time in ice hockey between a shot and a goal that the cry, "he shoots, he scores" rings out in every arena, game after game, with no variances.

This sameness is a burden to sportscasters who have not found synonyms. Doc Emrick, who has great ability to glide up to a dramatic call and then slide back down, is particularly good at this rhythm with the proper tone of excitement. Sam Rosen of the Rangers also has that knack on football as well. Howie Rose gets the job done right on Islanders telecasts. He also does Mets baseball on radio. They are versatile announcers. I heard Sam calling baseball some years back on ESPN; he did well, but Sam now concentrates on hockey and football.

In the old days of sportscasting, baseball was the most lucrative team assignment and still is. If one does Major League Baseball in a big city market, that's employment on 162 games, plus possible play-offs and a chance also at pre- and post-game shows surrounding the games, not to mention freelance work on other sports. Michael Kay does Yankee games and an afternoon radio show. In early days the pay for each sport wasn't as high as it is today, so some sportscasters worked on many sports all year round and did very well.

Gradually, though, leagues started to expand their seasons, extending schedules. As sports overlapped it became increasingly difficult for a sportscaster to diplomatically leave one's schedule of events to do another sports championship. Today, the networks mainly use their own stable of announcers. They don't do many games during the week but are paid well on the network weekend events and have to hope that their network retains its rights to the sport they cover. Otherwise, the succeeding network uses its own personnel. Only a few sportscasters with great name value are able to bolt from one network to the next. Most stations will permit a few announcers to leave them for major events like the Olympics where everyone gains in name value by the exposure. Agents usually write this possibility into contracts. Networks have their depth charts, though. Agents are always maneuvering to get their budding stars greater opportunities. Producers and directors have their favorites. Older sportscasters may be moved to lesser assignments regardless of their work quality. And if advertising hits hard times, high-salaried sportscasters may be replaced with lower-income future prospects. There are no guarantees in show business.

One other important note about techniques: On soccer, hockey, and even basketball, where identification is a major part of the calls, a simulcast of the TV call can replace the radio broadcast to save money. But there is too much descriptive talk for TV and one can't point out things on radio that video will show. It's not a good option for either TV viewers or radio listeners.

At Wimbledon in 2009, TV silence was very apparent as tennis analyst John McEnroe and play-by-player Ted Robinson rarely talked during the action except to exult on a great shot or serve or play. It was well done.

And coming down the homestretch of a football, basketball, or hockey game—or the last inning of a memorable baseball game—I enhance it more on TV by going to a more exciting radio-type call, bringing out the drama of the game as it reaches its peak.

31: Even Legendary Broadcasters Encounter Opinion Hazards

RED BARBER WAS at the World Series mike in 1947 when Floyd Bevens was pitching a no-hitter against the Dodgers at Ebbets Field in Brooklyn. The Yankees were leading 2–1 in the bottom of the ninth and Red was making his point by disregarding superstition and emphasizing the continuing "no-hitter" as Brooklyn pinch-hitter Cookie Lavagetto came up with runners on base—and Bevens just one out away from the no-hit game and a Yankee win.

"And here's the pitch. There's a line drive to right field, off the wall, here comes the tying run and here comes the winning run."

The unfavorable repercussions at Red's disregard for the baseball superstition were enormous from listeners, players, baseball people, and probably the sponsor as well. Red said he was just being honest, but his job was to enhance, not antagonize. Synonyms and other descriptions could have kept listeners informed and have been just as honest.

At the halfway point in the great 1956 Series duel between Don Larsen and Brooklyn's Sal Maglie, I spoke to Joel Nixon, the Maxon Advertising Agency producer for Gillette who was in the booth with me. "Joel," I said, "I want you to know I'm not going to use the words 'no-hitter' or 'perfect game' unless it happens, but I'll guarantee my words will let everyone know what's happening. Is that okay with you?"

"Absolutely," said Joel, "just make sure everyone knows." And that's what I did.

Obviously, Red and I disagreed on how to deal with the long-time baseball superstition—how to handle a potential no-hitter on a broadcast.

Both of us believed it should be made known to the public by our reporting. That was our responsibility as reporters. It also helped to build our audience—more casual listeners would stay with us to hear what would happen.

Where we differed was our method of doing so. Red believed it was foolish to believe that his talking about a "no-hitter" would jeopardize its happening. As an honest reporter, he'd have no part in side-stepping the potential feat, in fact would emphasize it as the game continued. And that's what he did. He decided to defy the baseball tradition.

I believed that my job was to make the facts known, but avoid irritating or offending the listeners who believed in this particular superstition. I could do this very easily by using alternative phrases or comments or synonyms to let people know exactly what was happening while keeping the special words "no-hitter" and "perfect game" available for a possible punch-line ending.

My system was to employ other words and phrases—and it worked.

"Eighteen in a row set down by Larsen." "Larsen has now retired all twenty-four." "The only hits and runs are by the Yankees." I repeated these phrases and their many related variations with excitement mounting in my voice. My broadcast was heard throughout the nation and on Armed Forces radio around the world.

I didn't receive one letter of complaint. No one wrote that any information was withheld. Instead there was an overflow of congratulations via telephone and mail. Radio still had a major audience and listeners were intent on hearing the details of what would turn out to be one of baseball's most historic calls.

And what a perfect way to use the punch lines I'd saved for the end of my broadcast. "It's a no-hitter, a perfect game for Don Larsen, Yogi Berra runs out there and leaps on Larsen, he's swarmed by his team-mates, and listen to this crowd roar!"

If you're wondering if I'm superstitious, let me put it this way. I find no proof that superstitions work, but I do have similar idiosyncrasies that I prefer to call "patterns of behavior."

I seem to work better with a certain pen, or suit, or pre-game meal, or medal in my pocket, or stone I've picked up by chance—all of which are subject to replacement by new keepsakes. This is so foolish that it shouldn't be in a book. I have been exceedingly lucky, though, main-taining a pattern of behavior does give me peace of mind. Fortunately, I'm not superstitious.

Well, okay, perhaps eccentric. I do know that a sportscaster's role is to please the public while informing them. In Brooklyn, Red set

Yogi Berra

the broadcast pace just as Vin Scully does now in Los Angeles. Red survived the superstition problem, but in his later years encountered one that he didn't see coming. Red switched boroughs to join the Yankees' broadcast crew, and he no longer controlled the pace as he had in Brooklyn. The times had changed and his Yankee colleagues were calling games with a more modern, energetic pace—raising their voices for great plays, big hits, home runs, adding emotion and vigor to their tones. Today more sportscasters are veering toward this more animated style. A few get downright hysterical over ordinary plays. Just remember, such overacting isn't tolerated at high-level jobs.

Red's soft, disciplined style when paired with the more excited styles of his boothmates, made some listeners feel Red didn't care as much about the game or the Yankees as he did about the Dodgers. That worried management, who view sportscasters as part of their selling team. When Red one day pointed out on camera all the empty seats at the stadium, the brass believed this was no way to please a sponsor or attract more paying customers.

Again, Red said he was just being honest. His assertion was correct, but it wasn't too long before the next vacant seat at the Stadium was his. That's a hazardous part of the job.

Red had some sympathizers with his frank approach. But viewing the empty seats was vivid enough proof without further elaboration. Those with a business stake in the team wanted discretion in dealing with negativity. Red's reputation as an all-time great remained intact, but his employment took a setback.

Vin Scully was the TV announcer during Larsen's perfect game along with Mel Allen. Vin was comparatively new to TV work at the time and very cautious in his calls. He believed that TV meant fewer words. I believed, having been a TV pioneer announcer beginning ten years earlier, that it wasn't the number of words—it was their use that counted. While words on TV should complement the picture, on radio, full description was vital.

The Gillette people used my radio call for promotion and it became a fixture on highlight reels and discs. Major League Baseball

Productions purchased a copy of the Scully-Allen TV tape from collector Doak Ewing to inaugurate the MLB Network and later in a series of Yankee "perfect game" discs on sale to the public. On their MLB album, I was pleased to note they also included my radio call along with the TV version. The radio and TV versions are also available at Doak Ewing's Rare Sportsfilms Inc. 1126 Tennyson Lane in Naperville, Illinois 60540. John Miley is also a pioneer collector who sometimes teams with Ewing. Both men have provided a great service by recording many sports broadcasts that are the only copies available on DVD and CD and are prized today.

In a piece for the January 14, 2009, edition of the *Los Angeles Times*, Diane Pucin asked Vin for his assessment of his work on the second half of the telecast. Vin said, "The approach in those days was, we were always told to be quiet, don't talk. Ball one, strike one, fouled back, don't say much else. Today, under those circumstances, we'd be talking up the drama, the tension, telling people who Don Larsen is, what he does. We were somewhat intimidated to talk in those days." That's the path that Vin took.

Vin was doing his third World Series, but was not a veteran TV announcer at this time. Red Barber was his mentor. I wasn't swayed by anyone who suggested a less talkative way to do things. In baseball telecasts, I'd cut out stock radio phrases—like "a swing and a miss"—still used by many on TV. I might comment on the ferocity of a swing or how the pitcher fooled the batter. When pitchers stopped winding up, I didn't continue "he winds up" when it became archaic. Larsen, in this game, did not use a windup, now a common practice.

The last part of the TV Don Larsen broadcast lacks the enhancement that Vin might have imparted had he departed from the poor advice to speak less. Vin happens to be the most lyrical of sportscasters and was deprived of enhancing this call as only Vin can do.

Radio calls are almost always used on highlight records, discs, or tapes because they're more descriptive and more exciting. My radio call of the Larsen classic gets constant replays, on both radio and TV.

32: The Team May Be Losing But The Broadcast Should Be Winning

IT'S MUCH EASIER to call a winning team, particularly if one is at home and the home team is in front. There's plenty of crowd roar and one's voice is echoing the excitement. Everybody's a hero, including the announcer—he's relaying the good news.

As long as a team is in contention, the sportscaster feels that, indirectly, he or she is in the game—every play has an importance. When a team no longer has a chance at the pennant and is just playing out the season, the local sportscaster is faced with two difficult tasks—the first is to keep an audience tuning in to the broadcast or telecast; the second is to make his or her words compelling enough to hold interest in a game when his club is out of the game early.

In some cities, interest disappears early in the season when it becomes apparent the team is too weak to win.

For many years when the Senators were early cellar-dwellers, I'd come to the ballpark in Washington each day prepared to tell updated human-interest player stories, discuss baseball topics, render opinions, and intersperse some humorous anecdotes so that the audience and I could share some entertaining moments together, regardless of who won or lost.

The fan letters kept mounting—I tried to answer them all—and I noted the general theme: "enjoyed your work," "kept me entertained

Clark Griffith

hour after hour," "loved your stories," "feel that you're a family member," "appreciate your views." That feedback let me know I was on the right track. The audience viewed me as their friend. Dramatic games didn't need bolstering, nor did meaningful games. When to stay serious and when to change the tone to a more light-hearted approach are part of one's judgment

When I went nationwide on TV and radio, I was prepared to focus on the drama of the game—or if it were one-sided, intersperse other topics along with the play-by-play.

Late in the 2009 baseball season, my wife and I were dining out; and when we left the restaurant, I turned on the car radio to get the local scores. The Mets were playing, Howie Rose was doing the play-by-play, assisted by Wayne Hagin. They're an excellent team—and I became so engrossed in hearing what they were saying that it came as

JOHN EDGAR HOOVER
DIRECTOR

Federal Bureau of Investigation
United States Department of Justice
Washington, D. C.

May 16, 1960

Mr. Bob Wolff
c/o Griffith Stadium
7th and Florida Avenue, N. W.
Washington, D. C.

Dear Mr. Wolff:

I want to commend you for the excellent
manner in which you broadcast the Senators'
baseball games. You have the faculty of
effectively describing the various plays during
the game which enables the listener to clearly
understand what is going on in the field of play.

I have heard a number of favorable comments
concerning the outstanding manner in which you
broadcast the games.

Sincerely,

J. Edgar Hoover

1960 FBI letter from J. Edgar Hoover

a surprise to hear the score now in the eighth inning. The Mets were
trailing, 11 to 3.

The Mets were finishing out a tough season filled with injuries and
disappointments, and were being clobbered this night—and yet I found
this a great broadcast. Howie and Wayne were enhancing a losing game.

I called Mark Chernoff, the WFAN executive who has put together
so many on-air winning combinations, asking for a tape of the broadcast—and here it is transcribed, edited for space, but not content. It's
a master class on how to make a broadcast a top-notch presentation

regardless of the score or the team's standing. We begin in the eighth inning of a one-sided game.

Howie: "This is the twenty-first of September and every once in a while its fun to look at some of the Internet musings about this date in Mets history. *Pay off pitch to Ross, pop in the air to shallow right field, Hernandez the second baseman called off by the right fielder Reed. Jeremy Reed playing shallow and makes the catch for the first out.* A couple of things happened this date worth noting, it was on September 21 eight years ago when baseball returned to New York for the first time after the attacks of September 11 and really one of the most unforgettable nights in the history of Shea Stadium, when the Mets and Braves got together and Mike Piazza hit the home run off of Steve Karsay in the eighth inning. The two run homer that brought the Mets from behind and gave them a 3–2 win. *Nate McLouth takes a fast ball high 1 and 0,* and the lasting image I had that night, Wayne, still think about it to this day eight years later, a couple of firemen that we showed on television celebrating, *the 1–0 outside, 2 and 0,* I thought it was so poignant that here just ten days after those uniformed firefighters who were in the stands that night, just ten days after they undoubtedly lost friends, comrades, who knows who, maybe even family, then in the midst of all the tragedy and all of the personal loss and anguish that the entire city and really the country felt, that, an event at a baseball game gave them reason to smile and to feel good, if only for a few fleeting moments.

"*3-0 pitch, a fastball down the middle, 3 and 1,* and I will never ever forget that image and how it was at that moment that I understood why baseball had to come back because after September 11, I don't know, personally I couldn't have cared less if they came back or not, *3–1 pitch fastball for a called strike two,* if they would have cancelled the rest of the season I'd have been all right with it until that moment when I saw all those uniformed firefighters and how they had cause to celebrate just ten days after the attacks. Mike Piazza could not have hit a bigger home run in his career ever; *pay off pitch to McLouth fouled back to the screen.*"

Wayne: "Being at that point with the Colorado Rockies we were in Phoenix, Arizona, when it happened, very early in the morning and

I remember Larry Walker called everybody on the team, he got the roster as it were for where everybody's room was and he called you and woke you up and told everybody what was going on in New York and around the country—*pay off pitch to McLouth lined foul into the seats down the first base line*—and in Washington D.C. and of course later we would find out about the plane going down in Pennsylvania, in fact Jason Doll was the United Airlines pilot and he lived in my neighborhood in Colorado, he had just helped my wife and a friend of hers five days before."

Howie: "And he was the pilot on that plane?"

Wayne: "And he was the pilot on that flight. who lived in a very small community. *Pay-off pitch to McLouth hit hard on the ground to first and a nice short hop pickup by Daniel Murphy who takes it to the bag for the out, two men away*, and it was only because I had actually gone into the radio station early to do some commercials like you and I will do at times, if we don't do it at the ballpark I came by the station in Denver and went on my way, it was about oh I'd say thirteen miles south of the city and I told my wife I was going to come back and I didn't, I went to the ballpark and called her on the way and that's why they went and asked Jason Doll if he could help out because they knew he was an airline pilot for United and he was available and helped them out."

Howie: *"Pitch to Martin Prado taken outside, high ball one."*

Wayne: "And he had some remarkable changes in his own life that he talked about that day five days later, a horrible tragedy."

Howie: *"Kelly Johnson now, pardon me, is batting for Martin Prado and takes low two balls and no strikes, Johnson a left hand hitter batting .220 with eight homers and 26 runs batted in."*

Wayne: "I'm still so very proud of what you and the Mets and the city of New York, what you guys did to overcome it."

Howie: *"2–0 fastball low 3 and 0.* Well, Bobby Valentine was unbelievable, for the few days that Shea was used as a staging area, I don't think the guy slept most of the interim period between the attacks and when they came back to play, *3–0 pitch fastball on the inside corner,* *strike one*, and he did everything and anything you could imagine to help at Shea Stadium. Boxing things, handing out things, he was just brilliant, *3–1 pitch fouled into the mitt of Josh Thole, 3 and 2*, inspirational is what Bobby was that week."

Wayne: "The city of New York was inspirational to the rest of the country because we all felt it in varying degrees. It wasn't in our backyards like it was here for you, but it was in our backyard in America, it was on our soil and we felt it wherever we were in this country."

Howie: *"Pay off pitch to Johnson inside and low, ball four."*

Wayne: "I can't tell you how proud I was to watch New York and I remember telling people who had never been to New York, who were with the Rockies, people in the neighborhood, and I said that city could withstand an awful lot and they are proving it."

Howie: "And so did Washington D.C. at the Pentagon we should never forget what happened there and of course that flight we talked about. It was just an incredible day we should never forget and even people say that well baseball has helped to bring it back to normalcy but there's no normalcy, the world has changed forever.

"Well that was all eight years ago tonight, when baseball returned to New York at Shea Stadium and Mike Piazza hit that dramatic home run. *Chipper Jones the batter, switch hitter, he has a three run homer and he takes it low 1 and 0, Braves leading 11 to 3 with two out, Kelly Johnson not being held on first.*

"On a much, much, lighter note, forty years ago today the Mets closed in on the National League East Championship in 1969 by sweeping the Pirates in a double header and that was a little bit bigger then it might sound considering they clinched three days later, *pitch on the way to Chipper a grounder back to the mound,, Stokes underhands to first in time.* We'll elaborate later as the side is retired here on the top of the eighth, no runs, no hits, a walk, one left, middle of the eighth, 11 to 3 Braves on the WFAN Mets Radio Network.

"Here's Angel Pagan leading off against Kenshin Kawakami, the first pitch a fast ball outside ball 1. I mentioned that forty years ago the Mets were closing in on the National League East they swept a doubleheader against the Pirates at Shea Stadium. *Here's the 1-0 pitch and that's taken low two and nothing,* well there wasn't panic starting to set in, it was getting a little uncomfortable because the Mets lost the first three games of that series to the Pirates, they lost a twi-nighter at Shea on Friday night, *2–0 to Pagan, fastball for a called strike 2 and 1,* and then on Saturday Bob Moose pitched a no-hitter against the Mets, so things got a little sticky but the Cubs kept cooperating because they lost just about every game for the last month, month and a half, *the 2–1 pitch and Pagan takes a fast ball high 3 and 1,* but in the twin games at that Sunday double header after the Mets had won the opener a lot of us in New York got a bit of an introduction to a guy who had been a legend in Pittsburgh named Bob Prince, *3–1 to Pagan and he pops it in the air to left field, not too deep, moving under it Reid Gorecki and he makes the catch for the first out.* Prince was the long-time Pirates broadcaster and between the twin games of the doubleheader at Shea, Ralph Kiner brought Prince with him to the 'Kiner's Korner' studio, they did an expanded interview and it was unbelievable to hear Bob Prince so reassuring to Mets fans, he had this gravelly voice I mean he sounded like he had rocks in his mouth and he said 'Oh don't worry Ralph you guys are gonna win this thing, don't worry about those last three games.' Now to a kid at home those words felt kinda soothing, you know. *Fernando Tatis swings and misses, nothing and one,* and you know you start to get overly concerned and then three days later they wound up clinching first place. So off of that one interview I always loved Bob Prince."

Wayne: "And remember he was the same guy who dove into the swimming pool from a couple of stories up at the Chase Hotel in St. Louis on a bet. He was a wild thing."

Howie: "That is one of the stories you can repeat on the air about Bob Prince. Ralph has regaled us with many over the years, *the 0-1 to Tatis popped in the air near first base and Adam LaRoche moves under it and makes the catch for the second out, two men away.*

"You hungry for a hot, juicy hamburger? Wendy's makes all their delicious hamburgers with fresh, never frozen beef. They are always hot and juicy and it's way better than fast food, it's Wendy's.

"11 to 3 Atlanta, two outs, nobody on, bottom of the eighth and now Cory Sullivan will bat for the first time, so as we originally figured the pitcher is batting sixth, they had it wrong on the score board and now we will have to adjust our scorecards, so here's Sullivan who is 1 for his last 19 and he takes a called strike nothing and one. You know I had a feeling that was gonna happen.

Bob Murphy used to have a saying, *0–1 curve ball for a called strike to Sullivan, nothing and two*, he said, 'that's why they put erasers on pencils' and idiots like me use ink. *Here's the 0–2 to Sullivan and he checks his swing at a change-up away and holds back it's one ball and two strikes. So Jeremy Reed is on deck and Stokes is batting in the sixth slot.* It is like spring training, isn't it Wayne?"

Wayne: "Oh, big time."

Howie: *"Here's the 1–2 pitch and it's a splitter in the dirt, two balls and two strikes. It's been a struggle lately with Cory Sullivan with a 1 for his last 19. Now the 2–2 pitch and a fastball just missed the inside corner and that runs it full to Cory Sullivan.*

"Here's the payoff pitch and it's popped foul into the seats behind third. Big crowd tonight 37,706 here at Citi Field.

"GEICO wants you to know that a fifteen minute phone call could save you fifteen percent or more on your car insurance. Call 1-800-947-AUTO.

"Three and two to Sullivan with two outs. Now Kawakami winds and the payoff pitch is hit in air, foul to the seats behind third.

Bob Murphy

"*Here's the payoff pitch to Sullivan and it's lined to right center field and that's a base hit headed towards the gap Diaz the right fielder backhands it in the alley, Sullivan is digging to second and he slides in ahead of the throw with a double. So Cory Sullivan is safe at second.*

"*Jeremy Reed is the batter. He takes the first pitch for a called strike. The second pitch is wide. The 1 and 1 pitch lined foul just outside the right field line. Here's the one and two pitch to Reed for a called strike three. That retires the side—no runs, a hit, no errors, one left, at the end of eight, it's 11–3 Atlanta on the WFAN Mets Radio Network.*

"*We head to the ninth inning with the Braves leading 11 to 3. Brian Stokes pitching to Kawakami who takes a called strike on the inside corner, nothing and one. Here's ball one. Kawakami's first outing in the bullpen was last week against the Mets. He chops one back to the mound, grabbed by a leaping Stokes who throws out Kawakami for the first out, one man away. Yunel Escobar coming up.* Braves have not had a hit since the third inning but I think you have to look at that and understand what their approach has been. *Slider for a called strike, nothing and one.* Let's say when they extended the lead to that 11 to 1 advantage they just started to swing at first pitches and not being selective at all and just frankly trying to move this thing along. *Here's the 0–1 another slider in for a called strike, 0 and 2.*

"Derek Lowe, apparently recovered from a finger blister, figures to win this game. Mets famously had a pitcher with blister problems back in the 1960s. His name was Nolan Ryan. *The 0–2 with a fastball high and away 1 and 2.* Back in the day he was given pickle brine to soak his finger in to toughen the skin and although, over the years the Mets trainer at the time Gus Mauch received most of the credit, *1–2 on the way, breaking ball low outside 2 and 2*, Gus Mauch is the guy who said 'soak your finger in this pickle juice and the skin will toughen up.'

"But the guy who told Gus about it was a fellow by the name of Lou Napoli, who, for many years, worked in the Mets press room. *2–2 pitch hit hard in the air to center, going back is Angel Pagan, he's under it. Angel makes the catch for the second out.* Lou Napoli was an amateur boxer who worked as a bartender in the Mets press room and there was Lou who gave Gus Mauch the idea about having Ryan soak his hand in the pickle brine because Lou said that's what boxers do. I don't know that Lou fought bare knuckle necessarily, you would think the boxing gloves would protect that, but I suppose having not been a boxer you know the friction inside the glove might rub and you know bring up a blister. So anyway a guy named Lou Napoli factored into that.

"Here's Reid Gorecki and he swings at the first pitch and misses a fastball, nothing and one. One and one breaking ball outside. 2–1 fastball swung at and missed, two and two to Reid Gorecki. Here's the 2–2 pitch and a fastball fouled back to the screen."

(Wayne contributed here by starting a story about a baseball personality named Joe Charboneau, a Rookie of the Year, who was a one-year wonder.)

Wayne: "Then he goes down to Mexico and is still trying to make some money. He came from a tough background and didn't have a whole lot of money so he went to Mexico and gets stabbed by a guy with a pen because he refused to sign an autograph."

Howie: *"2–2 fastball swung at and missed, strike three, side retired,* and the moral of the story is always sign."

Wayne: "Always sign and don't be anywhere near Joe Charboneau."

Howie: *"First strikeout for Stokes, Braves go in order, middle of the ninth, 11–3 on WFAN, the Mets Radio Network."*

You've heard the saying, "You can't beat the script." Well, this script was another Mets loss, but Howie and Wayne changed the game with their own script. They didn't plan it this way—they were clever enough to do so. This is the sportscaster's job and their work rates commendation.

The art of storytelling—impromptu, unrehearsed, audience-holding material—is a tremendous asset, particularly in baseball broadcasting where new material is a requirement for every game.

There's less need in the fast-action sports or games where the drama doesn't need story embellishments.

For an inning and a half of a one-sided game, Howie and Wayne held my attention and, hopefully, yours. The spoken word benefits from vocal enthusiasm, inflections, pauses, declarations, and laughter. Stories may be serious, humorous, revealing, or newsworthy—but the object is the same—winning is holding the audience. Doing this day after day brings enjoyment to the daily listener.

Most broadcast auditions contain excited calls of winning plays— they command attention. But keeping listeners and viewers tuned in to one-sided games or losing teams demands a sportscaster with a special knack—it's a more challenging aspect of the business and a great plus for the advertisers and the ratings. Some ability is needed on sports talk shows. Mike Francesa spends five and a half hours daily on the mike with a similar mission, holding an audience.

In the studio shows, however, the stations demand everything be put in writing to aid in adding video and prepare the program properly. That's a different art. The reading pace has to fit the time segment.

The Mets have an excellent TV crew as well, who also entertain while they report. On July 20, 2010, I wanted to see how Gary Cohen and Ron Darling handled adversity. I saw and heard outstanding TV in a game that from a competitive standpoint, ended in the first inning. Brash, outspoken Keith Hernandez, who knows the game, was off this night but is an excellent addition to Ron Darling's baseball analysis and Gary Cohen's outstanding play-by-play.

Mike Pelfrey, who entered the game with a 10–4 record, was battered by Arizona in the first inning for four runs, yielding four hits and two walks. Pelfrey appeared overmatched. Given a chance to come back in the second inning, the humiliation continued with three more hits by Arizona, two runs charged, and a yanking after an inning and a third. A nightmare performance for any pitcher, but particularly one who got off to such a fine start, only to enter a mysterious slump after his tenth victory.

The Diamondbacks kept adding runs and won the game 13–2, but Cohen and Darling never let down in their comments. They kept up a brisk pace and spent most of the second part of the game taking viewers' phone calls and answering their questions while the TV picture kept fans abreast of the "action."

Their chat with the fans was a pretty strong statement that it was now up to the TV duo to supply the evening's entertainment and they supplied just that.

New York time was well past midnight, the outcome of the game had long since been determined, when I finally decided to get some sleep. It was 13–1 Arizona after eight innings when I reluctantly turned off the set. In a one-sided Mets loss those TV guys put on a winning performance.

It is entirely possible to become a star in the sports, entertainment, or political fields more on exposure, power, or wealth than on personal magnetic appeal. Many of the world's richest businessmen or top university presidents don't have that magical quality, that award-winning sports cartoonist Bill Gallo calls "it."

Bill White

"It" has nothing to do with winning or character or doing a job well. "It" is difficult to define. It's a glow, a charisma that some have, some don't.

People may disagree, and rightfully so, on who has "it." Some who have it may be soft-spoken, others may be loud.

Hirers realize, however, that having "it" may attract an audience—listeners and viewers—and whether one likes or dislikes the person may be secondary.

It's true in politics. Ronald Regan had "it," Jimmy Carter didn't. Franklin Roosevelt had "it," but not Harry Truman. Barack Obama has "it," John McCain doesn't. And Sarah Palin may not be smarter than a fifth-grader, but she has "it."

Frank Sinatra had "it" in singing, so did Louis Armstrong and so does Tony Bennett. There are hundreds of other popular singers with hit records who don't have "it." Oprah doesn't sing or dance, but she has "it."

In movies, Cary Grant had "it." So did Clark Gable. Jimmy Stewart had "it," as did Henry Fonda. Tom Hanks has "it," so does Billy Crystal. In movies, though, remember actors and actresses are reading lines written for them, not revealing their own thoughts. As guests on talk shows, they have an opportunity to reveal their personalities.

In sports, John Madden had "it," Pat Summerall didn't, but had charm with his low-key approach. Howard Cosell had "it," so did Don Meredith. Modest Frank Gifford had appeal, but as the booth quarterback deferred to his partners to supply "it." Dick Enberg and Al Michaels also fulfill their roles without claiming the spotlight. So does Dick Stockton.

Phil Rizzuto had "it" as a Yankee announcer. He was unpretentious, down-to-earth, and it was fun to hear him get excited at a ball game. His more reserved partner, Bill White, also had "it" as part of the team. Michael Jordan and Magic Johnson had "it" in abundant fashion and LeBron James may develop "it." Derek Jeter has "it."

But some of the great superstars don't have "it," including Larry Bird, Alex Rodriguez, Tom Seaver, Kobe Bryant, Kareem Abdul-Jabbar, and Patrick Ewing. The lack of "it" hasn't hurt their stature or their bank accounts. They had appeal.

Today, unless one is the voice of a team or a commercial or cable network's top play-by-play man or analyst-commentator, most of the other TV sports segments around the country do not allow enough sports time to do more than give scores, highlights, or a few sports headlines and sound-bite interviews. Sportscasters doing talk radio or pre- and post-game TV shows have a better chance to develop a rapport with the audience and demonstrate a personality. Developing "it" on routine jobs is difficult to accomplish. And appeal should be natural, not contrived.

Having a special charm, however, can be an important factor to the hirer selecting who gets the job. Expressing oneself with solid, researched opinions in a graceful and entertaining manner makes one stand out from the crowd.

Remember, having "it" is strictly an opinion, not a tested fact. It's not a requirement for success, but a degree of charm can benefit any performer. One doesn't have to be luminous to be a star. Being liked as a person is a great plus.

Don't worry, though, if you don't have "it" as a sportscaster. It's not a job requirement. The headliners are those you're describing— they're playing the games. Your words, your emotions, are enhancing the enjoyment.

Most of those hired with special appeal are commentators who add another look to the production.

Of more importance in the sportscasting field is the ability to wear well—day after day, year after year. These sportscasters gradually become electronic friends—a part of the listener or viewer's life. They're liked, they're hired, and they solidify their positions as the years go by. Passing the test of time is important to a successful sportscasting career.

The legendary radio broadcasters occupied a far greater role in listeners' lives than modern telecasters, particularly in baseball and especially in play-by-play.

There's a reason for this. The radio guys were heard on every game, constant companions. In many cities, fewer games are on TV and in some cities, they're scattered over a variety of outlets—commercial TV, cable, regional and network. In some cities, announcers rotate. There's rarely one consistent voice.

The big difference, though, is that, on radio, the play-by-play man provides the picture with his description and comments. On TV, the picture speaks for itself. The sportscaster adds his excitement and identifications, plus there are fewer words needed to caption what the viewer is already seeing. That reduces his role.

Many of the old-time radio greats had personalities, pet phrases, and stylized calls that became part of their individual charm. Fans in the area accepted this individual style as the way games should be called.

On May 4, 2010, a broadcasting radio great, Ernie Harwell died of cancer at age 92. Ernie received fan devotion that few modern broadcasters achieve. An expert caller of games with a passion for the sport, his pleasant manner and rich, low voice made for comfortable listening. His humble desire to please his listeners without histrionics struck just the right chord. Ernie broadcast for a variety of teams, fifty-five years in all, but became a legend in Detroit where he was idolized as the voice of the Tigers for forty-two years.

Ernie made his mark—not as a personality, but as a person.

Personalities perform. Making it as a person means one is accepted as a friend. And that's how all Ernie's colleagues—and his fans—thought of him.

Attaining this status as a sportscaster is a noble achievement. Many sportscasters are admired, but tuning in to hear one's friend on the air is devotion only a special few achieve.

Location is important to pitchers and sportscasters alike. It should come as no surprise that there's an advantage to be seen and heard by the executives of major companies and their advertising agencies. If they are big sports sponsors, the sportscaster is auditioning every day as well as making friends with those in power.

In the early days, Mel Allen of the Yankees and Red Barber of the Dodgers became the first in the broadcast wing of the Baseball Hall of Fame. Vin Scully came along a bit later. Gillette's advertising agency, Maxon Inc., was in New York. They saw and heard the New York sportscasters every day.

The Red Sox's Curt Gowdy was also a Gillette favorite. Curt had previously been with the Yankees. The Boston-based company saw and heard him doing the Red Sox games. Anheuser-Busch, the brewer of Budweiser, had a full stable of St. Louis announcers to choose from. Chicago was a sportscaster contributor, Wrigley is a big name in sports, as was Pittsburgh with Westinghouse and Baltimore with the National Brewing Company. All of the men with sponsor backing fully deserved their accolades and assignments. Today Joe Buck is carrying on the St. Louis tradition, as is Bob Costas. There is an advantage of being seen and heard locally by a national sponsor.

Washington has only one big business—government. I realized my goals but had to take a more circuitous route to get there. Being seen and heard by major sponsors is easier if one is fortunate to be working in the same city where such a company has its headquarters. The big advertising agencies and network headquarters are in New York. Being Madison Square Garden's leading TV sportscaster on play-by-play for many decades provided a great agency exposure boost for me. Not only was I being seen and heard by people who handled the hiring, many also sponsored my shows in Washington.

When I started anchoring nightly sportscasts at News 12 Long Island, I learned quickly that all the young people working with me had been brought up in the art of pruning all their sports stories into the fewest words possible.

In New York, covering nine major league teams plus local schools, colleges, and national stories in three- or four-minute segments is far different than calling ball games that would average over three hours.

The time limit on TV studio sports shows meant condensing, not expanding. No surprise that twittering has caught on as communications, along with texting and all the abbreviated word usage based on phonetics—"u-no" what I mean?

Andrew Rappaport is the hatchet man for my essays at News 12 Long Island. He's the show's producer and he's merciless—"Cut ten seconds" is his usual cry. I now do this automatically and appreciate Andrew's guidance. At News 12 Westchester, when I also tape opinions in a quiet studio for my "Point of View," Jenna Russo and Nancy Pristash make sure to keep me revved up in the absence of crowd roar or a studio audience. Anchor and reporter Jamie Stuart mastered this art before he became a pro and Kevin Maher, another Syracuse grad, added another creative touch to our mix while anchoring sports. Photography has put less emphasis on writing skills. Our cameraman at News 12 Long Island, Dan Jacobsen, can tell a story with the right camera shots, with an impact that overshadows words. TV editing is a fine art that can make a story even stronger. TV producers want as many pictures as possible to tell stories. Mike Lechner had that knack when we worked together at News 12. Vinnie Scaffidi was an artist at that too.

Although the time constraint of TV studio sports shows—mainly scripted with teleprompters—demands compressing stories to get them in the allotted time, working in the field as a sports reporter or play-by-player requires ability to make one's points without written help.

In studio shows I started with the same wire stories available to everyone, but I changed the words around—not the facts, of course—to make my show sound more distinctive. "The Air Force was flying high today—on target for a 40–6 win over shell-shocked . . . " "Army bombed their opponent, while Navy torpedoed the visitors, with Tom Jones launching four touchdown missiles from his quarterback position."

Add in a little wordplay and the show has a breezier feel, an extra touch.

There was a football coach at that time named "Spook" Jacobs. I had a lot of fun with Spook as his team kept making "ghost-to-ghost" headlines.

33: Statisticians, Spotters, And Sports Records

I 'M CONVINCED THAT, among the reasons for my early success doing play-by-play, is that I always screened and selected someone to work with me as my booth assistant who would listen closely to every word I said and was ready to nudge me and whisper to me to correct any slip, if I made one. Frankly, I don't remember this ever happening, but it was a valuable safeguard. Accuracy was my trademark; and I wanted to make sure that, if I ever gave the wrong score or name, I'd correct it immediately like it was a slip of the tongue rather than let it lie there as an error.

Further, I wanted my assistant to quickly check the record book if a record was at stake, or if I needed to get more information from the official scorer—or even get to the officials' room to settle a perplexing question. My assistant had to do this without my urging him to do so. I was involved watching the play unfold, but these extras would make my description complete. After every game I broadcast, I checked all the local papers to make sure I had covered every story angle.

My booth assistants knew I was always looking for every newsworthy story and did not hesitate to pass me notes with pertinent observations knowing that there was time to include only a few select ones on the air. I didn't have to wait for a final stat sheet to check my accuracy, though. If my assistant wrote down a stat, that was it. Length of a punt, yards in a touchdown run, shooting percentages, made foul shots in a row, on and on.

There were always a director, producer, and about a dozen technicians watching and listening in the control room, but all were preoccupied with concentrating on their own jobs. They heard my words, but were more intent on fulfilling their responsibilities. I could not rely on them to whisper something to be corrected in my earpiece so I did not rely on that. They depended on me to be correct. With all these safeguards, and my intense preparation, I can't recall any mistakes in calling games. If I had, believe me, I'd still be brooding.

It was my own expense to have a personal assistant. I always paid him myself, including his travel and on-the-road expenses. After many years of footing the bill myself, I gradually got the networks, stations, or sponsors who hired me to put in spotting and assisting fees on their budgets and that now exists in the higher level jobs.

I also made a list of assistants on distant trips that I could call to work with me to save travel costs, and I discovered that this elite network of booth aides was also being employed by some of my colleagues. Before hiring them, I could now ask who else they worked for. Any assistance given to me was also made equally available to my partners in the broadcasting booth when a second or third broadcaster was added. When paired with other broadcasters, it was important that we helped each other as well, as friends and colleagues.

During my years in Washington, I worked with brainy aides like Dick Heller, Phil Hochberg, Eddie Shapiro, Les Sand, Howie Williams, and Maury Povich. There was a young man in Washington who listened to my air work for many years, but we never had the opportunity to work together. We met on many occasions at various sports events. Marty Aronoff started helping out sportscasters in Washington and elsewhere on many sports and became so much in demand that he left his government job after eighteen years to become a full-time sports statistician expert—a sports journalist to a who's who of top network sportscasters.

A partial list of those he sits beside and provides notes to includes: Jon Miller in baseball, Dick Stockton in basketball, Kenny Albert in baseball, Sean McDonough in college football, Mike Patrick in college basketball, Dave O'Brien in baseball, Mike Tirico in football, Dan Shulman in baseball, Gary Thorne in baseball and many others. That assortment of top sportscasters provides ample proof not only of the job importance but also of Marty's great ability.

The system hasn't changed, even with the rise of new technology. The stat man provides a continual pile of quick notes that one glances at quickly. He keeps the basketball score sheet with up-to-date information that one can check at a glance. In baseball, I'd keep my own scorecard. The sportscasters choose which notes they want to use, but the sportscasters work with the stat men like a pitcher with a catcher "they think alike"—the stat man knows what the sportscaster wants, and there's no delay in getting the information on the air.

Hubie Brown, Mike Tirico, and Marty Aronoff

In the control truck, there's also a stat man to put notes on the screen. Many graphics are prepared before the broadcast. The booth stat man and the stat man with graphics are connected with headphones, frequently assisting each other. Basketball stats are also being kept by a stat group in the arena. A stat monitor in the booth will show points, rebounds, assists, and other basic information; but staff assistants provide points in a row, lead changes, biggest leads, biggest deficits and many other newsworthy notes. They're the little extras that enhance the game calls.

In the early days, I screened and selected my own stat men. Occasionally on long road trips, I'd use experts in other major cities, many of whom were developing big reputations such as Jim Stamos, who did many network shows, and Paul Evans who worked with Marv Albert on the All-Star basketball game in Dallas in 2009. Paul worked with me many years ago. These booth assistants are a vital part of a smooth broadcast. Selecting the right people is part of the sportscaster's job.

Starting out, I often used sportswriters or injured players to assist. I found that some injured footballers oddly didn't recognize their teammates that well from a distance and eventually went back to my own people rather than gamble on someone who had not been pre-tested in a booth.

At Madison Square Garden, and on some on road games, too, I worked Knicks and college basketball with talented stat men including Sonny Hertzberg, Bill Raftery, Richie Regan, Lennie Lewin, Bob Rosen, and Harry Robinson. Norm MacLain assisted on Rangers hockey. All bright men and major contributors to the shows. Bill Raftery continues as one of the nation's top TV basketball analysts. Harry is still doing the job at the Garden. More than stat men, they became personal friends. Talented craftsman, they added to my confidence for each game. Confidence brings relaxation. I knew they listened to my words, always double-checking my accuracy. Sportscasting is a team effort. These sidekicks are like bench coaches in baseball, vital contributors to the success of the team.

Maury Povich was my stat man and young producer in Washington for baseball, then joined me in Minnesota with the Twins and even

Roger Angell

worked in some early mike time when I had to leave a late-running game to catch a flight to New York for a network show. Maury also worked the famous 1958 Colts-Giants NFL overtime championship football game with me. In 1956 for my first World Series I asked Herb Heft, the Senators' PR director, to join me. Herb later joined the Mets in the same capacity when they began six years later. Bob Neal was my broadcast partner on that World Series.

Most sports bios dwell heavily on statistics. For readers who enjoy story angles, Rich Marazzi and co-writer Len Fiorito came up with an impressive book about all the major leaguers from one decade—*Baseball Players of the 1950s*. Each profile unearths unusual content beyond the numbers, which always adds extra punch to the reading. These are the type of stories that have the most impact, unusual items that hold the audience's attention.

All these stat people have a great sense for what's newsworthy. The numbers they use all have meaning. And the numbers they make rightfully keep increasing.

Herb Heft

Some stadium facilities are better suited for TV than others. I found it essential to hear the crowd roar when I called the game as my voice rose and fell with the play. With a closed window, I'd see the bodies, but I couldn't hear the noise. I always tried to work with an open window or an open TV booth. If need be, I'd use headphones to hear the sound. With a closed window for football, it was difficult when it rained or snowed—the rain spattered against the window and the snow clung to it. Numbers on players became smeared in the mud. My earphones could pick up crowd roar to a small extent but I also had to hear my director and booth partner. When I selected football spotters, particularly on college games, my first question would be, "can you identify these players even if the mud wipes out their numbers?"

On outdoor games my only worry with regard to visibility was my distance from the field. And I've encountered the fog problem, not only outside but inside as well in arenas that host ice hockey and basketball.

Architects of sports venues usually don't consult with sportscasters about what they need. Architects are structural artists but not sportscasters. Communication in the early stages would help.

My best advice is whenever possible, particularly for football, have the public relations directors of the teams you are covering on the weekend send you two or three copies of game tapes so you can learn the players by body movements, as well as numbers. These tapes can be played at the TV station or at home. It's a great way to prepare regardless of the elements or the location of the booth. I did this whenever possible.

33: STATISTICIANS, SPOTTERS, AND SPORTS RECORDS

I must add this financial note about hiring stat men. In my early broadcasting days, when broadcasting fees were low and my bank account was even lower, I used friends to assist me in the play-by-play booth who just wanted to enjoy the experience. Soon after, I began payments to booth assistants. Kevin Maher, now the Sports Director and Anchor at News 12 Long Island, learned this craft at Syracuse University, where he also taught, and worked commercially at the CBS station in town, WTVH.

Kevin told me he did football games without any spotters. I since have heard that others attempt this as well. I salute Kevin's courage. I would never risk not getting a play right but that's the sportscaster's choice. I prepared to have this capability, but knew that just one missed number or wrong call or long hesitation would tear down my reputation for accuracy and quickness. One of my early students at St. John's, Carl Reuter, does a full schedule of high school and college sports for Madison Square Garden Varsity. Like Kevin Maher, Carl told me that the person he relies on for stats, notes and spotting is himself. He also told me that he follows one of my favorite techniques for being fast on calls, particularly football, by listing all the players' numbers in numerical order across his score sheet so he can quickly look down for the numbers of the runner and the tackler.

Originally, I used to put down line-ups: offense, defense, special teams, kickers, holders, captains, kickoff and punt returners and the rest. I still did that after I got more experienced, but found out that there's no time to search for a number so I had the numbers right at the top of my sheet and the rest below. I was delighted to hear that my old system still works. But like other sportscasters, this wasn't in any book I read, it was by trial and error until I found the best one for speed.

If Carl ever has to sneeze and blow his nose, does he ever fall behind in spotting the new players entering the game? He has to be not just quick, but courageous, too.

I used carefully selected booth assistants for baseball, basketball, football and hockey. I didn't need them for soccer, horse shows, dog shows, boxing or other events. If I was broadcasting the game of one college team I covered all season, one spotter was sufficient. Same with the pros if I knew the team well. But for the college *Game of the Week*, with large squads and teams I was watching live for the first time, I wanted the assurance of one spotter for each team. In one-sided games, when the winning coach would make changes to get each player a mention, I didn't want to disappoint parents waiting for those names to be called.

Kenny Albert, an ascending star for FOX TV who covers fast action sports like football, basketball and hockey, as well as baseball, finds that he can work well with one excellent spotter holding spotting cards for both teams. I recommend whatever system one has faith in, as the results are what count. On college games when I've already called one team and know the players, one spotter can suffice. It's all a matter of confidence. The sportscaster has to feel secure.

Kenny told me he also does what I do, memorize numbers, notes and body movements by watching game films, tapes, or discs in advance of calling live action. Some of the games he finds on satellite.

If one is correct and quick, that's what matters. Now it's become customary for college and pro games to furnish spotters if needed, and they expect to be paid. Public address announcers don't have assistants but are not involved in mentioning details of each play. I am a firm believer in the booth assistant system, but like many other aspects of sportscasting, there are no rules stating what one should do. It's individual choice by the sportscaster, and finances may enter into the decision.

I've always been more interested in stories and playing techniques than in numbers, but statistics are an important part of the games, in broadcast booths, in salary negotiations, and with the public. I try to use stats that have meaning. Some are used for measurement tools. On quick calls, I tend to use locations rather than exact footage. A broadcaster who declares "it's a twenty-five-foot shot" must be gifted with amazing eyes. It's an opinion, an estimate, not a fact.

With sports, along came records. Records remain long after the individuals who made them have left us. In the early days of sports, there were fewer record-keepers and certainly less double-checking than there is today.

Today, in the electronic age, old scribbled notes on papers and typewritten copies have been bypassed by the Internet and information-gathering technology. There is increased demand for more and more numbers for TV, radio, and press coverage. Today, records are kept and TV coverage is preserved. Newspapers hold on to past editions with digital files.

For many years, our son Rick was the editorial director of the official *Baseball Encyclopedia*, a huge book that has the records of all the major league players and managers and a Negro League Register. Checking the records of the early players was a formidable task. Rick enlisted the aid of the Society for American Baseball Research along with many distinguished baseball historians, to double-check all entries, and found to his dismay that some of the early listings didn't add up and could not be verified. What's worse was they were already printed in books or on award inscriptions.

Does one change them according to newly researched data or let it go? One prominent columnist voiced his views, "They're part of the record, it's too late to change them now, the statute of limitations has run out."

"It won't change their stature as players," Rick countered. "As the Official Encyclopedia this book has to be as correct as we can make it. There's no statute of limitations on truth. Honesty has to be our policy. Let's get to work."

From Babe Ruth on, I've seen most of the top home run hitters in action—some more than others—but I believe none had more game power than Mickey Mantle. In batting practice, some of the bloated musclemen of the steroid era could put on chemical distance shows that were memorable displays. Fortunately, today's heroes are again hitting homers without artificial help.

Mantle's versatility was astounding. No other slugger had his power from both sides of the plate, and no others could also put down a drag bunt, knowing if it rolled past the pitcher, it was a sure base hit.

Mantle told me on an interview that he was a natural righty. The only thing he could do lefty, aside from bunting, Mantle said, was swinging away. He felt he was stronger right-handed—he hit more line drives from the right side of the plate—but he lifted the ball higher lefty.

I broadcast two of what were considered in the press as Mantle's three longest home runs.

The first was off Chuck Stobbs of the Senators at Griffith Stadium in Washington in 1953. Batting righty against the southpaw pitcher, and aided by a gale blowing to left, Mantle cracked a rising line drive heading towards the bleachers. Griffith Stadium was built for pitching, not hitting. It was 405 feet down the left field line, then came a fence and the bleachers rose upwards 32 rows. At the top was the sponsor's sign, National Bohemian Beer, portrayed by "Mr. Boh." The liner nicked the sign, flew out of the park and disappeared from sight.

In all my years in Washington, I had never seen one leave the ballpark in left field. In fact, I had never seen what was beyond the bleachers, nor had anyone else from the broadcast booths.

The low press area for TV and radio at Griffith Stadium was constructed about fifteen yards up from the ground right behind home plate, and it was mpossible to see the area beyond the bleachers. The same went for the writers in the press box, which was higher up.

I remember calling this Mantle homer more with awe then with the rising voice I used on other calls. There was no time for embroidering. It was like an express train rushing by a station without passengers, gone in a flash. I played up "first to leave the park over the bleachers" and Mantle's might.

I mentioned that Josh Gibson, a legendary catcher with the Negro League's Homestead Grays, who also played in Griffith Stadium, had been written up as having accomplished this feat, but I hadn't seen it. Gibson died at an early age without being given the opportunity to be a major league catcher.

When the home run was hit, Red Patterson, the Yankees' energetic public relations director, left the press box in search of a witness beyond the bleachers to provide more details to the writers and broadcasters. Most important was the distance of the homer, needed before the press deadline and TV-radio signed off.

Red was applauded for coming back quickly with a story and a number. He gave the distance of the homerun as 565 feet, which I

Bob and Mickey Mantle

used on air in Washington as did Mel Allen, sitting just to my left, broadcasting back to New York. Red also gave his step-by-step account of how he had measured this, what happened after the ball left the ballpark and where it landed. This is from the story of the young "observer" who, like Red, had not seen it happen. Deadlines were met and Red's story became part of history.

In fact, it became so much history that the Yankees highlight record that year includes Mel Allen's recreation play-by-play based on Red's story of what happened after the ball went over the bleachers to where it finally stopped. Mel believed it to be true, although, like myself, he could not see it from the broadcast booth. To me "hit out of the ballpark" is the story, the rest is hearsay. But the announced distance of the "tape measure home run" (there was no tape measure) is referred to now without any mention of "estimated," "believed to be," or "calculated." It's now historical fact.

In 2010 Jane Leavy, a brilliant author, completed her terrific book, *The Last Boy: Mickey Mantle and the End of America's Childhood,* for HarperCollins Publishers. There's no more thorough researcher than

Jane, and it's fascinating to read the lengths she'll go to unearth the truth.

She interviewed over 500 people for the biography. The problem is that eyewitnesses have different opinions of what they saw or heard or think they saw or heard. This is more true in the years before television replay was available or used to get a second or third look.

But few search as painstakingly as Jane. It took years for her to finally track down the fourteen-year-old Washington observer who had produced, for a slight fee, the story about where the ball finally landed and a ball he said was the one Mantle hit. The youngster, now a seventy-year-old man, according to Jane, was inside the ballpark when Mantle hit it and "did not see the ball land on the fly in the backyard of 434 Oakdale Place and he never showed anyone where he had found it."

Jane took the investigation as far as it can go. She believes that the unverified story might have come close to the truth. It was a relentless effort.

But my eyesight and my later call of Mickey Mantle's left-handed home run off Pete Ramos in 1956 at Yankee Stadium did vary with Jane's opinion and research of its trajectory. My telecast of this game went back to Washington and other stations on the Senators' TV Network, but no tape was saved and there was no replay. Nor was a tape kept in New York. Unlike the line drive out of Griffith Stadium, Mantle hit one with a lefty uppercut swing. It took off, kept rising, and went soaring over the lower deck in right field, over the mezzanine and on its way over the third deck to baseball heaven until its flight was rudely interrupted by smashing into the Yankee Stadium façade, eighteen inches from a journey to outer space.

I kept describing its flight as "going up, still rising, still going up" and when it crashed, I said, "This was inches away from being the first ball hit out of Yankee Stadium. Still going upwards, I believe the total distance could have been 600 to 700 feet." No radio or TV tapes were saved, but the TV diagrams from the Yankee files tell the story. They're printed in the book. So is the *Daily News* back page picture. They confirm my ascension call.

And here are the words from the Yankees' popular beat writer, Joe Trimble. Of Mantle's gigantic swat, Joe writes in the New York *Daily News*, "It soared on and up as the crowd held its collective breath. As it climbed through the haze and headed for the heavens, it seemed

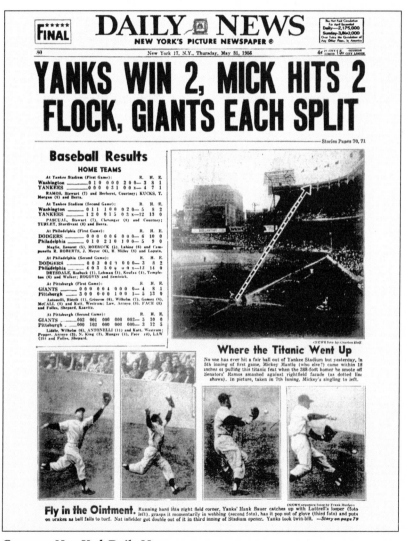

Courtesy *New York Daily News*

almost sure to clear the roof, but it struck the green façade (oxidized copper) just a foot and a half short—the longest ball ever hit in that direction since the Stadium was rebuilt in 1938."

"It's the hardest ball I ever hit left-handed," Mantle said between games. These words and the pictures in this book are from the back page of the *Daily News*, May 31, 1956, the day after the historic homer. The picture was by famed photographer Charles Huff, the diagrammer is unknown. They're printed with the *News'* permission.

Jane uses an illustration in the front and back of her book showing a diagram which indicates that the ball may have dipped down a bit before hitting the facade. Her source appeared to be United Press International, a company acquired by Corbis. Corbis took over their photo archives and gets a credit in Jane's book.

Having a difference of opinion with an esteemed writer like Jane Leavy is like a math intern challenging Einstein.

Corbis is well-respected for its digital imaging and rights providing.

I spoke to Ken Johnston, the Director of Historical Photography for Corbis. Ken deals with old-time photos and proved extremely helpful.

Ken told me that Corbis had taken over Bettman Archives, which owned United Press International's Archives. That's where the picture came from.

Ken said that no one knew who added the diagram or whether it was a baseball person, but added he had two different diagrams—

Flight of Mickey Mantle's homeruns, courtesy of *MSG*

33: STATISTICIANS, SPOTTERS, AND SPORTS RECORDS

one of the ball ascending, one dipping, and sometimes diagrams are selected for picture clarity rather then objectivity. They're more of a guide than verification. Diagrammers are not given credit by name.

The matter may be academic, however, because in 1963, Mantle hit another majestic homer into the façade off Bill Fischer of Kansas City that Mantle said was "the hardest ball I ever hit." Does being hit hard mean distance? Mantle's line drive shot in Washington might have rolled further on a flat surface, but the Yankee Stadium homers had higher trajectories. Mantle indicated to Jane the one in Washington had a 50-mile-per-hour tailwind and the one off Ramos was coming down more.

That would seem to put the one off Fischer into the longest-ball winner's circle except for these sharp-eyed observations from newspapers accounts used by Jane in her book.

The New York Times said that the ball off Fisher hit the façade "374 feet from the batter's box and 108 feet and one inch above the playing field." *The New York Post* said it traveled "at least 475 feet (that's over 100 feet more) sailing over the 367 marker, about 100 feet high, and was moving at a 45-degree trajectory." *Newsday* said it soared "380 feet and was five feet from the top of the façade." Five feet from the top would move this from first to third place for the longest. The *Newsday* quote is from Jane's book, as are the others.

The point is that opinions differ. That's part of baseball's fun, giving opinions.

So for the fun of it, let's consider a three-way tie for Mantle's longest homer. I was curious to get Jane's opinion on my ascending homerun call compared to the call published in her book, so I called her on the phone. I left word and she e-mailed her response. Jane's answer was, "Bob, we used this as endpapers because it was a better quality photo than the one from 1963. I did not dwell on the specifics of the 1956 home run because I knew I was going to spend so much time on the 1963 home run and did not want to be repetitive. So I say go with your eyes."

Her answer won my applause for unrivalled graciousness. She hit this one out of any ballpark, no measurement needed. No one can be fairer.

329

34: Sportscasting Teams

THERE WERE MANY factors in the tremendous growth of sports, but none greater than television which reached local or national audiences with selling impact. Advertisers could show their products and subscribers would pay to have their choice of cable channels. In the early days, one sponsor would sponsor an entire game. Now multiple sponsors are the financial backers. The athletes provide the show, and their salaries have made the stars multi-millionaires.

The invention of TV made it a new ballgame. Is there more growth still ahead? Global TV can capture worldwide consumers. The desire for increased sports on TV and radio using more sportscasters for play-by-play, pre and post-game shows, talk shows, panel shows and all the rest, including the analyst group, opened the doors for a large group of new personalities. These are big years in the sportscasting business.

It began with one sportscaster doing play-by-play for each event. That's now changed. The pairing of sportscasters has become the norm. The second announcer can add analysis, opinions, banter or judgments. They've become strong partners.

Some play-by-players stick with the basic information, while others become informative conversationalists.

The better the pairing, the stronger the team. There's an art to putting together the combination. Mark Chernoff, the WFAN operations manager and VP for sports programming for CBS Radio and WFAN, New York, has made a science of fitting two different types together. Mark tells me that contrasting personalities and voice play an important part in his selections, but some pairings just click, while others don't. They're auditioned together before any contracts are signed. Being knowledgeable in a variety of sports is important. It's good to have a track record of experience. Having a creative style is an asset, and a big name is an extra attraction but not a necessity. The duo not only has to get along well, they have to respect each other's viewpoint. Their discussions may become heated, but the audience must feel its friendly debate, not a competition.

These are not hasty decisions. Mark has a feeling for what works. Then he works at double-checking his initial reaction. He's known for his winning combinations. When former NFL football star Boomer Esiason was paired with Craig Carton on WFAN's morning show, it was assumed that Boomer would be the lead announcer. Mark had heard Craig enough on a show outside of New York to know that Craig had excellent sports knowledge along with a descriptive, higher voice that commanded attention. What would Boomer's reaction be to working with him?

On TV panel shows it's Boomer's presence that is always known. He doesn't hold back. On this radio pairing, Boomer serves as much a moderator as an opinion maker. He lets Craig make his points without interruption and then makes his, but it's not a fight. It's two friends having a friendly discussion. Mark Chernoff sensed this would happen and it does.

The play-by-play sportscaster usually gets his or her name spoken first, but it's the second man who is often the personality. Dick Enberg helped to make Al McGuire a star on basketball some years ago. Al's naturalness and unique basketball expressions stole the show and Dick, a fine craftsman, played the straight man role, while also calling the game.

John Madden and Pat Summerall were football's hottest pairing. John's down-to-earth, discerning analysis, delivered with gusto, was terrific when contrasted with Pat's pleasant, unruffled, low-key call.

Football has many great pairings today. Familiar praise-worthy combinations are Joe Buck and Troy Aikman. Pam Oliver does well on her sideline duties. Jim Nantz and Phil Simms are polished and pleasant, Al Michaels and Chris Collinsworth…there are so many duos who, together, complement each other well. Getting the right partner can affect a career. Partners have to like each other and take pride in the pairing. There may be more good pairings in sports than there are in private life.

Jon Miller and Joe Morgan spent twenty-one years together on ESPN baseball and Joe Buck and Tim McCarver have staked a yearly claim to baseball's World Series coverage so long as FOX holds the contract.

An oddity about sportscasting is that, as a conveyer of sports news, not a maker, one is immediately accorded a special status. Fan letters, autograph requests, speaking engagements are a by-product.

There seems to be something about being seen or heard that triggers people's curiosity. They want a closer look at these people who keep entering their homes electronically. A lot of people stop and look at these personalities in person as if they're finally meeting long-time friends they've been listening to or watching for years. An autograph becomes proof, particularly with an inscription.

It's flattering to receive accolades in the mail or in person, knowing that doing one's daily job actually has an affect on others. Since I started out as a professional and ever since, I've spoken to so many of my colleagues on the air, on the phone or at sports events. With rare exceptions, they don't sound any different, look any different, or act any different than the other people I meet everyday. Their voices, their looks are like anyone else. Very few automatically command attention. Occasionally a beautiful voice is recognized or a remarkable personality. But when the red light goes on, the tone, the look, the speech rhythm, the authority, the word flow, the emphasis, the entire person takes on a different glow. When the game's over, normalcy returns. We all go back to being people.

This isn't an act. Just like athletes, when the game begins, we're up for it with complete concentration. This is a natural reaction to the business. As a performer, one bears down. It means one's ready.

One doesn't have to work at this. It just happens by itself. And it doesn't take long for the ex-athletes to make the move to performer. Athletes do this the moment the game is underway. When they move into TV or radio, and the action starts, they react the same way. The whole body comes alive. They're ready, too.

35: Sportscasting Organizations And A High School Sports Venture

THERE ARE TWO organizations designed to assist sportscasters—the National Sportscasters and Sportswriters Association based in Salisbury, North Carolina, and the American Sportscasters Association, headquartered in New York.

Neither has union power or pressure to negotiate issues or financial matters, but both are of assistance to sportscasters and sportswriters as central forums to discuss problems and solutions in the field. They're fraternal groups with common goals.

Both organizations bestow honors and awards—all of which can be beneficial to the recipients in boosting their résumés from a promotional standpoint. To belong officially, just join the organization.

The older one is NSSA—which began when an enterprising restaurant owner in Salisbury decided to honor a sportscaster and sportswriter each year in a publicity venture. The idea took hold, and since that time the group has bestowed awards yearly on state sportscasters and sportswriters and national winners. There also is a NSSA Hall of Fame.

To become a member, the fee is $40. There's a delightful homey atmosphere at the yearly award ceremonies, held at the railroad station in Salisbury. The awards are coveted by the who's who in sportscasting and sports writing, with a large roster of big-name winners. Their dinners are lively, memorable affairs. A few years ago, I was honored by being inducted into their Hall of Fame, while at the same time won a sixth award as New York State Sportscaster of the Year and also received the Powerade Award for Best TV Sports Story of the Year.

The main contact during these years was energetic Barbara Lockert who made sure that the award celebration days were filled with stimulating discussion and events. Local townspeople are assigned to be chaperones for all the arriving sportscasters and sportswriters. For many years my wife, Jane, and myself have enjoyed the warm hospitality of Joe and Wilburn Taylor. Today the NSSA executive director is former state winner Dave Goren.

Of more recent vintage is the American Sportscasters Association, a big city operation. Their leader is ASA chief Lou Schwartz whose promotional award dinners in New York have featured celebrity big-name guests as presenters. ASA also puts out a newsletter of their activities. Their 2009 release of the top fifty all-time sportscasters received national attention. Joining ASA costs $50.

Both organizations would welcome deep-pocketed sponsors to help the largely volunteer workers fulfill their lofty goals of increased fraternal activity and provide the finances required for maintaining the Hall of Fame shrine for their luminaries.

As for high national honors, baseball has its broadcast wing in its Hall of Fame, the Ford Frick Award—and basketball has a Hall of Fame Award named for Curt Gowdy. Curt and I are the only two sportscasters to be honored in both the baseball and basketball halls.

The Baseball Writers Association of America uses its power to set and enforce press box rules, takes charge of seating during post-season competition, and its membership votes on Hall of Fame and annual award winners.

Hockey and football also have media awards which are prized. Winning any of these awards is very special to any sportscaster or sportswriter.

I also was excited about induction into the Madison Square Garden Walk of Fame, the Sigma Nu fraternity Hall of Fame, the National High School Athletic Coaches Association Hall of Fame, the New

York City Basketball Hall of Fame, and the Westchester and Rockland Counties Halls of Fame. It's a wonderful feeling to have one's past recognized. In the present, Jane and I take great pride in what our children and grandchildren are accomplishing. We've been blessed.

High schools are known in their town or region but are not known nationally. Some small towns, away from big cities, draw big football crowds to their high school games, but in the more populated areas, such as New York, with nine professional teams competing for fans, high schools and colleges take a backseat. With more TV exposure, high school events should draw more fans and more family support.

On Long Island for example, with around 150 schools playing about fifteen boys and girls sports, it's difficult to build audiences for any one school or sport.

Yet, there's a family emotion in high school sports that can't be overlooked. High school sports are the athletic acme for about 95 percent of the competitors. Most will never again receive the cheers,

MSG Walk of Fame

the applause, or the local headlines they earned in school. Very few are able to continue garnering acclaim in the college ranks, getting into the pro ranks is a rarity, and getting to the majors means defying all odds. It's no wonder parents and grandparents treasure all the headlines the youngsters make in high school, for most the highlight of their sports careers.

As national advertisers fall off, local advertisers turn to cable and local sports events are watched with a passion.

Madison Square Garden Varsity makes it possible to watch their kids on TV.

And regardless of the size of the school, these games are exciting and emotional. A great pass or catch or run or goal draws cheers at any level. So do cheerleading squads and marching bands. Girls' sports have finally had a chance to flourish. And many high school sports bring about college athletic scholarships.

Cablevision has news, weather and sports TV stations all around the New York City area: News 12 Long Island, News 12 Westchester, News 12 Hudson Valley, News 12 Bronx, News 12 Brooklyn, News 12 New Jersey, and News 12 Connecticut. All of their sports departments are now gathered under the MSG Varsity umbrella, sharing sports stories together. MSG Varsity also includes high school educational topics, marching bands, cheerleading, sports discussions and other features relating to school sports activity.

Over a hundred jobs have been filled for this new enterprise. Mike Lardner, the network's executive vice president, has selected on-air people, play-by-play callers, producers, directors, cameramen, technicians, marketers, publicists, and office workers to get this coverage underway. The most modern technology is being used, variety is being stressed in programming and youth is being served. Theresa Chillianis is the Senior Vice President and General Manager of this thriving business.

Jared Greenberg, who had professional TV and radio experience while in high school and college at Hofstra, is already a skilled pro in his mid-twenties. He's paired with perky Shawna Ryan, a young veteran and owner of a degree from Columbia and a master's from Northwestern, for an evening sports program.

I work for MSGV parent Cablevision, so have an emotional interest in the company's success, but have been impressed with the production and the creativity. Recently, I watched their high school band competition, which was excellent. High school activities include programming that has not been utilized before. This could start a new trend in the sports field.

36: The Overlooked Art Of Interviewing

INTERVIEWING IS THE most overlooked art in sportscasting. Those who get this job on TV, after a few years, are treated as specialists, very much as game show hosts are. Fortunately, those with the more inquiring minds and a pleasant conversational style stay in demand, but fewer get the chance each year as TV formats keep changing.

The basic requirement for this job is the ability to recognize a newsworthy story. Then one must know how to get beyond surface chitchat to dig it out and unearth this, even in TV's ever-quickening pace.

Howard Cosell reveled in the shocking first question. This produced immediate audience reaction, but did not win awards in the etiquette department. Most good interviewers understand that the interviewee has to have faith in the interviewer before opening up with disclosures. This means that a gentle opener is the best way to begin.

If the interviewee has just won a big game, had a great moment, or received an honor, the opening comments are a time for exultation. Then comes the first question to set the stage—knowing that it's the follow-up questions that are the vital ones. This means listening to the initial answer and then trying to pin down the truth. The art is in the follow-up. "You admitted you made a mistake—what do you believe should be done with your records?"

The reason there's so little training in this art is because nightly TV sports shows, on almost all stations and networks, are limited to the sameness of scores and highlights. When sound bites are used, they're usually stock answers to stock questions. In essence, all they prove is that one got the star or coach on camera. There's no time for probing questions for newsworthiness.

In TV's early years, the least experienced interviewers were given the job of doing sideline interviews—very few were skilled at asking questions.

Today, to add extra frills to ball games, sideline reporters are on camera for their thirty seconds or one minute of glory to report on an injury or interview a coach on his way to the locker room at half-time. Too often, nothing specific comes out of this. The coach is consumed with the game and the questions are not probing.

Many of the present sideline reporters have the ability to look for angles or question coaches on decisions that have been made in the game—but don't have the time to explore anything in depth. It's hit and run TV.

In the early days of TV, talk shows abounded, but there are fewer every year now. Most talk shows which continue are those dealing with problems of society—Maury Povich has kept his verve for many years. Continuing are Jerry Springer, Dr. Phil, the "judge," shows but an old standby—the Larry King show has ended its run. Popular Oprah Winfrey has had a long reign. Ellen DeGeneres supplies smiles and energy. Meanwhile, sports talk shows have stayed in fashion.

Johnny Carson had the knack of combining humor with his interviews. David Letterman has an inquiring mind with his questions. Craig Ferguson, who follows Letterman on CBS, is a visual comedian who makes use of facial expressions for laughs but doesn't stray from cocktail comedic chatter with his guests. Jimmy Fallon does much the same. Jay Leno works harder at comedy than interviewing. Interviewers who aren't prepared, or at least curious, miss golden opportunities to hold attention.

The most important factor in being a successful interviewer is actually being a quick-witted conversationalist, employing a less formal and more intimate style—friends just conversing. It certainly helps to have an inquiring mind. This is an open field for capable questioners.

A great opportunity in sportscasting is using time with teams in pre-season training in the major professional sports to get to know the players better. They're more relaxed, and have ample time on their hands to answer any and all questions, not just the standard mass interview stuff. Personal one-on-ones are far more revealing. Rehashing the past season, thoughts for the future, and ever-present predictions are overused stock topics.

Training time was a golden chance for me to film or tape conversations with the athletes on their personal lives, their families, their opinions, their beliefs "time for humor pieces, serious ones" all with one intent—to have timeless appeal and hold an audience. Some were spur of the moment, but there were ample hours to research, to prepare the direction I wanted to take, and to tape timely shows for use at the start of the season or beyond.

All I promised Madison Square Garden and News 12 Long Island in advance was that my shows would be different and entertaining—that nobody else was going to the training base with that specific mission in mind. I returned with sufficient material for long-length specials.

I discovered that then Mets catcher Todd Pratt had earned an earlier living working in a pizza shop. Figuring this may have contributed to his quick hands, we showed him in action in a pizzeria twirling pizzas in midair—excellent finger control. I found a Yankee catcher who also had quick hands and could demonstrate his dexterity performing magic tricks.

Biographies, needling sessions among players, action clips of batting, fielding, and catching, and location visits with players in recreation hobbies—the underlying goal of each segment was to have fun. As an extra plus, the personal relationships developed with the players made reporting easier all year. Shows with new angles remain a wide open area for future sportscasters. You have to convince your boss of its value—but if it's done well, it perpetuates itself year after year. Interviews with interesting topics last longer than those based on stats which lose timeliness quickly.

I've done thousands and thousands of interviews—pre-game, post-game, in game, on radio shows, TV shows, specials and the like—and have never used notes. But it's vital to do research first if possible. That way I know what I want to find out and that guides my questioning.

Hopefully, one arrives prepared, well-rehearsed in the background of the guest. Without need for notes, you're relying on your natural curiosity and can use your questioning to satisfy that curiosity.

Questions should be short. An incomplete answer leads to a follow-up question and maybe more—this is what brings out the gold—the ultimate truth. End the interview in a convivial manner—with a laugh or smile if possible.

It's the guest who does the revealing if the questions are good ones—remember you're a questioner, not an adversary. You want the friendship and the trust to continue.

One day I was scheduled to interview Ted Williams on camera in the Washington ballpark. Ted had arrived for a promised interview with me after a difficult day just before that in Fenway Park. He had thumbed his nose at those in the press box, spit on home plate as he crossed it, and was fined $5,000 dollars.

Ted vowed to never do another interview with anyone—writer, broadcaster, radio, or TV. But earlier in the season, he had promised me he'd do a telecast when he came to Washington.

"Ted," I said in the dugout before the game, "you promised to go on with me, but I read you would never do another interview. I view you as a good friend, so if you want to bow out of this show, I'll understand. If you do go on though, I'll have to ask you about your actions in Boston or I'll lose my credibility as a reporter. It's your decision. Either way, it will not interfere with our friendship."

Ted asked, "Where will the show be done?"

"On the field, in front of the Washington dugout."

"What time?"

I told him, then inquired, "Ted, how about the questions?"

"Bob," he said, "ask anything you want."

I did the interview. Ted expressed remorse for his actions and then said, "Bob, I just want to add, I'm doing this show with you because you've always been fair to me, and I want you to know how much I appreciate it."

I used that interview and one with Mickey Mantle to sell my syndicated baseball TV conversation series, not only in Washington but to major markets for pre-game shows including the Yankees and the Red Sox.

One of my most prized interviews is one with owner George Steinbrenner before he stepped out of the Yankee spotlight.

George was great copy, and captured press space with ease. Hardly a week went by without the Boss appearing on the back page (or front) page of a New York paper. Building World Series Champions was his passion and he made that dream come true.

George made spur of the moment decisions in building his championship teams. He was demanding, impetuous, hated to lose, fired

With Ted Williams

36: THE OVERLOOKED ART OF INTERVIEWING

Walter Winchell, Mickey Mantle

quickly, then rehired, a charming charitable man who wanted his staff to be available day and night so he wouldn't lose time in tracking them down. George was an emotional leader—in his early days he was involved in football and believed that emotional fervor in football might boost baseball's less emotional realm.

An interview with the Boss could provide terrific newsworthy material, My job was to make it happen without jeopardizing his trust in my fairness. Spring training was the ideal site for this one-on-one exercise.

In my mind I planned the direction of our conversation—knowing that he was well aware of my tactics, my strategy, and my goal. To me it would be a fun battle of wits. We were both ready for the mental game.

We arrived early, sat in the dugout at St. Petersburg, no other reporters present. George was wearing a baseball cap that read Top Dog.

I began with a couple of soft lobs right down the middle so he could speak about his team. He answered in glowing terms, of course.

Then I mentioned how the Mets, just down the road, were improving, and were proud of their pitching staff, which they considered the best in the majors.

"Well," George jumped right in, "they're good, I'm not sure about being the best, we'll have to wait and see. They've got good management over there, but we've got some great pitchers too.

"You know, the Mets have finished low in the standings and they've had top draft choices to take pitchers like Gooden and players like Strawberry to help them grow. We've been lucky with late draft choices like Don Mattingly, but our scouts do a fine job in getting talented players who were overlooked."

"George, you've had an earlier interest with football and know the importance of emotion in that sport. Do you try to bring emotion into baseball?"

George now spoke a bit louder with more emphasis. "I like players who show emotion and I get emotional about my team. I heard a union boss say that I had a second-rate operation. No one is going to get away with remarks like that about me. We run a first-class franchise, everybody knows that, and we pay top dollars."

"George, when you get together with the other club owners, do you discuss the rising cost of players?"

"No, I'm aware of collusion, we have a lawyer right with us. But I'm not going to be held up by some agent telling me how much I should spend. Nobody's going to tell me how to run my ball club," said George, now in mid-season form. "But the system isn't fair. I'll pay any amount of money if a player tells me he'll hit .350 and does it, or a pitcher says he'll get me twenty wins and comes through.

"I'll pay for performance, but the players make no guarantees. They want to be paid based on what they did in the past. Other businesses pay for present results. It's all a gamble in baseball. That's not fair." (A strong point by the Boss.)

"George, I know how involved you are with the city, but what are these rumors that you're considering a move to New Jersey?"

"Bob . . . have you stayed up at night working on these questions? I've known you a long time. I know how you do it!"

After a prolonged silence, I asked, "George—is that your answer?"

George broke out in unbridled laughter—and so did I.

The conversation ended—the laughter continued.

The mental battle was exhilarating fun. We each knew what the other was doing and thinking. It concluded, as always, with mutual respect. For television, it had on-air appeal, entertainment and unexpected levity at the end.

Some time later, I sent George a tape of that show. I prize that interview and I share with you his response letter that I treasure.

Baseball has had its share of colorful personalities. None who created more air time and print space than the Boss. He was the master. I miss our invigorating get-togethers and the excitement he brought to our jobs. It was flattering to learn that George also enjoyed our time together.

• • •

The ability to win on merit—to be given that opportunity—is what we all seek in the American way of life. The greatest reward for all sportscasters is applause, the response of listeners or viewers regardless of where any assignment may be. Applause brings instant gratification, but it's not like building a business for the future. The show can go on with a new cast. That's show business.

Somewhere, at some time, all sportscasters have experienced a vote of approval. That's success as a sportscaster—even if the rating is only in one's own home.

My hope is that this book can assist sportscasters in this quest.

New York Yankees

GEORGE M. STEINBRENNER III

TAMPA OFFICE
LEGENDS FIELD
1 STEINBRENNER DRIVE
TAMPA, FLORIDA 33614
(813) 281-9001

June 29, 2006

Bob Wolff
News 12 Long Island
One Media Crossways
Woodbury, New York 11791

Dear Bob:

What a wonderful surprise it was to receive not only the VHS tape of our interviews but also your *Legend to Legend* DVDs. You can be sure that I will treasure both of them.

I too have cherished the time spent during our interviews. You were always the consummate professional - prepared, courteous and very forgiving. I'm glad that you didn't take my sidestepping topics or issues that I wanted to avoid personally. My father (a master at so many things, including evasion) taught me how to deflect topics I didn't care to discuss. It's now part of my DNA.

Thank you dear friend for thinking of me. I am so glad that you're still enjoying, what is sure to be, one of the most celebrated and astounding career in sports casting.

May you continue onward . . . .

Best regards,

George M. Steinbrenner III

Letter from George Steinbrenner

Acknowledgments

MARK WEINSTEIN, THE sports-savvy senior editor at Skyhorse Publishing, well-versed in the art of publishing, initiated this book idea with me some years ago.

Sportscasting is a different sort of occupation. Sportscasters become famous locally, regionally, or nationally as a link between the athletes who play the games and those who watch or listen to the results. Movie and stage stars use a writer's lines to grab the public spotlight. Sportscasters use their own words in game or studio action. That's a basic difference.

When Mark and I discussed the book again, I told Mark I'd now be delighted to take on this project because I felt the time had come to reveal how others can get these exciting jobs, and more important, how to do them and keep advancing to the top. This meant my shattering some myths along the way, drawing from my personal experiences as the longest-running professional TV and radio sportscaster in history.

To aid in my compilation and organization of data, I needed a bright, conscientious person with strong editorial ability and sports knowledge. Ann Bernzweig, executive assistant to Pat Dolan, President of News 12 Network, agreed to work with me after office hours, which made it possible for me to add to my TV and radio assignments as well. I'm grateful to Ann for her brainy, tireless and cheerful assistance.

For double-checking facts, Mark Weinstein showed his stuff—great job there—and there were also contributions from Rob Del Muro, Phil Schwartz, Kevin Maher, Jamie Stuart, Carl Reuter, and Kenny Albert.

I also used the counsel of my son, Rick Wolff, VP and executive editor at Grand Central Publishing, who's also an author, broadcaster, former professional baseball player and coach.

On the executive side, Irving Mitchell Felt, Joe Cohen, and Mike McCarthy at Madison Square Garden, Pat Dolan at News 12, and Navy Comander Hugh Haynsworth all played significant roles in my career.

Fortunately, my wife and partner since 1945, Jane, has always been patient with my sportscasting life, and handles all the practical necessities in our household while I'm broadcasting games, doing studio shows, or also writing a book. Her latest concession is allowing me to keep these pages on the dining room table while I edit them. If you taste gravy on your fingertips, please consider this an extra bonus. I told Jane that after publication, we'll return to normal life. I know, however, that sportscasters don't live normal lives. But none of us are complaining. It's nice to get paid when all we have to do is talk.

There's great artistic ability in taking an excellent picture. I know that the interest in this book's pictures is focused on who's standing beside me. That's my interest, too. There are a few solo shots, however, mostly to show location or an event.

When the present Madison Square Garden opened, I asked two talented young photographers to assist me on picture projects. Both kept moving on to the top, but took time to contribute to this book. My thanks to award winners, George Kalinsky, the official photographer at Madison Square Garden, and Barton Silverman, who gets the choice sports assignments at The New York Times.

Other talented contributors include Don Wingfield, who snapped most of the pictures during my Washington days. In New York, Louie

Requema and Al Coqueran. And thanks to the PR departments of the networks for many other shots. NBC-TV, CBS-TV, ABC-TV, DuMont TV, Madison Square Garden Network and News 12 Long Island.

There was also the *Daily News*, the *New York Times*, the Mutual Broadcasting System, WTTG, the Pathfinder, Bob Herzog, Norman Driscoll, Reni, George Havens, Wallace Kammann, Karas, Richard Collins, John Maguire, Tore Heskestad, David Mintzer, GFI Photo Reproductions, and many others from my personal Bob Wolff Collection.

I'm grateful to all the contributors. I'm well aware that when I'm photographed chatting with stars like Babe Ruth to Derek Jeter, I'm just a guy holding the mike. Can this be considered a job?

About The Author

Bob Wolff is the longest running broadcaster in television and radio history, now in his ninth decade behind the microphone. The only broadcaster in history to call the play-by-play championships in four major pro sports (World Series, NFL Championship, NBA Finals, and Stanley Cup Finals), his historic calls include Don Larsen's legendary perfect game in the 1956 World Series and the 1958 NFL Championship Game between the New York Giants and Baltimore Colts (known as The Greatest Game Ever Played). Wolff was the television and occasional radio play-by-play voice of Madison Square Garden since 1954, and was saluted by the Garden with a 50-year special called, "Bob Wolff's Golden Garden Anniversary." In addition to his college games and special events schedule, Wolff was the TV play-by-player of the Knicks first two championships, and called the Knicks for 27 years, the Rangers for 20 years, the Holiday Festival for 29 years and the National Invitational Basketball Tournament (NIT) for 25 years. He's enshrined in both the baseball and basketball Halls of Fame, has been honored with induction into Madison Square Garden's Walk of Fame, the National Sportscasters and Sportswriters Hall of Fame the Sigma Nu fraternity Hall of Fame, and numerous others. In 2009, the TV home booth at Nationals Park in Washington was named in his honor. Still sportscasting TV and radio, he lives with his wife, Jane, in South Nyack, New York.

INDEX

A
ad-libbing, 219
Aikman, Troy, 332
Albert, Kenny, 322
Albert, Marv, 37, 91, 110, 183, 210
Allen, Maury, 218
Allen, Mel, 3, 36, 61, 75, 252, 279, 281, 296, 325
American Sportscasters Association, 334
Andariese, John, 149
Andrews, Erin, 214
Aparicio, Luis, 283
appeal, 2
Aronoff, Marty, 316
Arries, Les, Sr., 67
Auerbach, Red, 50
Auerbach, Zang, 67

B
Banforth (Commander), 48
Barber, Red, 86, 281, 293
Barnett, Dick, 181
Baseball Writers Association of America, 335
Batchelder, Johnny, 103
Bathgate, Andy, 264
Beck, Bruce, 118
Berle, Milton, 223
Berman, Chris, 37, 57
Berman, Len, 145, 183
Best, Neil, 130
Bevens, Floyd, 293
Blazejowski, Carol, 14
Bob Wolff's Sports Clinic, 67
Bob Wolff Productions Inc., 140
Bradley, Bill, 181
Breen, Mike, 57, 212
Brennaman, Thom, 278
broadcast partners, 53, 331
Brown, Hubie, 149, 185, 211
Buck, Joe, 246, 332

C
Candelaria, John, 255
Caray, Chip, 275, 277
Caray, Harry, 57, 212
Carson, Johnny, 95
Carter, Gary, 263
Carton, Craig, 214, 331
Carvellas, Jim, 129
CBS Network, 13, 22, 66, 75, 127, 203, 212, 321, 331

Cervasio, Tina, 13, 214
Chernoff, Mark, 17, 300, 331
Clark, Scott, 145, 183
Cohen, Gary, 211, 308
Cohen, Mike, 246
Cohn, Linda, 13
Coleman, Michael, 12
Collinsworth, Chris, 332
Condon, John, 173
Cone, David, 264
Cook, Eddie, 95
Coombs, Jack, 19, 28
Cooper, Scott, 249
Cosell, Howard, 83, 85, 180, 286, 310, 338
Costas, Bob, 57, 121, 210, 246, 251
Crispino, Mike, 149
Cronkite, Walter, 238
crowd roar, 153
Curry, Jack, 115

D
Darling, Ron, 211, 308
Davidson, John, 37
Dean, Dizzy, 2
DeBusschere, Dave, 181
DiMona, Joe, 55
Dockery, John, 119, 214
Dolan, Pat, 11, 167
Dressen, Chuck, 264
Dudley, Jimmy, 57
Duke University, 19, 36
Dunn, Jackie, 160
Dunphy, Don, 75, 286
Durocher, Leo, 89
Dutch MacMillan and the Duke Ambassadors, 24

E
Eckert, Meredith, 183
Edwards, Doug, 71
Edwards, Ralph, 45
Emrick, Doc, 210
Enberg, Dick, 37, 149, 310, 331
Erving, Julius, 264
Esiason, Boomer, 213, 331
Evans, Paul, 318
exposure, 156, 158

F
Feinstein, John, 218
Feller, Bob, 51, 68
Fenster, Milt, 164, 246
Finley, Charlie, 134
Fiorito, Len, 319
Fletcher, Tom, 27
Foreman, George, 107
Fowler, Chris, 214

Fox, Donna, 13
Fox, Nellie, 283
Francesa, Mike, 17, 121, 211, 308
Franklin, Pete, 118
Frazier, Walt, 57, 149, 181
Frick, Ford, 124

G
Gallery, Tom, 132
Gallo, Bill, 309
Game of the Week, 3, 74, 81, 89, 91, 132, 139, 143, 150, 168, 196, 229, 279, 322
Garagiola, Joe, 3, 132, 148, 211, 226, 251
Garroway, Dave, 33
Germino, Hugo, 28
Gibson, Bob, 255
Gibson, Josh, 324
Gifford, Frank, 310
Gilbert, Rod, 214, 264
Gillespie, Earl, 58
Gillette Safety Razor Company, 80, 287
Godfrey, Arthur, 61
Gold, Bill, 66, 72, 278
Goss, Bailey, 61
Gowdy, Curt, 15, 251
Grauer, Ben, 71
Gray, Jim, 119, 214
Greatest Game Ever Played, The, 185
Greenberg, Jared, 337

H
Hagin, Wayne, 59, 149, 211, 299
Hall, Halsey, 63
Harmon, Merle, 142
Harmon, Phil, 144
Harwell, Ernie, 312
Haynsworth, Hugh, 49
Helfer, Al, 75
Heller, Dick, 14
Hemond, Roland, 134
Herbstreit, Kirk, 128
Hernandez, Keith, 211, 308
Hernon, Pat, 232
Heyman, Jon, 211
Hochberg, Phil, 14
Hodges, Russ, 42, 66
Holzman, Red, 182
homerism, 3, 189
Hoyt, Waite, 58
Huff, Charles, 328
Husing, Ted, 75, 90

I
interviewing, 338

J
Jackson, Keith, 210

Jackson, Phil, 181
Jacobs, Spook, 314
Jacobsen, Dan, 314
Jessup, Bill, 28
Jiggetts, Dan, 14
Johnson, Dave, 211
Johnson, Gus, 213
Johnson, Walter, 54, 68
Johnston, Ken, 328
Jonas, Paul, 159
Jones, Kimberly, 214

K
Kamzic, Nick, 132
Karpin, Howie, 145
Kasten, Stan, 63
Kay, Michael, 37, 149, 213
Kellogg, Clark, 212
Kirshner, Rob, 144
Kornheiser, Tony, 180
Koufax, Sandy, 256
Kraft, Barney, 67
Kubek, Tony, 148, 266

L
LaFontaine, Pat, 264
Larsen, Don, 82, 183, 272, 293, 297
Last Boy, The (Leavy), 325
Lavagetto, Cookie, 293
Layton, Eddie, 242
Leavy, Jane, 326, 328
The Last Boy, 325
Lechner, Mike, 314
Leiter, Al, 264
Leonard, Jack E., 69
Ley, Bob, 57
Lichtenstein, Irv, 73
Lieberman, Nancy, 14
Liguori, Ann, 145
Lindemann, Carl, 132
Lockert, Barbara, 335
Lopez, Al, 264
Lorenz, Bob, 115
Lucas, Ed, 145
Lucas, Jerry, 170, 182

M
Madden, John, 127, 150, 180, 213, 310, 332
Madison Square Garden Network, 121, 186, 241, 251, 269, 287
Maglie, Sal, 293
Maher, Kevin, 13, 314, 321
Malone, Bill, 16
Mancuso, Mike, 145
Mantle, Mickey, 323
Marazzi, Rich, 319
Marchiano, Sal, 145
Martin, Billy, 265
Martin, Ned, 15
Martinez, Buck, 276
Mason, Donna, 69
Mattingly, Don, 264

351